Way More! FREE $TUFF From the INTERNET

Patrick Vincent

CORIOLIS GROUP BOOKS

Publisher	Keith Weiskamp
Editor	Ron Pronk
Proofreaders	Michelle Stroup and Jenni Aloi
Interior Design	Rob Mauhar
Cover Design	Bradley O. Grannis
Layout Production	Rob Mauhar
Publicist	Shannon Bounds
Indexer	Lenity Mauhar

Trademarks: All brand names and product names included in this book are trademarks, registered trademarks, or trade names of their respective holders. Some of the clip art used in this book is from the Corel GALLERY, version 1.0.

Distributed to the book trade by IDG Books Worldwide, Inc.

Library of Congress Cataloging-in-Publication Data

Vincent, Patrick
    Way More FREE $TUFF from the Internet / Patrick Vincent
        p. cm.
    Includes Index
    ISBN 1-883577-27-6 : $19.99

Printed in the United States of America

10 9 8 7 6 5 4 3 2 1

To Hailey Morgan Vincent, the most patient three-year-old ever.
The book's done, sweetie; now we can go to Disneyland.

Here are a few of the author's favorite E-mail messages from readers, who offer their opinions of *Free $TUFF from the Internet*. We even let Mr. Vincent include his responses, which might have been a mistake....

I just purchased the book today and cannot put it down. As a new Internet user, this is the first publication I read that I could totally understand. I am still fumbling my way around, but am learning more each day. If you have any suggestions, or are planning an update to this book, please reply —D.S.

Your wish is my Alt+Shift+Command. The next book is called FREE $TUFF from the World Wide Web, *and will be available mid-year, 1995. There are a few other titles lined up for publication soon after, but they hinge on whether I'm released from Happy Acres by then. The nurses finally let me have my computer back, and told me that next week I may even be able to have visitors.*

Your book makes sense of many confusing Internet topics. It is well organized and humorously written. I'd like to see your team tackle a book about Mosaic, including as much of the help/configuration files as possible. —Joe D.

I appreciate the comments, and have in fact recently gang-authored a book with PC Guru Jeff Duntemann and Mac Wizard Ron Pronk (their true full names) called the Mosaic EXplorer Pocket Companion. *If you're looking for my name on it, look way down at the bottom. Jeff and Ron told me it was a matter of listing the names alphabetically, though that's what they said about why I was given such a small office with no window.*

I just got your book.... This is absolutely incredible!!!!! This place [the Internet] is unlimited in getting any kind of info anyone wants to whenever!! —Duffy M.

Thanks Duffy!!!!! I know you're excited, but easy on the exclamation key!!!!! And save a little caffeine for the rest of us!!!!!

I feel that *FREE $TUFF from the Internet* will not only be helpful for education but also helpful...in personal endeavors.... I feel that there is just so much in this book that it is well worth the purchase. —R.H.

It's also guaranteed to freshen breath, whiten teeth, and generally make you more attractive to the opposite sex.

RE: "Let us know what you disliked, as well." THE INK! The stench that emanates from your book, the asthma attack it produces in people who are allergic, and the fact that it must be read contained in a sealed, metal-glass-topped box. —C. L. W.

Since FREE $TUFF from the Internet *is intended for recreational use, I guess I should have included a warning that it not be smoked, inhaled, snorted, or ingested in any way. Rest assured that this oversight will be corrected in future editions.*

Regards from Malaysia! Just a note to say I am thankful for the info you've written to enable people like me who're quite new to the Internet to surf it more easily. Do you mean that I can write to President Clinton and expect a reply? —L. H. W.

I guess that's between you and the President. All I can say is that if you are going to write him, make it fast. His address is subject to change— perhaps to something like former.president@nobody.appreciates.me.

Thanks to everyone who sent me mail. I've tried to respond to each note, but with two kids, two books I'm currently writing, and only 24 hours in a day, I may have missed someone. Thanks for the feedback!

Preface

In the Beginning

A neighbor asked me a few months back what I do for a living. When I told her I'm a writer, she was fascinated. But when I told her I write books about the Internet, her fascination changed to disapproval. "That's nothing but pornography," she said. Really. Needless to say, our relationship hasn't been quite the same since.

Such is the bad rap the Internet has taken lately. Once the darling of the media, the Net has recently received a few bruises, giving some people the delusion that it's little more than a haven for pedophiles and degenerates.

Does the Internet contain pornography? Sure, but so does your local library and bookstore, if you know where to look. And on the Internet, most kids don't know where to look, and frankly they have no idea how to view any of the R- and X-rated stuff that's available. Let's keep it that way. Anyway, don't let the small percentage of "bad" outweigh the overwhelmingly large amount of "good" contained on the Net.

WAY MORE FREE $TUFF from the Internet was written to show PC and Macintosh users what an incredibly valuable resource cyberspace can be for the whole family—including the kids. Get past the hype and one truth remains: the Internet is fun! Imagine suddenly having access to thousands of games, books, puzzles, recipes, pictures, movie clips, sound bites of your favorite bands, animation, and more. On the Internet, you don't have to imagine it—it's real, and it's waiting for you.

And it's free.

And *WAY MORE FREE $TUFF from the Internet* shows you how to get it.

I've received hundreds of email messages since my first book, *FREE $TUFF from the Internet*, was published in 1994, including compliments, criticisms, suggestions, and questions about the book and the Net in general. In *WAY MORE FREE $TUFF from the Internet*, I've tried to answer as many of the questions as possible.

I've also taken a lot of the suggestions I received for improving the book and incorporated them into *WAY MORE FREE $TUFF from the Internet*. The results are:

- Lots more free stuff for Mac users
- File sizes so you know what you're downloading
- More email addresses
- Tons of Web sites
- Free updates to the book online
- Helpful FYIs and reminders scattered throughout the chapters
- Way more free stuff listed at the end of each chapter

Acknowledgments

I learned early on as an editor and proofreader that when it comes to writing a book, there's no such thing as a solo project, and *WAY MORE FREE $TUFF from the Internet* wouldn't have gone past the idea stage if it weren't for several talented, obsessive, helpful, and generally wacky people:

- **Ron Pronk** If any other name deserves to be on the cover, it's editing and Mac guru Ron Pronk. To Ron, editing is not just a job, it's a way to take out his pent-up hostilities on unsuspecting authors.
- **Lisa Vincent** Most wives would be hard-pressed to put up with the lunacy of being married to a writer. Then again, Lisa's a little loony herself.

- **Jean Vincent** If I hadn't been able to borrow Mom's house for a month of intense organizing, I'd still be plowing through my pile of notes and outlines trying to breathe some life into this project.

- **Dr. Terry Welsh** When Mom sold the house and moved in with Aunt Terry, I came along as part of the furniture. Thanks Terry, for letting me hide out for a couple of months.

- **Jenni Aloi** and **Michelle Stroup** Without Jenni and Michelle's tag-team approach to proofing my jumbled manuscript, this book wouldn't have been nearly as fun to write—nor as fun to read.

- **Rob Mauhar** Rob's contribution as a layout artist cannot be overestimated. Rob was able to transform some crude text and photos into a great-looking book.

- **Dr**. **Bradley Williams** I don't know what Dr. Williams put in those accupuncture needles to get Lisa back on her feet, but it worked—and made a believer out of me.

- **Sat-Kartar Khalsa** This may be a first, where an author thanks his masseuse for helping him complete his book, but Sat-Kartar kept me from having to write lying down when the pain in my back became a real pain in the butt.

Finally, thanks to the 100,000+ readers of *FREE $TUFF from the Internet* who grabbed the attention of my publisher and made this sequel possible.

Any Comments?

Will there be a *WAY, WAY MORE FREE $TUFF from the Internet*? Ya got me. Let me hear what you think of this one, first. Tell me what you like and dislike, and I'll try to answer any questions you might have. I can be reached at:

pjvincent@coriolis.com

Patrick Vincent
Glendale, Arizona
October, 1995

Contents

Way More Free Stuff

Computers   57

Education   77

Government and Politics   139

Health and Nutrition   157

International   215

Internet Resources   227

Kid Stuff   245

Language and Linguistics   265

Law 285

Movies and Television 305

Music   323

Science and Nature   339

Sports and Leisure 365

Travel 387

Index 403

Introduction

The Communication Revolution

What a difference a few years make. It wasn't that long ago when most people hadn't even heard of the Internet. Sure, it'd been talked about in university and scientific circles since the 1960s, but to mainstream America and the rest of the world, it was just so much science fiction. After all, until recently, most people didn't even have access to a personal computer and modem, and even if they did, Internet connections were too expensive, computers were too slow, and cyberspace was, well, too *boring* to bother with anyway.

As I said, though, what a difference a few years make. Computers got faster, modems became commonplace, and seemingly overnight the Internet took center stage in a communication revolution. While Cold War bombs are being dismantled and the military complexes around the world are being downsized, the Internet—really just an old warhorse by-product of the Cold War era—is growing exponentially.

At last count, there were over 30 million users wired to the Net, with an additional 10,000 plugging in every day. And for the first time in history, personal computers are outselling televisions in a $185 billion per year industy. You don't have to be hit over the head to realize something's going on.

In the last couple of years, there's been a wave of tsunami proportions of companies scrambling to provide Internet access to individuals and small organizations. These Internet Service Providers (or ISPs) offer a variety of services—from electronic mail to the World Wide Web—to anyone with a home computer and a telephone line.

Using easy-to-navigate point-and-click software, these ISPs have taken the seemingly complex and made it simple. What once was the lone stomping ground for computer-savvy propeller heads has become a wide-open forum for anyone with a modem and limited skills at the keyboard. Once for the few, the Internet is now for everybody.

Cyberspace Today

Today, the most popular U.S. Internet providers are America Online, CompuServe, and Prodigy. While they've only allowed their subscribers full access to the Internet since early 1995, the *Big Three* (as they're known) have subscribers totaling over 7 million users. And now with the Big Three about to become the *Big Four* as Miscrosoft lures its Windows 95 users to its Microsoft Network online service, millions more will soon be surfing cyberspace.

And the U.S. isn't the only one on the crest of this revolution. America Online and CompuServe are both battling a plethora of Internet providers for market share in Europe, as well, and there are literally thousands of small ISPs around the world offering computer users seemingly unlimited—and cheap—access to the Internet.

Where It's Going

What's next for the Internet is anyone's guess—and if you tried to guess, you'd probably just be wrong, anyway. After all, who could have imagined the Net's explosive growth even five years ago? Three years ago, most people had never even heard of the Internet. Today you can't pick up a magazine or newspaper without reading about it. One year ago, the World Wide Web was a fledgling niche in the Net, with relatively few users able to access it. Today, the Web is the fastest growing portion of the Net, with users—numbering in the tens of millions—accessing it.

The Internet Basics

To get the most out of this book—and the Internet itself—you'll need to take a quick lesson in Net 101. The Net tools listed below—offered by any ISP that promises *full* Internet access—will let you surf the Net in style.

Electronic Mail

Electronic mail (*email*) is the lowest common denominator of the Internet. If you can send and receive email, you already have access to a huge amount of information on the Net. I've included dozens of email addresses throughout this book for you to write to for giveaways, catalogs, games, brochures, and lots of other fun stuff.

You'll also find addresses to subscribe for getting online magazines, newsletters, and gossip on your favorite topics. Caution: email is *addictive*; before you know it, you'll be spending more time reading your mail than eating or sleeping.

A lot of the email addresses I include in *WAY MORE FREE $TUFF from the Internet* are for *mailing lists*, sort of online clubs you join to discuss your favorite subjects. Usually when you subscribe, you're sent information about the mailing list and its rules, frequently asked questions and answers about the list (*FAQs*), as well as information on how to cancel your subscription. Be sure to save this file on your computer in case you ever want to unsubscribe. It may seem like a waste of disk space now, but it'll save you a lot of headaches later—like when you come back from vacation and find 300 email messages waiting for you in your mailbox.

File Transfer Protocol

File Transfer Protocol (*FTP*) is a system for downloading (and uploading, but for the purposes of this book, you don't need to worry about that) programs and files stored on computers all over the Net. This book contains tons of games, books, business applications, pictures, and more you can access and download by FTP.

Many FTP sites across the Internet—and all of the ones in this book—offer files through *anonymous* FTP, which means anyone can access them even if they don't have an account on that system. Simply type *anonymous* if you're prompted to provide a username, then your email address if you're asked for a password. (That may seem a little strange, but it works.)

Not too long ago, using FTP was a complicated lesson in frustration. Users needed to memorize cryptic commands and type in long addresses to download programs. These days, most FTP software uses point-and-click interfaces to make navigating into the depths of an FTP site much easier.

Keep in mind that there are millions of other people on the Internet using FTP, and traffic jams sometimes occur when lots of users try to access the same site at once. Occassionally—especially during peak hours—you'll get an error message saying there are too many users trying to access a site, and to try again later. This is the Internet's equivalent of a busy signal. Be patient, try later, and don't get frustrated.

Also, pay attention when you *do* connect. Many Internet sites have *mirrors* (identical sites located around the world) you can access that may be closer to where you live, and which are often listed when you first enter a site. The closer the site you access, the faster you'll be able to navigate it and download files.

Gopher
Gopher, one of the most popular on-ramps to the information highway, is a menu-based system that lets you browse through collections of information and databases scattered around the Net. Once you've found what you're looking for, retrieving documents is as easy as pointing and clicking.

World Wide Web Browsers
The World Wide Web (*Web*) is the newest and most exciting innovation to come to the Internet in years. Using a Web browser, such as Netscape or Mosaic, Net surfers point and click their way around the Web—the Internet's graphical side, complete with sound, movies, pictures, and more. And Web browsers can be used to access Gopher and FTP sites, as well. Just type in gopher:// or ftp:// followed by the Internet addresses included in this book to use your Web browser to surf the Net.

Compressed Files

To keep things moving as fast as possible on the Net, most files and programs you download are compressed to make them smaller and easier to download. Once you've downloaded a compressed file, you need to uncompress it before running it.

PC users can use PKUnzip for DOS or Winzip for Windows to extract "zipped" files. Either is available for free at many sites around the Internet, including:

- **DOS:** FTP to igc.net/pub/igc/viewers and download pkunzip.exe (28 K)
- **Windows:** FTP to oak.oakland.edu/simtel/win3/archiver and download wz60wn16.exe (321 K)
- For a Windows 95-compatible version of Winzip, FTP to ftp.outer.net/winzip and download winzip95.exe (331 K)

For Macintosh users, uncompressing files is a bit more complex, mostly because the Mac uses several different compression schemes. I highly recommend that you purchase a copy of StuffIt Deluxe, because this commercial package can uncompress virtually all compressed formats, including ZIP files. The shareware version of StuffIt is much more limited.

Most files on Macintosh archives are stored in a text-encoded format called BinHex. You can easily identify these files because they have an .hqx file extension. StuffIt Deluxe can automatically decode BinHexed files, and so can Compact Pro.

Even after you decode a BinHexed file, you might still need to uncompress it. If a Mac file has a .cpt extension, the compression was created by Compact Pro. Both StuffIt Deluxe and Compact Pro can uncompress these files. If the file has a .sit extension, the compression was done by some version of StuffIt, so you'll need StuffIt to uncompress the file. The more current the version of StuffIt you have, the more likely you'll be able to uncompress the file.

If, after you decode a BinHexed file, the resulting file has the extension .sea, you're in good shape. This is a self-extracting archive created either

by StuffIt or Compact Pro. All you need to do is double-click on the file name to uncompress it.

Here's where to find the various uncompression and decode utilities you'll need to use for Mac files.

- BinHex 4.0 This is the most popular utility for unBinHexing encoded files. You can find it at these locations:

   Web: mrcnext.cso.uiuc.edu/~deej/index.html
   FTP: ftp.sunet.se/pub/mac/info-mac/cmp

- StuffIt Lite: This is the shareware version of StuffIt. It's BinHexed, so you'll need to download BinHex 4.0 first, in order to decode the file. You can find StuffIt Lite at these locations:

   Web: www.aladdinsys.com/
   FTP: ftp.204.147.235.101/pub
   FTP: ftp.sunet.se/pub/mac/info-mac/cmp

- Compact Pro. Use this program to uncompress Compact Pro (.cpt) files.

   FTP: ftp.sunet.se/pub/mac/info-mac/cmp

If you have StuffIt Lite, you can also use the cpt.sit converter to convert .cpt files to .sit files. The converter is available on the Web at www.aladdinsys.com.

Know Your Name and Address...

Keep in mind that many of the Internet addresses you type in are case sensitive. If you see an address like **Alpha.CC.UToledo.edu**, be sure you enter it *exactly* as written, with *Alpha* initial capped and *CC* and *UT* in uppercase. If you don't, many programs won't recognize the address and you'll be stuck in the Information Highway's version of the breakdown lane.

Share and Share Alike

WAY MORE FREE $TUFF from the Internet is jammed with tons of programs for you to download, all of which are free to try out. And while many of them are free to keep (*freeware*), many others are *shareware*, a marketing concept that lets you try before you buy. If you don't like the program, delete it and pay nothing. If you like it, send in the registration fee.

I Think I'm Coming Down with Something

Funny things can happen to a computer infested with viruses, though you won't think it's too funny if it happens to you. Be sure to practice safe computing and scan your programs before running them. While most of the programs you download have already been inoculated at the sites they're stored at, don't take anyone's word for it. Talk to the experts where you bought your computer to find out which scanning software is best for your system, then use it.

For Mac Users Only

One of the recurring suggestions I received from readers of *FREE $TUFF From the Internet* was to include more Macintosh software. In fact, with a few readers it was more of a veiled threat. Well, with this book, I've tried to make amends. Any topic that begins with the Travelin' Mac icon describes software that runs on Macintoshes only. So, if you're a Mac user, you can quickly spot software for your system by flipping through the book and looking for this icon.

Get 'Em While They're Hot

It's an exciting time to be in cyberspace, and the Internet's changing all the time. Every day, software and Net sites are being added by the thousands.

The bad news is that as the Internet grows, some sites occasionaly disappear. What's here today is sometimes gone tomorrow.

The good news is that my publisher, Coriolis Group Books, has its own Net site (coriolis.com) that you can access via FTP or the Web to get free updates to my books. If you're having trouble locating something, check there first. If a new address is not listed, email me and I'll point you to the goods.

Surf's up! What are you waiting for?

pjvincent@coriolis.com

Way More! FREE $TUFF

*They couldn't find the artist,
so they hung their picture.*

Anonymous

Arts and
Culture

A Treasure Chest of World Art

Egypt, China, Japan, India, Cambodia, and Thailand are just a smattering of the countries represented at the World Arts Treasures Web site. This collaboration between the J.E. Berger Foundation and the Swiss Federal Institute of Technology, established to help add a little culture to Internet explorers' lives, is definitely worth checking out.

It's hard not to be impressed with the seemingly endless displays in this online museum, which offers hundreds of images from a variety of different civilizations and cultures. French Internauts will be happy to know this site is also available in their native language.

More art than would ever fit into one museum is yours for the viewing at the World Arts Treasures.

How

World Wide Web

Where

sgwww.epfl.ch/BERGER/index.html

Priceless Pixels

Not all the best paintings are hanging in museums. Okay, most of them are, but that doesn't mean it's the only place you can see them. Here's a site that has borrowed the best of the best from the art world and put them on the Net for your viewing (and downloading) pleasure. Check out Van Gogh's *Starry Night*, Dali's *Persistence of Memory*, and many other masterpieces.

How

Gopher

Where

twinbrook.cis.uab.edu

Another STARRY NIGHT on the Net.

Go To

The Continuum

The Boardwalk

Art for the 21st Century

It used to be that Paris was the home of suffering artists destined to spend their days painting bowls of rotting fruit. But modern technology has changed all that. Thanks to cyberspace, aspiring artists can now suffer anywhere—even Toronto, home to Internet artist Colin Baker.

Actually, I'm not sure how much Colin is suffering—he seems to have scraped together enough for a color scanner and an Internet connection. And this collection of his paintings has certainly surpassed the obligatory bowls of fruit. Instead, his work takes on more of an outer space theme. I'm sure you'll find them as out of the ordinary as they are out of this world.

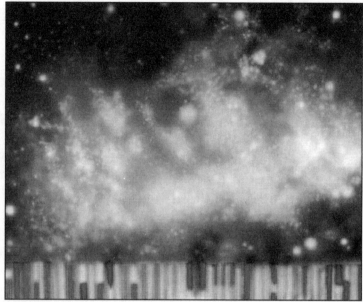

LARGE MAGELLENIC CLOUD, by Colin Baker.

How

World Wide Web

Where

www.interlog.com/~cwcjb/home.html

A Brush, a Canvas, and a 450-Meg Hard Drive

Contrary to what you may think, not all modern artists are busy stringing brassieres across the Grand Canyon or covering themselves in chocolate syrup—though I'd be the first to say there is certainly a need for those types of expression. The truth of the matter is that the computer is fast becoming the canvas of choice for many of today's would-be Picassos and Rembrandts. And in many circles, it's becoming the tool of choice for displaying the finished product.

Here's a sampling of try-before you buy software packages to help you design and market your soon-to-be masterpieces:

PhotoShow Pro is a multi-image viewer of JPG, GIF, BMP, TIFF, TGA, and an alphabet-soup of other picture formats. You can create slide shows of open files, create thumbnails, and alter images. There's even a built-in editor for creating customized icons. (If you're a Macintosh user, check out JPEG View, which I mentioned in the *Computers* chapter.)

Graphic Manager Plus helps you manage bitmap, metafile, icon, and run-length encoded (RLE) graphic files. You can load an entire directory of different images of varying sizes then review or remove selected at the click of a button. This one comes with good online help, as well.

WinMorph for Windows turns your computer into something right out of a science fiction novel—or a Hollywood special-effects lab, anyway. This program lets you transform one image into another—just like you've seen in such movies as *Terminator 2*, as well as countless music videos. This one comes with a nice demo and some bitmaps to get you started, or you can use your own images.

WinJPEG lets you convert images to BMP, GIF, PCX, TIFF, as well as many other formats. You can convert images one at a time, or turn your computer into an assembly line and convert images in batches.

How
FTP

Where
oak.oakland.edu

Go To
SimTel/win3/graphics

Download
photosho.zip (438 K)
gphmn1_2.zip (282 K)
winmrf16.zip (288 K)
winjp276.zip (296 K)

Electrifying Art on the Internet

The Electric Gallery is an online masterpiece of stunningly spectacular art from around the world. Divided into six "wings," this Web site displays dazzling examples of folk art, works from Haiti and the Amazon, portraits of jazz and blues legends, and more. This site is constantly updated, so check back often for the latest works from up-and-comers and experienced masters alike.

THE TANRILLA, **downloaded from The Amazon Project at the Electric Art Gallery.**

If you don't have time to stick around, that's okay, too. Downloading a catalog of all the art in the gallery can be done by clicking on *Catalog*, or you can order a catalog on diskette.

How

World Wide Web

Where

www.egallery.com/egallery/

Special bonus: You can even play a 19-second audio clip of B.B. King singing *The Thrill Is Gone* while you explore the Jazz & Blues Wing. Does your local museum offer *that*?

Grab It, Capture It, and Print It

Here's a handful of programs to help you turn online works of art into online works of wallpaper and other displays of bits and bytes. Print Screen 1.3 for Windows, Capture for Windows, and GrabIt Pro 3.1 all let you capture images on your monitor and save them in a variety of file formats. Trying them is free, so drive each of 'em around the block to see which works best for you.

How

FTP

Where

ftp.csusm.edu

Go To

pub/winworld/convert

Download

grabpro.zip (147 K)

capture3.zip (33 K)

amps13.zip (141 K)

Not Just for Cuckoos

Throw your traditional idea of the cuckoo clock out the window before accessing this site. Johann Georg Laubles has put his own slant on these Germanic time-pieces—with some wildly interesting results.

Johann calls his creations the German an-swer to the SWATCH wristwatch, and he couldn't be more on the mark. These fully functional clocks are true works of art, as fun to look at as they are, frankly,

Cuckoo clocks aren't just for hanging at Grandma's house anymore.

annoying to listen to. Don't believe me? Download the audio file and you'll hear what I mean.

How

World Wide Web

Where

deep-thought.biologie.uni-freiburg.de/~clock/

 Downloading these images from Germany can be slower than going through Customs, but all are well worth the wait—and you won't have to pay any duty on them either.

Let Your Fingers Do the Walking

Sometimes, locating specific information on the Internet is harder than applying for a home loan—and can be twice as tedious. That's why it's nice to find sites like the Arts Gopher Yellow Pages that have already done the legwork for you. No matter what artistic discipline you're interested in—with the possible exception of Jell-O wrestling—you'll find an Internet link here where you can get more information.

Let your keyboard do the walking in the Arts Gopher Yellow Pages.

A few of the links you'll find here include:

- Art and Architecture at Carnegie Mellon
- The Ceramics Gopher
- *Art Com* Magazine
- Film Review Database
- Smithsonian Art Gallery

New links are constantly being added here, so be sure to check it often. Who knows, before long they just might have that Jell-O link.

How

Gopher

Where

gopher.tmn.com

Go To

Arts Wire

Arts Gophers of the World

Arts Gopher Yellow Pages: By Artistic Discipline

Can You Say Monet? I Knew You Could

As if new parents didn't have enough to worry about, here's something else to keep them tossing in their sleep. According to some experts, your baby may not be getting enough artistic stimulation. What's a parent to do? Before you set Junior in front of the TV to watch *Inspiration of Painting with Jerry Yarnell*, you first might want to check out the Baby's Art Gallery on the Web.

Infants exposed to high-contrast images, like those available here, throughout their early months show increased weight and height, as well as improved muscle coordination and self-esteem. Young infants are strongly drawn to black-and-white images in their first six months. These images were created with just that in mind.

They're never too young to start appreciating the arts.

How

World Wide Web

Where

www.infohaus.com/access/by-seller/Babys_Art_Gallery

Coloring the Information Highway

Kids love computers at least as much as they love to color, so combining the two was about as natural as combining peanut butter and chocolate—or in my daughter's case, ketchup and anything.

9

It's never been so easy to stay within the lines.

Here's an online coloring book that lets kids color up to six different drawings with the click of a mouse. Simply select a color, then point and click to fill in each area. When the drawing's finished, you (or preferably your kids) can print it or save and download it as a GIF.

How

World Wide Web

Where

robot0.ge.uiuc.edu/~carlosp/color/

The pictures used here were taken from Coloring Book 3.0 for the Mac, which can be downloaded from this site (coloring-book-30.hqx). Who say's there's nothing for Mac users out there?

Don't forget that the Big Three online access services—America Online, CompuServe, and Prodigy—all provide Internet access, including the World Wide Web. To access the Web, log on to your service, then:

AOL—Keyword *Web* from the Go To menu
CompuServe—Go *Web*
Prodigy—Jump *Web*

Clipping Away

If the only thing keeping you from becoming a great artist is the fact that you couldn't draw a straight line to save your life, have no fear. This is the computer age, where clip art is king. So if you can't be a great artist, you can at least fool your friends, provided they're gullible enough.

Now isn't that pretty?

These collections of clip art may not turn your boring word-processing documents into masterpieces, but they'll definitely help dress them up. You'll find hundreds of images on every conceivable subject, and then some. Some of these freeware images are a little strange, bordering on rejects from a Rorschach test. Others are a lot of fun and will go a long way toward sprucing up your documents. You'll have to decide which is which.

How
FTP

Where
ftp.csusm.edu

Go To
pub/winworld/graphics

Download
clipart.zip (695 K)
cliplib1.zip (363 K)
cliplib2.zip (939 K)

Sign Here, Please

If you consider large, obnoxious billboards to be works of art, then you'll think you're riding on the Freeway to Heaven at this site. While it doesn't have billboards in the usual sense, it does let you create huge, multiple-line

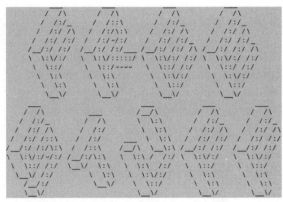

Annoy your friends by attaching a customized signature to your email messages.

messages and designs called "signatures" that many of the more obnoxious Internet correspondents include at the end of way too many E-mail messages. Having said that, I shudder at the thought of what I'll be finding in my E-mailbox. So much for honesty.

Simply enter your text and select a design. This free service does the rest and even lets you copy the results to your computer. Is this really art? I guess it depends on your definition. If you consider art to be novel, fun, and just a little annoying, this site's right on the mark.

How

World Wide Web

Where

www.inf.utfsm.cl/cgi-bin/figlet

Double Vision

If you barely survived the random-dot stereogram craze with your vision intact, here's a freeware program that will finish you off. With RanDot 1.1, you can create your own stereograms for viewing online or for printing.

Similar to many drawing programs, RanDot lets you choose shapes, text, fonts, and more to include in your masterpieces, then generates a stereogram at the click of a mouse. The documentation's a little fuzzy—pun

Stereogram extraordinaire created by the author.

intended—but play around with it and in no time you'll be as cross-eyed as the rest of us. Next stop, the optometrist!

How

FTP

Where

oak.oakland.edu

Go To

pub3/simtel-win3/graphics

Download

randot11.zip (247 K)

Fancy Fonts for Fun and Fame

Personally, I've never paid too much attention to the type of font my word processor is using, but I'm told that many people take this seemingly trivial thing *very* seriously. I guess it's not what you say or how you say it, but how it looks once it's on paper.

The graphic arts crowd will appreciate getting its collective hands on the fonts available here. And don't look for any run-of-the-mill fonts stored

either. Instead you'll find fonts with names like Wilshire, Sling, and Paghetti, and, as they say, much, much more.

These hard-to-find TrueType fonts designed specifically for the professional graphics artist will turn your common piles of papers into first-rate posters, brochures, and promotional letters, not to mention they'll make your teeth whiter and make you more popular with the opposite sex. Who could pass up such a deal?

How

FTP

Where

ftp.csusm.edu

Go To

pub/winworld/ttfonts

Download

startt.zip (1.3 MB)

 Monster download alert! This is one big file, so keep a good book nearby.

Picture Perfect

The poor but proud connoisseur of the arts will appreciate this site. When it comes to sheer volume, this Gopher archive is hard to beat. You'll find hundreds of images of all types for downloading, viewing, and anything else that comes to mind.

 Remember, shareware is *not* freeware. Try it out, and if you like it, be sure to follow the developer's instructions on how to register the software.

It's like having your own personal art gallery—something I've always dreamed of—but without the armed guards and velvet ropes. The number of allowable connections at one time is limited, so getting in can be a hassle, but it's worth trying until you do.

How

FTP

Where

wuarchive.wustl.edu

Go To

multimedia/images/gif

Also, be sure to view the JPEG and ASCII directories while you're here.

Holy Toledo! Culture Comes to the Heartland

When you think of art don't you immediately think Toledo? I know I do. Surprisingly—at least to those of us who don't know better—the Toledo Museum of Art is considered by many to be one of America's greatest art museums—not to mention one of its best-kept secrets. Until now.

Reap the rewards of accessing the Toledo Museum of Art.

You'll find treasures from ancient Egypt, Greece, and Rome, as well as an exceptional collection of paintings, sculptures, tapestries, and graphic

arts from around the world. Some of the paintings displayed are by such masters as El Greco, Rubens, Van Gogh, Degas, and Monet. So leave the Louvre to the French, and come on over to Toledo.

How

Gopher

Where

Alpha.CC.UToledo.edu

Go To

Campus And University Information

Art Museum—Toledo Museum Of Art

Images

ASCII and You Shall Receive

When it comes to finding the lowest common denominator for art on the Internet, you can't get much lower or more common than ASCII. These "pictures" are made up of letters, numbers, and other keyboard symbols grouped together to depict images ranging from corporate logos, cartoon characters, and even photographs. You'll also find maps, illustrated poems and stories, and much more.

How

Gopher

Where

twinbrook.cis.uab.edu

Go To

The Continuum

The ASCII Art Bazaar

Browse through the ASCII FAQs documents stored here to learn more about ASCII animation.

Virtual Art for Virtual Art's Sake

This electronic sampler of the Krannert Art Museum's permanent collection contains dozens of thumbnail images, including sculptures, paintings, African and Asian art, and Greek and Egyptian pottery, along with detailed information about each exhibit.

In addition, the Krannert Art Museum Explorer takes you on a hyperlinked behind-the-scenes tour of the museum, with in-depth biographies of featured artists and a look at how curators, conservators, art historians, and scientists all work together to learn more about the ancient objects on display and the people who created them.

How

World Wide Web

Where

www.art.uiuc.edu/kam/

Lorado Taft's THE BLIND, on display at the Krannert Art Museum and on the Internet.

FREE $TUFF from the Internet

Link Up to KIDLINK

The KIDLINK Gallery was created to showcase the
artwork of 10- to 15-year-olds from around the world.
While this site primarily houses art created on computers, anything goes—within reason.

Sure, the art displayed here will help your
kids learn about other countries and cultures,
but the bottom line is that it's fun to explore and
link up with other kids around the globe.

**A self-portrait of a budding
artist at KIDLINK.**

How

Gopher

Where

kids.ccit.duq.edu

Go To

KIDART Computer Art Gallery
KIDART Gallery Artworks!

Be sure to explore some of the other links here to learn more about other
KIDLINK projects.

Your Wish Is Granted

The final curtain may soon be closing on the National Endowment for
the Arts, so this entry may be better suited for the *History* section. On the
other hand, nothing ever blazes through the United States Congress, so
the NEA may not be going anywhere anytime soon. Who's to say? One
thing's for certain, though: With over $14 million in grants approved in
1995 for California artists alone, it's obvious I'm in the wrong business.
I'm seriously thinking of becoming a street mime and applying for a
grant of my own.

In the meantime, follow the money while the battle rages on and see
what (at least partially) the fuss and controversy are about. You'll get a

state-by-state breakdown of the most recent grant dollars approved by the NEA and the artists they were awarded to.

How

Gopher

Where

gopher.tmn.com

Go To

Arts Wire

Every Arts Wire Gopher

NEA Grant AWARDS: State by State Listing

What a View

Now that you've downloaded all the great art described in this chapter, you'll probably want to view it. Here are a couple of shareware programs you can check out to make it just a little easier:

- VuePrint for Windows lets you view and convert JPG and GIF images.
- WinJPEG lets you view and convert BMP, GIF, IFF, JPG, PCX, PPM, TGA, and TIF images for Windows. WinJPEG also lets you create slide shows for hands-free viewing.

How

FTP

Where

oak.oakland.edu

Go To

pub3/simtel-win3/graphics

Download

vuepri40.zip (291 K)

winjp276.zip (289 K)

Where to Find Way More Goodies

If you're into astronomy, you can find thousands of images from space. Check out the "Sites and Sounds of Space" and "In a Galaxy Far, Far Away..." topics in the *Science and Nature* chapter.

NWHQ, a hypermedia magazine of art and literature, is available online. It's described in the *Books & Literature* chapter. Also be sure to check out the post-Nagasaki bombing photographs available at *The Nagasaki Journey*, which is mentioned in the *History* chapter.

One of the newest and most interesting art exhibits is "The World's Women On-Line!" This exhibit features images by more than 500 women artists from around the world. You can find it on the Web at www.asu.edu:80/wwol.

If you want to create your own Web page, you'll also want to include some graphics. You'll find lots of images, backgrounds, and icons at these Web sites:
• www.unt.edu/icons.html

• www.jsc.nasa.gov/~mccoy/Icons/index.html

• www.infi.net/~rdralph/icons

To view JPEG, GIF, and PICT images on your Mac, you'll probably want to use JPEG View. You can find out how to download this utility in the *Computers* chapter. For kids who like to draw on the Mac, check out the Kid Pix drawing program described in the "Picture This" section of the *Kid Stuff* chapter. Hundreds of JPEGs, PICTs, GIFs and other artwork are available in Mac compressed format via FTP at ftp.sunet.se:80/ftp/pub/mac/info-mac/art-info/_Graphic.

For free updates to this book via FTP or the Web, go to: coriolis.com

Way More! FREE $TUFF

There are no dull subjects.
There are only dull writers.

H. L. Mencken

Books and Stuff for Writers

The Internet By Any Other Name...

When Paul Black's search for online information on Emily Dickinson came up empty in early 1995, he took matters into his own hands in a serious way. The result: the Emily Dickinson Home Page, with links to many Net resources about the prolific-yet-private poet.

Emily Dickinson Page

Poetess extraordinaire Emily Dickinson, desperately in need of a little sun.

While still in its infancy, this site shows lots of promise in becoming a comprehensive repository of information related to Dickinson's poems, her work, and life. You'll find links to Dickinson mailing lists, archives of her poems, fan clubs, reviews of books by and about her, and more.

How
World Wide Web

Where
lal.cs.byu.edu/people/black/dickinson.html

Down to the CORE

The English poet and critic Samuel Coleridge defined *prose* as words in their best order, and *poetry* as the "best" words in the best order. You'll find both and more in *CORE*, an electronic journal of poetry, fiction, essays, and criticsm.

Each issue is filled with thought-provoking essays, poems, and interviews by some of the brightest up-and-comers on the literary front. While science-fiction buffs will have to stick to *Star Trek* reruns for their literary fill since sci-fi is strictly *verboten* here, other literary buffs won't be disappointed.

How

Gopher

Where

gopher.etext.org

Go To

Zines

CORE_Zine

Honk if You're Horny

Somebody—not me—once said that each generation has its sages. Ancient Greece had Socrates, we have bumper stickers. While you may feel that bumper stickers have as much to do with wisdom as Tang has to do with oranges, others (myself included) beg to differ. What other form of writing allows you to express such profundity in so little space—and can be read while careening along the highway at 60 miles per hour? Taglines—deep and not-so-deep messages, slogans, thoughts, and sayings tacked onto the end of email messages—are the Internet's version of the bumper snicker.

This archive of over 55 *thousand* of the best taglines was collected from email messages zooming along the Information Highway. While billed as a pleasant way to waste an afternoon, it'll take you a lot longer than that to wade through all the info stored here. For those who want the abridged version, try the *Today's 100 Random Taglines* link.

How

World Wide Web

Where

www.brandonu.ca/~ennsnr/Tags/

Don't forget that many Internet addresses are case-sensitive, so be sure to type them *exactly* as shown.

The MacWeek in Review

Ziff-Davis, the publisher of *MacWeek* magazine, can be pretty selective when it comes to doling out free subscriptions. But you don't have to be a manager of a multimillion-dollar computer company to get a *MacWeek* subscription. All you need is a Web browser because the current issue of the magazine is always available on the Web. So now you, too, can keep abreast of the latest events taking place in the Macintosh community.

How

World Wide Web

Where

www.ziff.com/~macweek/

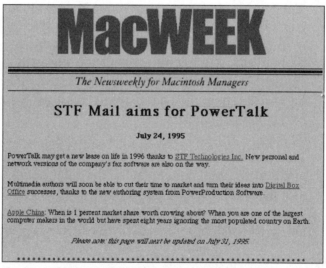

Check out this site to find out whether Apple's having a good week.

All-American Literature

You don't have to be a Native American to enjoy the Native American Literature mailing list. Anyone interested in the culture, history, and politics of American Indians will appreciate the topics covered here.

You'll get the latest information and discussions about any aspect of literature by, about, or for Native Americans. You'll also find great book reviews, information about publications, talks, conferences, and general chit-chat about Native American literature.

How

Email

Where

listserv@cornell.edu

Message

SUBSCRIBE NativeLit-L *Your Full Name*

Greetings from the Web

Did you miss Grandma's birthday again? It may be too late to say it with flowers, but it's never too late to say it in cyberspace, thanks to the Build-A-Card Web site. Build-A-Card lets you create greeting cards online that you can send across the Net to be viewed on the Web.

Follow the instructions to add clip art and text, then save your card as a GIF or send the URL to Grandma and let her view your greeting online.

Is that a slide rule in your pocket or...oh, never mind.

Grandma *does* have Web access, doesn't she? If not, at least now you
know what to get her.

How

World Wide Web

Where

infopages.com/card/

Read 'Em and Weep

Whether you're trying to increase your reading speed, find books to read
online, or keep track of the books in your library, this site has freeware
and shareware to help you out. You'll find dozens of programs, including electronic books, catalogers, poem generators, and more. Has reading always been this fun?

Here's a sampling of what's available:

- *Alice in Wonderland* and *Aesop's Fables* in WinHelp format
- Automatic poem generator
- Booklet printer
- Book cataloging program
- Reading tutor

How

Gopher

Where

gopher.ed.gov

Go To

Educational Software

IBM Computers and Compatibles

Download

ALICE.ZIP

AUTOPOET.ZIP

BOOKLET.ZIP
BOOKLIST.ZIP
READFAST.ZIP

If you're accessing the Internet using a Web browser, don't forget to key in the prefixes *http://* for Web sites, *gopher://* for Gopher sites, and *ftp://* for—you guessed it—FTP sites.

Red Alert for Interactive Publishing

Looking for trends in online publishing? How about exponential, explosive, no-end-in-sight, just-the-tip-of-the-iceberg growth for starters? If you're looking for a little more depth, maybe *Interactive Publishing Alert* is for you. This twice-monthly newsletter tracks recent developments in the electronic newspaper and magazine field, and provides in-depth analysis on the latest online trends.

Each issue addresses such topics as publishing on the Web, online advertising and marketing, and attracting women to online publications. While far from free, this site does offer complimentary highlights and excerpts of current issues.

How

World Wide Web

Where

www.netcreations.com/ipa/

Things That Go Bump in the Night

If you had nightmares after seeing *Casper, the Friendly Ghost*, this site will appeal to you about as much as a date with Linda Blair. If your tastes run more toward *The Amityville Horror*, move a little closer to the campfire and listen up.

Late each night, when the moon is full (and every other night for that matter), you'll hear a scratching on your Internet mailbox where an online ghost story will mysteriously appear. Nobody's sure how they get there, and anyone who has ever tried to find out has never been heard from again. So turn down the lights and get ready to panic as you read these eerie stories by the dim flickering glow of your computer monitor. Did you hear something?

How

Email

Where

ghost-stories-request@netcom.com

Message

subscribe ghost-stories

Net Books, Unofficially Speaking

Just how many different Internet books are there currently in print, anyway? 239 by this list's count, though I'd venture to say that number's pretty conservative. And the number keeps growing—counting this book, there's at least one more on the market. Find out about the latest Net books from this comprehensive-as-they-come list of Internet publications.

You'll find reviews, prices, ordering information, and more at this site, updated monthly or so. If you want the absolutely most recent list, there's information on how you can automatically receive the list via email whenever it's updated.

How

FTP

Where

rtfm.mit.edu

Go To

pub/usenet/news.answers/internet-services/book-list

An Experiment in Creativity

NWHQ, a hypermedia magazine of art and literature, features works from an international range of artists and writers. More than a literary magazine, *NWHQ* is a publication made up *of* independent artists *for* independent artists, and is devoted to free expression and the distribution of artistic ideas. *Suuuure*, you say. And how much is all this free expression gonna cost me? Oh, ye of little faith!

Art or literature? Only the "publishers" know for sure.

Through a match-made-in-heaven collaboration between online artists and creative computer pros, *NWHQ* built this free multimedia gallery of literature that uses the hypertext format of the Web to its fullest. Is it a library or is it an art gallery? I'm still trying to decide.

How

World Wide Web

Where

www.knosso.com/NWHQ/

Write It Down

Who says letter writing is dead? Maybe, as in my case, it's suffering from a state of seriously prolonged unconsciousness, but don't go burying something when there's still a pulse. If your letter writing habit is terminally ill, here's a program that might put a little life back into it.

While Envelope & Stationery Graphics Designer 1.0 won't write thank-you letters for you (maybe in the upgrade), it *will* let you customize your letterheads to create fun, wild, and wacky stationery that's something to write home about.

How

FTP

Where

ftp.csusm.edu

Go To

pub/winworld/labels

Download

ffdelp.zip (553 K)

He's a Poet and Doesn't Know It

It used to be that struggling writers had few outlets for their work. Short of the local coffee house, where they were almost guaranteed to receive a face-to-face encounter with humility—hold the diplomacy—wannabe poets and authors had very few venues for sharing their creations with the public.

Ah, the Internet—and the Patchwork mailing list in particular—comes to the rescue. Patchwork was created to give writers a vehicle for sharing their poems and prose with the rest of the world. Subscribers are encouraged to post their original works to the group, many of which will respond with comments and suggestions.

Anything goes, but members are asked to keep their submissions clean, which rules out my recurring Heather Locklear/Eggo Frozen Waffle dream. I guess you'll just have to wait for the movie.

How

Email

Where

patchwork-request@nox.cs.du.edu

Message

subscribe *address, if different than one used to send request*

Remember, shareware is *not* freeware. Try it out, and if you like it, be sure to follow the developer's instructions on how to register the software.

Dear Diary

Diaries aren't just for young girls to record who's the cutest boy in the fifth grade. My grandfather kept a diary religiously for over 30 years. What probably seemed to him at the time as nothing more than brief synopses on the happenings of a typical day, were to me fascinating glimpses into the life and times of a man I would otherwise not have known very well.

These days, you don't have to put your thoughts on paper; there are several E-diaries you can use to record your own thoughts, experiences, and observations. Here are a couple to try out:

- Daily Notes for Windows 1.3
- Dear Diary 2.6

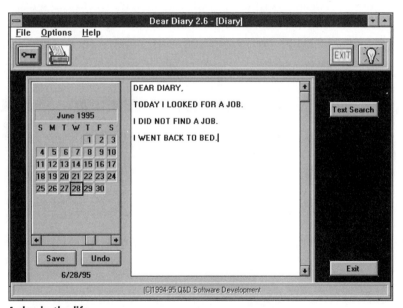

A day in the life.

Dear Diary comes with password protection—sort of an online version of a lock and key. Remember, though, forgetting the password could mean losing your entries, so be careful.

How

FTP

Where

ftp.csusm.edu

Go To

pub/winworld/pim

Download

am_dn13.zip (184 K)

diary26.zip (659) K)

Point, Click, Read

These electronic books may be hard to curl up with, but they're certainly fun to read. Much more than being electronic files of your hardcopy favorites, these classics were created in WinHelp format, which takes advantage of Windows hypertext links to allow you to move through the

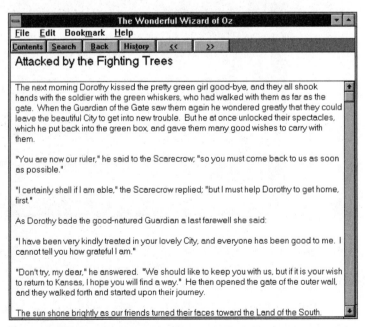

Dorothy and the Scarecrow are off to see the Wizard on the Internet.

stories in a nonlinear fashion to help you find specific passages in a pinch. Classic literature enters the 21st century—500 pages, no waiting!

Some of the books included here are *The Wizard of Oz*, *Aesop's Fables*, and *The Devil's Dictionary* (Ambrose Bierce would have no doubt considered the Internet to be the electronic manifestation of the devil—in short, he would have loved it.)

How

FTP

Where

gatekeeper.dec.com

Go To

pub/micro/msdos/win3/misc

Download

devils10.zip (376 K)

wizard.zip (102 K)

aesop12.zip (335 K)

A Bookworm's Golden Apple

If Aristotle or Hippocrates were alive today, don't you wonder what they would say about archives like this one at Virginia Tech, which gives you such quick access to their works? Oh, you'd probably hear something like *"If we had faster modems and more RAM, it wouldn't take us so long to download these stupid @#$% files!"* Philosophers are *never* satisfied, and always a little testy.

In addition to essays by these great thinkers, you'll find hundreds of articles, poems, and books by such writers as Yeats, Poe, and Thoreau, as well as over a hundred others.

How

Gopher

Where

gopher.vt.edu

Go To

Information for Students

Electronic Books

Don't Be So Literal!

There are Pulitzer prizes for journalism, literature, and music, so don't you think the Pulitzer committee should start handing them out for Internet books? When they do, I'll be ready to pick up my check—or maybe it'll be a debit. Anyway, I hope the ceremony doesn't conflict with my Nobel Peace Prize ceremony. Hah! You laugh *now!*

Regardless of the winner, here's where you can read all about the major literary prizes. There are lists of Pulitzer, American Fiction, Booker, Whitbread, and Nobel Prize winners for literature. Those who aren't faithful followers of fine fiction and nonfiction might think these lists should win the Nobel Prize for Useless Trivia, but if you appreciate a good book, you'll want to check these out and make sure you didn't miss any of them the first time around.

How

Gopher

Where

simon.wharton.upenn.edu

Go To

Lit Lists

The Media Circus Is in Town

Whether you want to email the *Anchorage Daily News* to complain about grizzly bears in your garbage cans or *Macworld* about bugs in your programs, The Media List is your one-stop directory for email addresses to major and minor media outlets.

You'll find hundreds of listings for newspapers, magazines, TV and radio stations, and other media venues you can gripe to electronically. Be sure to include your name, snail-mail address, and phone number if you want a publication to print your letter. To paraphrase Hemingway, the joy is not in griping, it's in having griped.

How

Gopher

Where

farnsworth.mit.edu

Go To

Digital Information Infrastructure Guide (DIIG)

DIIG: Interesting and Useful NII Information

A List of all known email addresses of Media organizations on the Net

If you'd rather receive the list and updates automatically via email, write to *majordomo@world.std.com* with the message *subscribe medialist*.

That Sounds Familiar

John Bartlett must have been the world's greatest eavesdropper, and this site proves it. You'll find thousands of familiar and not-so-familiar quotations by history's greatest writers, thinkers, and philosophers.

The best site on the Internet for finding just the right phrase, but don't quote me on that.

Bartlett spent a lifetime compiling these passages, phrases, and proverbs from ancient and modern literature and tracing them to the mouths and pens of hundreds of sources, including Socrates, Elizabeth Browning, and Daniel Webster. Wouldn't it have been easier just to paraphrase?

How

World Wide Web

Where

www.columbia.edu/~svl2/bartlett/

E-Zine Along on the Internet

Tired of stealing outdated back issues of magazines from your doctor's office previously read by God knows who? You'd better try this site. While it may not include the most popular magazines you've ever read, the text is at least guaranteed to be noncontagious, which is more than you can say about that dog-eared copy of *Field and Stream* you picked up in the waiting room.

Look for current and back issues from some of the best and most bizarre ezines on the Net. I guarantee you won't find these on the local magazine stand. Here are a few examples:

- *Britcomedy Digest*
- *Cat Machine*
- *The Celebrator Beer News*
- *geekgirl*
- *The Interactive Yellow Pages*

How

Gopher

Where

gopher.etext.org

Go To

Zines

ze-zine-list

Blistering Bookworms

Okay, maybe I need to get out more, but to me, few things are better than the feeling you get from devouring a great book. And when I find out that the author has several others waiting on the shelf for dessert—well, don't get me started. Here's a mailing list for avid readers like *moi* to exchange lists of their favorite and least favorite books and authors. While individual books aren't discussed here, you will find other bookworms who have the same literary sweet tooth as you.

How

Email

Where

majordomo@world.std.com

Message

subscribe blister

Where to Find Way More Goodies

For more reading material online, look for *ArtCom* magazine mentioned in the *Arts* chapter, *Careers* magazine mentioned in the *Business and Careers* chapter, the *Congressional Quarterly* and *Washington Weekly* mentioned in the *Government and Politics* chapter, and *Science Magazine*, mentioned in the *Science and Nature* chapter. Also be sure to check out *The Word Detective*, a bimonthly newsletter covering the origins of words in a fun and light way, mentioned in the *Languages and Linguistics* chapter.

If you're interested in writing for children, be sure to check out the Children's Writing Resource Center, mentioned in the *Kid Stuff* chapter. If you just want more information on helping your children learn to read, visit The Media Literacy Project, mentioned in the *Education* chapter.

MacShareNews, a guide to shareware and other Macintosh information, is mentioned in the *Computers* chapter. Another good resource for Mac users is TidBITS magazine, mentioned in the *Internet Resources* chapter.

For free updates to this book via FTP or the Web, go to: coriolis.com

Way More!
FREE $TUFF

This is the only country in the world where businessmen get together over twenty-dollar steaks to discuss hard times.

Honey Green, on the United States

Business and Careers

The Internet Is Now Hiring

Hey, whaddaya doing sitting around reading this when there's work to be done? Then again, if you're having trouble finding work to be done, maybe *Career Magazine* can help. *Career Magazine*, an interactive networking resource for the '90s, is designed to meet

CAREER MAGAZINE **helps job hunters in the '90s.**

the individual needs of job seekers, human resource managers, and career-minded professionals.

Some of the features of this online career resource include:

- A fully customizable job-searching database, with hundreds of new professional, technical, and managerial job openings daily
- Detailed company profiles
- Interactive forums that provide a way for job seekers and employers to meet online
- News and feature articles for job seekers
- Classifieds of employment and career management products and services, as well as a directory of executive recruiters—searchable by industry.

How

World Wide Web

Where

www.careermag.com/careermag/

If you're using Netscape (version 1.0 and higher) to browse the Web, you can save yourself some keystrokes by skipping the *http://* prefix. Netscape assumes that if there's no prefix, you're accessing the Web.

Get Back on Schedule

Your restaurant cashier has a dentist appointment and the cook needs to pick the kids up from daycare. What's a manager to do? There's not much you *can* do except put on the apron and get in there yourself. And who said owning your own business wasn't glamorous?

Maybe Scheduling Employees for Windows won't help you much this time, but it just might help you avoid these kinds of conflicts in the future. This application is designed to help managers schedule workers and monitor time and wages. You can even display graphs detailing the time and wages for each employee.

With Scheduling Employees, you can enter up to 100 workers per department, with up to 99 departments. That's a total of 9,900 employees that you can track. Whew! If you ever need to deal with *those* kinds of numbers, write to the program's author and maybe he'll send you a free bottle of Rolaids (but don't count on it).

How

FTP

Where

ftp.csusm.edu

Go To

pub/winworld/calendar

Download

sew200.zip (350 kilobytes)

Whoz on First?

Most contact databases that I've seen for the Mac are either professional packages or require Hypercard. WHOZ-WHO is a new contact database for the Mac that's attractive, easy-to-use, and *fast*. This shareware program is independent of Hypercard, and lets you search for names, addresses, or virtually any text that might appear in a record. You can also

sort the database by different fields, print selected records, and enter memos or reminders for each contact record.

The author has written three versions—one for gray-scale PowerBooks, one for Power Macs, and one for 68000 Macs and color PowerBooks— so you can download the version that's tailor-made for your system.

How

FTP

Where

micros.hensa.ac.uk

Go To

micros

mac

finder

a

a195

Download

a195whoz-who-101-gs.hqx (805 K—for gray-scale PowerBooks)

a195whoz-who-101-ppc.hqx (1 MB—for Power Macs)

a195whoz-who-101.hqx (800 K—for 68000 Macs and color PowerBooks)

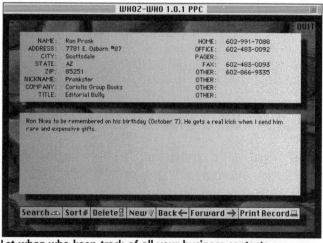

Let whoz-who keep track of all your business contacts.

Give Your Business the Internet Advantage

How well you succeed in business usually depends on how well you know your competition, not to mention what you know about your market that your competition *doesn't* know. More than ever before, success these days depends on information. Many businesses are now logging onto the Internet to get the valuable information they need to stay ahead of the other guys.

The Internet Business Advantage mailing list is a great intro to using cyberspace to help your business. In addition to valuable discussions about how the Internet can help your business succeed, IBA also serves as a daily business newswire, reporting high-quality, hard-hitting information about all aspects of online commerce. If you don't subscribe to IBA, you can bet that one of your competitors does.

How
Email

Where
info@wentworth.com

Message
subscribe iba *your e-mail address*

Your Best Bet for Job Searches on the Net

In case you haven't figured this out yet, let me be the first to break it to you: The Internet can be confusing. No, really, it's true. Combine with that the frustration and pressure that comes with searching for a job and you're really dealing with a mess. *Job Search and Employment Opportunities: Best Bets from the Net* can help. This comprehensive online resource guide is designed to cut through the confusing and sometimes overwhelming amount of information about job opportunities and employment found on the Internet.

Best Bets from the Net will show you where to get the latest job postings, places to submit your resumé electronically, and career information resources that are available to help you plan and execute a successful job

search. If you're new to the Net, this guide will also help get you started with information about the most common Internet tools, and will give you some tips on navigating through the maze of information that's available.

How

Gopher

Where

una.hh.lib.umich.edu

Go To

inetdirsstacks

Job Searching & Employment

Look Inside Your Mailbox

Ah, newsgroups and mailing lists: The heart of the Internet. Regardless of your interests, you can bet there's something here for you. Here's a sampling of mailing lists you can subscribe to if you want to share your business-related problems and solutions:

Biz-Wire addresses issues involving business and the creation of businesses. All aspects of commercial endeavors are welcome, as are announcements and press releases.

How

Email

Where

listserv@ais.net

Message

subscribe BIZ-WIRE *Your Name*

Internet Advertising is a forum for business people interested in learning new ways to advertise on the Internet.

Where

listserv@netcom.com

Message

subscribe internet-advertising *your_email_address*

Job List is used for posting and reading entry-level jobs from companies, government agencies, and universities for college graduates. Multi-level marketing companies, franchise opportunities, and third-party recruiters need not apply.

Where

listserv@sun.cc.westga.edu

Message

subscribe job-list *Your Name*

Moonlight 1 is for those night owls interested in moonlighting from home using their computer. Topics include operating a business on a shoestring, starting up a business, and dealing with home-office issues. In addition, *Moonlight With Your PC*, a free electronic newsletter on the How-Tos of successful moonlighting, goes out to the list once a week.

Where

listserv@netcom.com

Message

subscribe moonlight-l

That's Classified Information

No one will deny that thousands of jobs, services, and products are advertised on the Internet, but what good does all this do if you can't find the listings? Between the hundreds of newsgroups and commercial sites containing all this information, it's amazing anybody ever finds what they're looking for.

Don't forget that many Internet addresses are case-sensitive, so be sure to type them *exactly* as shown.

Finally, though, the classifieds are entering the computer age via the Internet. Here's a mailing list that lets you decide what kinds of ads you'll receive. Unlike a traditional mailing list, you can customize the types of messages that are sent to your address. Just follow the instructions below to choose the categories you're interested in, and you'll only receive ads matching those categories. Here's a list of categories to choose from:

Employment
D01-Other
D02-Permanent Jobs
D03-Temporary Jobs
D04-Seasonal Jobs

Business Opportunities
B01-Other
B02-Multi-Level Marketing (MLM)
B03-Franchises
B04-Distributorships

Home Services
C01-Other
C02-Repair/Contractors
C03-Cleaning
C04-Nanny
C05-Gardening/Landscape
C06-Moving

Business Services
A01-Other
A02-Telecommunications
A03-Instruction
A04-Legal Services
A05-Resumes
A06-Translation
A07-Consulting

Computers
F01-Other
F02-Hardware

F03-Software
F04-Printers
F05-Monitors & Video
F06-Modems
F07-BBS & Web Site
    Announcements

Animals
G01-Other
G02-Pets
G03-Livestock

Real Estate
H01-Other
H02-Houses
H03-Apartments
H04-Commercial

Autos & Vehicles
I01-Other
I02-Automobiles
I03-Motorcycles
I04-Trucks/Trailers
I05-Boats

Audio & Video
J01-Other
J02-Cameras & Camcorders
J03-Stereo Equipment
J04-TVs
J05-VCRs

General Merchandise
K01-Other
K02-Furniture
K03-Jewelry
K04-Clothing
K05-Exercise Equipment
K06-Antiques & Collectibles

Personals
E01-Other
E02-Men Seeking...
E03-Women Seeking...

Miscellaneous
L01-Other
L02-Airline Tickets
L03-Event Tickets

How

Email

Where

pangaea@eworld.com

Message

#subscribe
#category xxx,yyy,zzz

Make sure you only list the category ID numbers (not the actual category names). You may subscribe to as many categories as you wish. Here's an example of what should go in the message body:

#subscribe
#category a05,b03,c02

It's Gonna Cost Me How Much?!

The sticker price doesn't look too bad, and you might be able to squeeze the monthly payments into your budget, but how much is that new car *really* going to cost you? Crunch the numbers and find out with the Annual Percentage Rate Program for DOS.

You'll get a breakdown of the way the monthly payments combined with the accruing interest jack up the total cost. After you've put your eyeballs back into their sockets, maybe you'll realize this isn't such a good deal after all.

```
                        DISCLOSURE INFORMATION
            AMOUNT FINANCED          =        10,000.00
            FINANCE CHARGE           =           800.00
            TOTAL OF PAYMENTS        =        10,800.00

 PMT STREAM
   NUMBER          PMT AMOUNT        NO. OF PMTS        PDS - DAYS
 _____       _____        _____        _____
     1              300.00               36                1        0


          ┌─────────────────────────────────────────────────────┐
          │   ANNUAL PERCENTAGE RATE   =      5.0648 %            │
          └─────────────────────────────────────────────────────┘

    VIOLATION    The APR is overstated by:                2.4352 %


          Do you wish to calculate another APR (y/n/p=print)?   y
```

Read the fine print and don't sign anything until you've run the numbers through this APR calculator.

The software package also includes a real-estate construction financing program in case you don't want to live in your new car.

How

Gopher

Where

gopher.ed.gov

Go To

Educational Software

IBM Computers and Compatibles

Download

apr32.zip (121K)

The files here are compressed, but might not include the ZIP extension. Not to worry; simply rename the files with .ZIP tacked onto the end (for instance, calendem.zip) and they'll unzip fine. There are dozens of other programs stored here, as well. Read the Directory of Contents located at this site for more details.

If you're accessing the Internet using a Web browser, don't forget to key in the prefixes *http://* for Web sites, *gopher://* for Gopher sites, and *ftp://* for—you guessed it—FTP sites.

Business Bests

There are plenty of "Best of the Internet" lists spread across the Web to help you find the wildest, weirdest, and most controversial cybersites. But knowing the best place to download recipes or audio clips of punk bands isn't going to help the bottom line of your business.

Here's a site devoted to finding and reporting the best business-related Internet sites. With such categories as Government, Manufacturing, and International Business, this site is devoted to serious professional material. In short, you won't have to wade through garbage to get to the valuable information you need to maximize your business use of the Net.

There are also notes on all resource links, so you won't have to access each link to find out if it's for you. You'll also find some fun leisure links and information on globetrotting. C'mon, it can't be *all* work and no play.

How

World Wide Web

Where

kronos.twsu.niar.edu/cta/saleem.htp

Go Figure

When it comes to finding great try-before-you-buy business software, you can't go wrong on the Net. And here's proof: Judy's TenKey, a flexible online calculator, will make your Windows calculator look like an electronic abacus.

Judy's TenKey includes a scrolling tape to record your calculations, which you can save, print, and resize. You can also modify tape entries—causing the tape to recalculate—or reuse previous entries in new calculations. Plus, the display is fully customizable, so you can optimize it to fit your needs.

And it's easy to calculate monthly payments, expected investment growth, inflation adjustment, and more. The scrolling tape feature is perfect for statistical calculations, including average values, sums, or even standard deviations (as opposed to your substandard deviations—who says I didn't pay attention in algebra?).

How

FTP

Where

ftp.csusm.edu

Go To

pub/winworld/calculat

Download

10key301.zip (183 kilobytes)

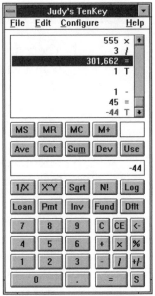

It all adds up: The Net is the place to find great business software.

This site includes dozens of other calculators of all types. Read the calculat.ndx file for more information.

Track That Package

With more than 3 billion parcels and documents delivered annually worldwide, United Parcel Service is the world's largest package distribution company. And, they're taking their business into cyberspace.

The UPS Web site lets users download rate charts, track packages, and get information about all the services offered. Internauts can also access press releases, get email addresses for online customer service, and read up on the history of UPS and what's to come.

How

World Wide Web

Where

www.ups.com/

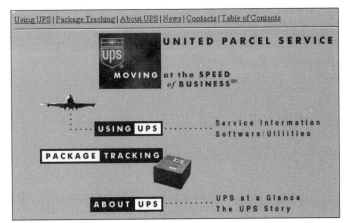

UPS, the tightest ship on the Internet.

That's an Order

Wasn't that package supposed to be here today? Or was it tomorrow? Or did I forget to order it in the first place? Help! If you get confused trying to remember the whos, whats, whens, and wheres of your business orders, OnOrder for Windows can help. OnOrder tracks your orders so you'll always know what packages to expect and when to expect them. Plus, OnOrder helps blaze the paper trail by printing envelopes, labels, and reports.

Also at this site, you can download a copy of Invoice-It, which you can use to create sales invoices.

How
FTP

Where
ftp.csusm.edu

Go To
pub/winworld/database

Download
onord10.zip (67 kilobytes)

invit200.zip (75 kilobytes)

OnOrder helps you keep your shipments straight.

Psst, What's the Password?

ATMs use them, long-distance companies have them, even my garage door needs one. I'm talking about access codes, of course, and they're a staple of life these days. Without the right access code at an ATM, for instance, you might as well have a zero balance in your checking account. And these days, more and more companies are using access codes and passwords to protect sensitive data stored in their spreadsheet programs.

So what happens when you forget your password? I can't help you with your checking account, but at least there's some hope for your spreadsheets. Here's a program to help you recover lost passwords for your Excel, QuattroPro, and 1-2-3 spreadsheets.

Remember, shareware is *not* freeware. Try it out, and if you like it, be sure to follow the developer's instructions on how to register the software.

How

FTP

Where

gatekeeper.dec.com

Go To

/pub/micro/msdos/win3/excel

Download

excrak.zip (272 kilobytes)

Cyberspace Is Open for Business

The fact that information can make or break a business is nothing new, but the speed at which we can gather information *has* undergone a revolution. It's not necessarily what you know, but *when* you know it. Here's a Gopher site that offers links to many valuable business resources on the Net to help you get the information you need—fast. Some of the links include:

- Babson College - Entrepreneurship Gopher
- Bureau of Labor Statistics
- Business & Economic Information
- Business Sources on the Net
- Consumer Product Safety Commission
- National Trade Data Bank
- Small Business Administration
- Social Security Administration
- Dept Commerce Economics and Statistics Administration

How

Gopher

Where

gopher.well.sf.ca.us

Go To

Business in Cyberspace: Ventures (and Resources) on the Matrix

Reprints, Reminders, and Resumés

Here's a variety of programs and utilities to help you organize your business, your life, your universe. They'll also help you keep in contact with your clients, and—when the stress gets to be too much—create and update your resumé.

- **Rockford 3.5** is an easy-to-use shareware program that helps you design and print business cards. While you're here, be sure to download a copy of BusinessCard for Windows to help you organize and keep track of your contacts' business cards.
- **Remind** is a freeware utility that lets you display reminder messages when you start Windows.
- **The Right Resumé** helps you create top-notch, one-of-a-kind, all-powerful, smokin' resumés and cover letters.

How
FTP

Where
ftp.csusm.edu

Go To
pub/winworld/pim

Download
bcr220.zip (181 K)
rckfrd35.zip (202 K)
remind25.zip (55 K)
trr10a.zip (1.1 MB)

Bank-CD Rate Scanner

When you're considering purchasing a CD, where do you go to get the best rate? With rates changing continually as banks and other financial institutions jockey for position, your guess is as good as mine. But why guess? Now, shopping for the best CD rate is easy, thanks to the Internet and the Bank-CD Rate Scanner. This Web site gives you up-to-the-minute rates on CDs being offered around the U.S., and even provides links to FDIC-insured suppliers.

Rates vary across the country and can change at any time, depending on a bank's need for deposits, so no individual bank offers the best rate all the time. With the Bank-CD Rate Scanner, you can travel the country to find the highest rates—all without leaving your computer.

How

World Wide Web

Where

www.wimsey.com/~emandel/

Where to Find Way More Goodies

The Optimist mailing list provides listings of available positions around the U.S., with special emphasis in the Silicon Valley and Multimedia Gulch areas of California. Look for it in the *Computers* chapter.

If your business engages in international commerce, you might want to download Metric Conversions, a software package that does just that. Look for it in the *Education* chapter, which also tells you how to get a free copy of the *Money For College Directory*. The Women Undergrads in Computer Science Web site, also mentioned in the *Education* chapter, is devoted to giving women the resources they need to learn more about undergrad and graduate degrees in computer science, and describes internships and scholarships available.

The FinanceNet Gopher site provides daily listings of government assets for sale, including aircraft parts, office furniture, communications and lab equipment, automated data processing equipment, and more. It's described in the *Government and Politics* chapter, which also tells you how to access the Federal Deposit Insurance Corporation site for information on institutions insured by the FDIC, regulations governing which deposits are insured, consumer-oriented publications, and lots of statistics.

Be sure to see the *Internet Resources* chapter to find out about the Internet FAX Server, which allows you to send faxes around the world, for free.

If you do business abroad, make sure to review the *Languages and Linguistics* chapter, which tells you where to find dozens of software packages designed to help you learn foreign languages. And the *Travel* chapter provides several resources for helping you travel abroad, especially the Commercial Airlines of the World Web page, which keeps you abreast of goings-on in the airline industry.

For free updates to this book via FTP or the Web, go to: coriolis.com

Way More! FREE $TUFF

A computer lets you make more mistakes faster than any invention in human history—with the possible exceptions of handguns and tequila.

Mitch Ratcliffe, Technology Review

Computers

Don't Change That Channel

With over 30 gigabytes of files, 130 phone lines, and 15,000 users, Channel 1 is one of the largest BBSs in the United States. Now Internauts can save themselves a long-distance call by accessing this huge collection of information through the Web or by FTP.

Once you log into this Web site, just click on *BBS* to register. Don't worry, there's no charge for using the site up to 30 minutes per day. If you want more, there's plenty of pricing information. Also, be sure to click on FTP to download some of the utilities, games, and programs available to PC and Mac users alike.

How

World Wide Web

Where

www.channel1.com/

If you don't have a Web link, you can FTP to Channel 1 at ftp.channel1.com. Go to the /pub subdirectory and you'll find lots of free software to download.

Don't touch that dial! You're tuned into Channel 1.

Bite Into This Apple

At first, this site didn't look like it had much to offer. In fact, it had all the makings of a big letdown. But the Apple Support and Information FTP site contains loads of help, therapy, and rehabilitation in the form of patches for dysfunctional Mac programs, utilities, and their users. So much for first impressions.

You'll find plenty of software updates, press releases, and product information here. There's also lots of help for developers, as well as a listing of phone numbers—for those moments of frustration when you just *have* to talk to a human being. And when all else fails, follow the FAQ links to get helpful tips on what else this site offers.

How
FTP

Where
ftp.info.apple.com

Go To
Apple.Support.Area

The Information Gateway

Here's a novel idea: If you want the best information about the products you use or are thinking of buying, talk to the people who are already using them. Nah, too obvious. Still, that's the idea behind the Gateway 2000 mailing list.

Created and maintained by those who use Gateway 2000 products, this list discusses the good, bad, and ugly of the products offered by this computer mail-order giant.

How
Email

Where
gateway2000-request@sei.cmu.edu

Message

subscribe gateway2000

 A digest form of this mailing list is also available. See dealer for details, mileage may vary.

Back Me Up

Maybe you're not Evel Knievel, but if you're like most computer hackers, you do play daredevil with your data—and you may not even realize it. It doesn't take much to lose a file, as you've probably already, unpleasantly, discovered. A small power surge—sort of the electronic version of a hiccup—can wreak plenty of havoc. One cup of coffee spilled on your computer is enough to do the damage. Now that's a real java jolt.

Colorado Backup Lite can help you recover from accidents and just plain "how could I have been so stupid" behavior. This Windows backup utility enables you to make quick backups to diskette or tape at the click of

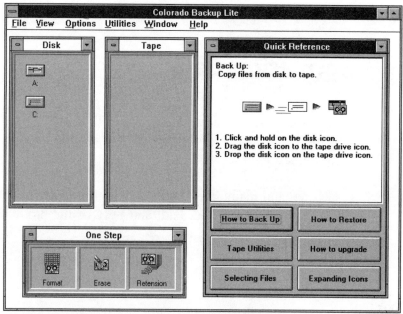

Why take the chance? Back it up with Colorado Backup.

a button. And restoring files is a breeze, too. Of course, you have to actually *run* the program to make it work.

How

FTP

Where

ftp.csusm.edu

Go To

pub/winworld/backup

Download

cbwlite.zip (866 kilobytes)

Feed a Cold, Nuke a Virus

Are you practicing safe computing? If you're downloading files without scanning them for computer viruses, you're walking an electronic tight-rope without a net—make that an ethernet. It doesn't take much to lose everything stored on your computer, and with many viruses, even your backups can be destroyed.

Each year viruses cause businesses around the globe millions of dollars in lost data. If you don't want to become part of these statistics, try one of these virus scanners—before it's too late. These cyberversions of germ warfare will go a long way toward innoculating your computer against serious infection.

Virus scanners search your PC for known and unknown viruses in memory, the partition table, the boot sector, and all subdirectories, as well as your diskettes. Don't ask me how they work; I'd explain it about as well as I'd explain the Polio vaccine. Just be glad they're on the job.

How

Gopher

Where

gopher.ed.gov

Go To

Educational Software

IBM Computers and Compatibles

```
Scanning memory for critical viruses.
Scanning for known viruses.

Directory C:\ contains 23 files.

No viruses found.
```

Just checking. This computer gets a clean bill of health.

Download

scan91.zip (129 kilobytes)

scan95b.zip (145 kilobytes)

If your files don't include the ZIP extension, rename the files when you download them and you won't have any trouble uncompressing them.

Share the News with a Mac User...

One of the overwhelming complaints Macintosh users have is that, when it comes to shareware and freeware programs designed for their systems, the well tends to be pretty dry. Open the floodgates, because now this lament couldn't be less true—as long as you know where to look.

MacShareNews is a free electronic publication that keeps readers abreast of what's happening in the quickly growing market of Mac and Newton (or is that Newt?) shareware.

How

Email

Where

steg@dircon.co.uk

Subject

msn-request

Message

subscribe msn *Your Name*

Don't forget that many Internet addresses are case-sensitive, so be sure to type them *exactly* as shown.

...Or Just Go to the Web

If you start to think that the gatekeepers of Internet software archives have never heard of the Macintosh, you'll feel better after you check out the Web. For instance, the HENSA database provides links to more than 2,000 shareware and freeware programs for the Mac, most of which are utilities and system patches—although you'll find loads of games, screen savers, and educational software here too.

Although you access HENSA using a Web browser, this database is actually a great set of Gopher and other database search utilities for locating Macintosh software. The HENSA database divides its contents into "Finder Software" (whatever *that* means—it has absolutely nothing to do with the Mac OS Finder) and HyperCard stacks. When you click on either of these hypertext links, you'll be given additional options for downloading software.

But your best bet is probably to click on Finder Software and then click on the "Package Code" icon to get a Gopher list of all software folders tracked by the HENSA site. Then read the Full index list file to find programs that you want to download. There, now; don't you feel just a bit more important?

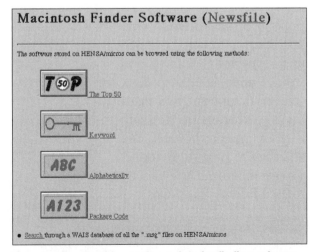

One of many possible starting points for finding software tracked by HENSA.

How

World Wide Web

Where

micros.hensa.ac.uk/micros/mac.html

Go To

Finder Software

HyperCard

The two most popular FTP and Web sites for Mac software are the University of Michigan archives (FTP to mac.archive.umich.edu/mac/ or point your Web browser to www.umich.edu/~archive) and the Stanford University archives (FTP to sumex-aim.stanford.edu/info-mac). But good luck getting into these. Both archives are more popular than your high-school homecoming queen, and the sites limit the number of users who can access them at one time. The HENSA site, on the other hand, is less crowded during U.S. daytimes and just about anything that you can find at the other two sites you can also find here. You can also access HENSA via FTP at: micros.hensa.ac.uk.

Time for a Change

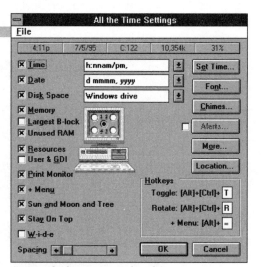

Too much time on your hands?

These days, you'll be hard-pressed to find anyone who just wears a "watch." Instead, they're wearing "information storage units" that keep track of everything from your heart rate to the barometric pressure to your cholesterol level. Oh, and they tell the time, too, if you can figure out how—in up to 24 different time zones.

So why should your Windows clock be any less powerful? All the Time, a freeware replacement for your Windows clock, displays the time and date, monitors your computer's memory and disk space, helps you manage your open applications and printer, and more. It even comes with several different WAV files for its alarm feature. As for checking your cholesterol level...well, you'll have to do that on your own time.

How
FTP

Where
ftp.csusm.edu

Go To
pub/winworld/clock

Download
att33all.zip (412 kilobytes)

Watching the Web

One word you'll never hear anyone use to describe the Web is *stagnant*. To the contrary, the Web is the ultimate "work in progress," and never remains the same even from one hour to the next. On the plus side, that means there's always something new to be discovered; on the downside, there's no guarantee that what you find today will be there tomorrow.

But every obstacle also represents an opportunity—just ask Specter, Inc., makers of WebWatch for Windows. WebWatch helps you keep track of changes in your Hotlist and Bookmark files, as well as any of your other HTML documents, by scanning your documents for links that have changed.

To download a copy, access this site and click on *WebWatch Product Information*. Next, click on *download the 32 bit version* or *download the 16 bit version* to get your own shareware version.

How
World Wide Web

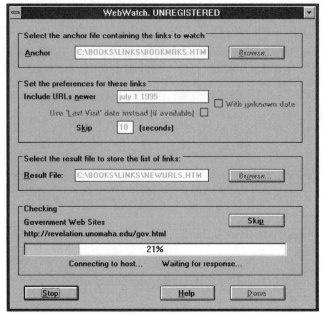

Here today, gone tomorrow. WebWatch will help you keep track of hyperlinks on the Web.

Where

www.specter.com/users/janos/specter

Download

ww10c_16.zip (92 kilobytes)

ww10c_32.zip (132 kilobytes)

The 32-bit version works with Windows 95, Windows for Workgroups 3.11, and Windows 3.1 running Win32s; the 16-bit version works with any Windows 3.x version.

Forever the Optimist

You might think that the Optimist mailing list would be devoted to those who believe the proverbial glass is always half full, but you'd be 100-percent wrong. This list is actually run by a software-design recruitment company that provides listings of available positions around the U.S., with special emphasis in the Silicon Valley and Multimedia Gulch areas of California.

So whether you're interested in programming in Pittsburgh, MIS in Mississippi, or development in Denver, the Optimist mailing list just might provide the hope you need of landing that perfect job.

How
Email

Where
listserv@netcom.com

Message
subscribe optimist-l

Who's Calling, Please?

No computer is an island, at least not if it has a modem. And you probably wouldn't be reading this book if your computer was "online challenged." But these days, modems are for more than transferring files. Some modems even double as answering machines, so now your computer can even help you duck calls. How's that for progress?

But somebody had to take things a step further, and here's the result: Caller ID for Windows lets you assign specific WAV files to different incoming calls, so you'll know who's trying to phone you by the sound of the ring. You can assign one sound file to your office, another to your spouse's work number, another to Erika's Swedish Massage Emporium... let's just say the possibilities are endless. And now you'll always know when your mother-in-law is calling. Had enough? Of course not, so try out some of the other modem programs listed below.

How
FTP

Where
ftp.csusm.edu

Go To
pub/winworld/comm

Download

callerid.zip (1.3 MB)

callid.zip (57 K)

traxx32.zip (355 K)

The Installment Plan

Installing software is relatively easy, but uninstalling can be confusing, tedious, and downright tortuous. And while many programs now come with uninstall features to help clean up the messes they sometimes create in your INI files, they're often far from thorough. After all, what software vendor really wants you to *stop* using their programs?

Inst-all.exe can help. This freeware Windows utility records your system's directory structure and its WIN.INI and SYSTEM.INI files, then compares the originals to the modified versions after you install any new software to make restoring the originals a snap.

How

FTP

Where

oak.oakland.edu

Go To

pub3/simtel-win3/install

Download

instn321.zip (33 kilobytes)

If you're accessing the Internet using a Web browser, don't forget to key in the prefixes *http://* for Web sites, *gopher://* for Gopher sites, and *ftp://* for—you guessed it—FTP sites.

How Slow Can It Go?

Ever have one of those days when your computer system just doesn't seem to have that old "boot up and go"? These system-monitoring utilities won't cure the problem, but they'll go a long way toward helping you diagnose it—just what the doctor ordered:

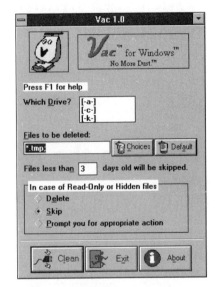

Real-Time Performance Monitor for Windows provides a graphical display of several performance parameters, including:

- Free virtual memory
- Active tasks
- Free system resources
- Free RAM

Vac for Windows is an easy-to-use hard-drive clean-up utility. Just one click and Vac deletes temporary and backup files—or any other files you want to get rid of, for that matter. Vac will also skip new files and system files, and you can configure it to prompt you when it comes across read-only and hidden files. Vac also records the names of files that have been deleted and how much space has been freed.

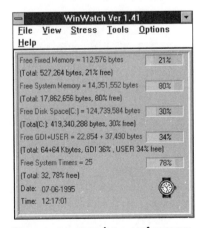

Does your system have performance anxiety? Find out with these handy utilities.

WinWatch displays available Windows resources—like fixed memory, system memory, disk space, system resources, timers, and other important system information and test tools indispensible to Windows programmers.

How

FTP

Where

ftp.csusm.edu

Go To

pub/winworld/memtools

Download

rtpm111.zip (31 kilobytes)

vac101.zip (269 kilobytes)

watch141.zip (251 kilobytes)

Get with the Program

Way back when Bill Gates was just a paltry multimillionaire (I did say *way* back), he and his cohorts whipped together a little collection of programs called Windows. And while there are a lot of devoted Windows users, many others are less than thrilled with the graphical interface. In fact, some of the more masochistic PC users still prefer suffering the pain and humiliation of working in DOS.

If you fall somewhere in between these love-or-hate extremes, check out this site, which contains dozens of replacements and add-ons for the Windows Program Manager.

You'll find utilities for modifying and randomizing your wallpaper, controlling your color schemes, launching programs, changing the startup logo, posting notes on your screen, and oh-so-many more.

How

FTP

Where

ftp.csusm.edu

Go To

pub/winworld/progman

Download

Too many to list. Check out the PROGMAN.NDX file for descriptions of the files.

The Screen You Save May Be Your Own

What's the sense in having windows if you can't dress 'em up? Here's an FTP site with loads of Windows screen savers to make bears dance, your monitor melt, display fireworks that rival a Fourth of July show, and lots more.

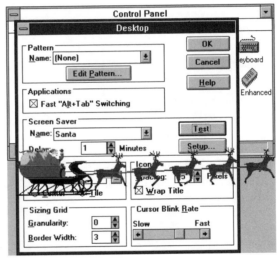

Ho! Ho! Ho! Merry Screen Savers!

How

FTP

Where

ftp.csusm.edu

Go To

pub/winworld/screen_saver

Download

Too many to list. Read the screen_s.ndx file for a complete listing.

71

I Think Icon, I Think Icon

I'll let you in on a little secret. Windows comes with lots of icons that most people don't even know about. In addition to the icons stored in the PROGMAN.EXE file, check out the ones in MORICONS.DLL.

Not a bad start, but for serious iconophiles and icoholics, you can't beat the *thousands* of icons available at this site. You'll find icons for sports nuts, train buffs, and more. There are even icon editors and icon management tools to help you create your own mini works of icon art.

How

FTP

Where

gatekeeper.dec.com

Go To

pub/micro/msdos/win3/icons

Download

Hey, I just work here. You're on your own at this site, although I will tell you to scan through the INDEX file to find out what's available.

Hands Off!

Computers have become such a common fixture in the home these days, families that used to fight over the bathroom now fight over whose turn it is to get online. But how do you keep the kids from fooling around where they don't belong? When you find the ultimate solution, let me know.

I haven't seen any security programs that are 100-percent fool-proof, but here are a few programs that go a long way to solving the problem. These programs enable you to lock others out from different areas of Windows, lock your terminal, and create passwords to keep little hands away from where they don't belong.

How

FTP

Where

ftp.csusm.edu

Go To

pub/winworld/guard

Download

chastity.zip (506 K)

lock.zip (104 K)

metz-lck.zip (218 K)

seclau.zip (42 K)

Zip It Up

Files on the Net are almost always compressed in some format for easier storage and fast downloading. One of the most common compression schemes is the ZIP format used by PKWare's PKZIP and PKUNZIP. But these two compression/uncompression utilities only run from the ancient DOS prompt. No self-respecting Windows user should have to suffer that indignity.

Enter WinZip, which brings the convenience of Windows to ZIP files without requiring PKZIP—WinZip's DOS-based cousin. It features an intuitive point-and-click drag-and-drop interface for viewing, running, extracting, adding, deleting, and testing files in ZIP archives. This is an essential tool for every Internaut running Windows.

How

FTP

Where

ftp.csusm.edu

Go To

pub/winworld/compress

Download

winzip55.exe (283 K)

Essential Macintosh Utilities

Robert Lentz maintains links to some of the best and most up-to-date shareware available for the Macintosh—especially utilities that make Internet and Web surfing easier and more fun. Here you'll find links to Web browsers, movie players, graphics viewers, and more. My picks for some of the essential utilities for Mac users include:

- **Sound Machine** and **SoundApp** allow you to play sound files, including sound links at Web sites. The two programs have different strengths and features, so you should consider downloading and experimenting with both.

- **JPEG View** is the essential graphics viewer for GIF, JPEG, PICT, BMP, and MacPaint files. The Preferences dialog boxes give you dozens of options for viewing and manipulating graphic images.

- **ZipIt** allows you to save and uncompress files in ZIP format. With this utility, Mac users never have to feel left out of the Windows/DOS world of compressed files.

- **uuUndo** Is a fast little utility that decodes the Uuencoded files commonly posted to newsgroups and other Unix servers.

- **Sparkle** lets you view and convert between MPEG and QuickTime movie formats.

How

World Wide Web

Where

http://www.astro.nwu.edu/lentz/mac/net/mac-web.html

Download

Just click on the links to the programs you want to download.

Perhaps the nicest feature about this site is that it's almost always easy to get into, and it constantly sifts through the thousands of available shareware utilities to display links to only the best of the best.

Self-Made Programmers

I recently read a study that ranked occupations in the United States according to pay, stress, danger, work conditions, and chances for advancement. Based on these criteria, the researchers compiled a list detailing the best and worst jobs.

At the bottom of the barrel was lumberjack, with construction workers faring only slightly better. I couldn't find Writer of Internet-Related Books anywhere on the list, although I imagine if there had been such a category, it would have fallen somewhere in the middle—on a good day: The pay's not bad but there's not a lot of room for advancement, and it tends to be rather dangerous around deadline time, depending on the editor.

With that said, guess which occupation was at the top of the list? Would you believe computer programmer? Here's a list that gives programmers the forum to pat each other on their collective backs. The Software Entrepreneurs mailing list is devoted to the interests of software entrepreneurs, including shareware programmers. If you count yourself among this career group, you'll want to subscribe to this list.

How
Email

Where
softpub-request@toolz.atl.ga.us

Message
subscribe entrepreneurs mailing list

Where to Find Way More Goodies

What can I say? Every chapter in this book has something for your computer. In particular, check out the *Internet Resources* chapter for information and software for getting the most out of your Internet online time. The *Government and Politics* chapter also explains how you can download the Terminator file deletion utility, which is similar to an electronic shredder that makes recovering deleted documents virtually impossible. Use this one with caution.

One of the best places to find the most updated Internet and computing resources for the Mac, as well as a great collection of links to other Mac sites, is Ric Ford's MacinTouch Web page. To access it, point your Web browser to www.macintouch.com/~ricford.

For free updates to this book via FTP or the Web, go to: coriolis.com

FREE $TUFF

*I keep trying to think,
but nothin's happenin'!*

*Curly, One quarter of
The Three Stooges*

Education

Have You Converted?

The extent of my knowledge of the metric system is that a 10 K race is a little over 6 miles, 90 kilometers per hour rounds out to about 55 miles per hour, and four liters of beer converts to one heck of a hangover. What more do I need to know?

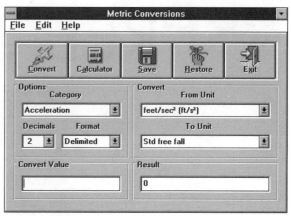

How do you measure up?

If Metric Conversions is any judge, I still have a long way to go. This shareware program will help the metrically challenged, like me, convert mass, volume, acceleration, pressure, velocity, and lots more. You'll even get help converting such non-metric units as fortnights, lunar moons, and horsepower. Talk about your thrill-a-minute shareware. Why didn't I put this in the *Games* section?

How

FTP

Where

ftp.csusm.edu

Go To

pub/winworld/convert

Download

convrt25.zip (72 kilobytes)

> Remember, shareware is *not* freeware. Try it out, and if you like it, be sure to follow the developer's instructions on how to register the software.

If You Can Read This...

Someone once said that getting children to *want* to read is half the battle of educating them. Okay, it was me who said that, but that doesn't make it any less true.

The Media Literacy Project, part of an ongoing research project at the University of Oregon's College of Education, is moving onto the Internet. You'll find valuable information and resources for educators, students, parents, and others interested in electronic media and their influence on children. Here's just part of what's currently available:

- A listing of media-related associations, organizations, and centers
- Schedules for conferences, workshops, and other events related to media literacy
- Programs of academic study or special course offerings related to media study at all levels of education

In addition, there's a huge listing of books, journals, newsletters, media resources, and related Gopher sites.

How

Gopher

Where

Interact.uoregon.edu

Go To

Institutes, Projects and Centers
Media Literacy Project

Your Education's in the Mail

Education by mail. Tell me the truth: Doesn't this concept make you immediately think of a degree in refrigeration repair? Well, you've been watching too much afternoon television. So put the clicker down and pay attention. The Internet includes dozens of electronic mailing lists

devoted to education, none of which has anything to do with your air conditioner. Here's a handful of the best:

Classroom Connect is designed for teachers who use the Internet in the classroom. It lists pointers to online lesson plans, grant resources for bringing telephone lines and computers into schools, education-related projects, and dozens of great Internet sites you can use in the classroom.

How

Email

Where

info@wentworth.com

Message

subscribe crc *your email address*

H-High-S is for high-school teachers, administrators, and other educators interested in tapping into the educational resources available on the Net. This list provides an ongoing discussion of curricula, instructional strategies, and educational resources, with particular emphasis on the use of computers, multimedia, the Internet, and other new technologies.

Where

listserv@msu.edu

Message

subscribe H-High-S *Your Name, Affiliation*

A.Word.A.Day is the online equivalent to the popular calendars/dictionaries cluttering up office desktops. This mailing list automatically sends you an English vocabulary word and definition each day, with the hopes that by year's end you'll be speaking like Winston Churchill—or at least Thurston Howell III.

Where

wsmith@wordsmith.org

Subject

subscribe *Your Full Name*

(The body of your message is ignored.)

GLO (Greek Letter Organizations) discusses issues related to college fraternities and sororities. In addition to history and trivia about the college Greek system, you'll also be subjected to—er, find—lots of information on current issues regarding frats and sororities (or should that be "sors"?).

Where

glo-request@merrimack.edu

Message

subscribe *Your Name, email_address*

home-ed-politics discusses the political issues surrounding home-based education, including federal and state legislation, how public schooling influences teaching in the home, and more.

Where

listproc@mainstream.com

Message

HELP

IAMS (Internet Amateur Mathematics Society) is open to all eggheads and egghead-wannabes that have a soft spot in their craniums for math puzzles and problems.

Where

iams-request@hh.sbay.org

Message

subscribe iams

Don't forget that the Big Three online access services—America Online, CompuServe, and Prodigy—all provide Internet access, including the World Wide Web. To access the Web, log on to your service, then enter:

AOL—Keyword *Web* from the Go To menu
CompuServe—Go Web
Prodigy—Jump Web

Dear Uncle Sam, Send Money

You don't have to be valedictorian of your graduating class or the high-school football star to receive a college scholarship. Actually, those prizes make up only a fraction of the scholarships awarded each year. If your parents are divorced, if you were raised on a farm—even if you can trace your lineage to a cab driver or two—there just might be a scholarship out there with your name on it.

Check out this site to find out how to get a free copy of *Money For College Directory*. This comprehensive guide includes thousands of unusual, little-known, and hard-to-find scholarships, along with instructions on how to apply.

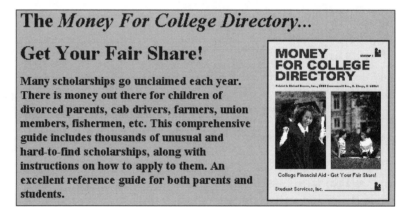

The *Money For College Directory...*

Get Your Fair Share!

Many scholarships go unclaimed each year. There is money out there for children of divorced parents, cab drivers, farmers, union members, fishermen, etc. This comprehensive guide includes thousands of unusual and hard-to-find scholarships, along with instructions on how to apply to them. An excellent reference guide for both parents and students.

The MONEY FOR COLLEGE DIRECTORY is helping make college more affordable for everyone.

How

World Wide Web

Where

www.studentservices.com/mfc/

I Am Woman, Hear Me Code

Women who work in computer science already know what many women currently studying the field may not realize: There ain't many of you out

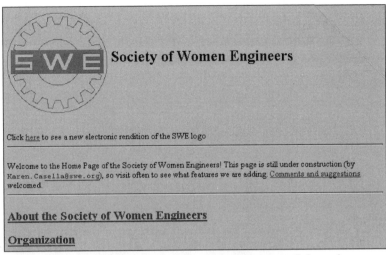

The Society for Women Engineers is just one of the many links at the Women Undergrads in Computer Science Web page.

there. Long dominated by the male species, the computer-science field is now providing skyrocketing job opportunities—especially for women.

Here's a Web site devoted to giving women the resources they need to learn more about undergrad and graduate degrees in computer science, internships and scholarships available, organizations and mailing lists devoted to women in computer science, and lots more.

How

World Wide Web

Where

infomac1.science.unimelb.edu.au/cielle/women/wucs.html

Software 101

For me, getting organized for school was half the battle. The other half consisted of trying to find a date to the prom. Between the two, I had little time for such trivialities as classes and homework. While I doubt the Internet could have helped me with the latter, I definitely could have used it to get my high-school and college acts together.

Here's a site to download lots of shareware for students, including:

Student Organizer is a database that helps you keep track of courses, grades, assignments, and more.

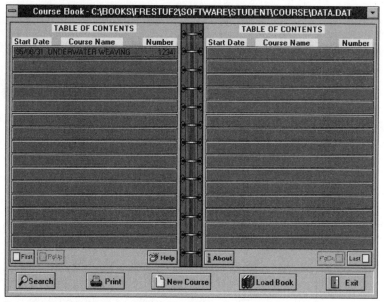

Stay on course with the student organizer.

Math Drill generates 100 math problems that you must complete within a certain time. You can even set it up for different levels and times.

College Bound Advisor is designed to assist the college bound with the countless odds and ends involved in applying for college, financial aid, and more.

How

FTP

Where

ftp.csusm.edu

Go To

pub/winworld/educate

Download

am_so12.zip (407 K)

mathdril.zip (353 K)

wincb21a.zip (968 K)

Gopher a Good Education

Sure, your kid's barely in preschool, but it's never to early to think about how hard it is to afford a good college education. No need to panic, though, if you're already tucking money away for Junior's ultimate education. What, you haven't started?! Okay, start panicking. Once that's out of your system, check out the U.S. Department of Education Gopher site. You'll find lots of information on financial aid and grant programs, free booklets on preparing your kids for college, and much more.

You'll also find helpful information on the Individuals with Disabilities Education Act (IDEA) Amendments of 1995. These amendments are designed to improve IDEA, the 20-year-old law that helps America serve more than 5.4 million children with disabilities.

How

Gopher

Where

gopher.ed.gov

The Internet Angle

Okay, let me see if I got this straight: The geometric mean m of two numbers p and q is such that m^2 equals p times q, and hence m, p, and q are in a geometric progression. Uh oh, I think I just pulled something in my brain. While I'm waiting for the paramedics to arrive, I might as well point out that you can check out The Geometry Forum Web site for more of this kind of enlightening punishment.

Funded by the National Science Foundation, The Geometry Forum serves as a math education center for students around the world. You'll find links to the Problem of the Week, Ask Dr. Math (he's definitely not me),

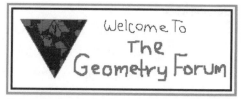

Geometry has never been so fun—and will never be again, I'm afraid.

and newsgroups and mailing lists devoted to geometry. There's also lots of software available to download, links to education resources, and archived mathematics discussions and information. Now, tell me again—the sum of the sides of an equilateral stripogram is directly contortional to the temperature of a cold day in July times the product of....

How

World Wide Web

Where

forum.swarthmore.edu

Education and Disabilities Resource

Equal opportunity for education isn't a privilege, it's a right. Don't let a disability keep you from reaching your highest academic potential. Look to the HEATH Resource Center for help.

This Federal clearinghouse on information about education and persons with disabilities provides up-to-date information on education, training, funding, and legislation for disabled students.

How

Gopher

Where

bobcat-ace.nche.edu

Go To

ACE Departments
HEATH Resource Center

An Apple for the Teacher

The Apple Macintosh is one of the most popular and widely used types of computers in schools—of all levels. And Apple the company knows how important it is to make sure Apple the computer remains an educational mainstay. So the company has

Virtual learning on the Apple Virtual Campus.

created a virtual educational community to help Mac users—both teachers and students—share and exchange educational information.

The Apple Virtual Campus is an offshoot of the company's home page on the Web. It's also a good example of Apple's commitment to education. When you go to this Web site, you'll find links to dozens of resources and other Macintosh user groups that focus on education. An Apple a day really can keep ignorance away.

How

World Wide Web

Where

www.info.apple.com/hed/home.html

The Doctor Is In

Long waits, short visits by doctors, and lousy hospital food were the overwhelming complaints I heard in an informal poll I conducted on American medicine—which consisted of three people, counting myself. Hardly scientific, but what it lacked in accuracy it made up for in falsehoods.

Enter the Association of American Medical Colleges, a non-profit organization committed to improving the nation's health and knowledge of health through the advancement of academic medicine and research.

This comprehensive Gopher site provides access to AAMC publications, newsletters, directories, policy documents, conference announcements, meeting schedules, and more, providing AAMC members with a single, easily accessible entry point to a wide variety of information. It also doubles as a launching ground to other academic medical associations, organizations, educational institutions, and other Internet resources.

How

Gopher

Where

gopher.aamc.org

Now You're Talking

Teachers talk at Teacher Talk.

Ever wonder what teachers talk about when they're not in the classroom? Me neither, but here's a site that will give you a clue, just in case it ever does cross you mind. Teacher Talk, a Web-based conferencing system, is open to K-12 teachers interested in discussing education-related issues with other teachers around the world.

Using one of the most advanced Web-based conferencing systems, Teacher Talk offers users an extremely easy-to-use interface for sharing ideas, engaging in debate, or comparing paychecks with other teachers around the world. Some of the topics discussed in Teacher Talk include:

• School reform
• Parental involvement

- Technology and schools
- Social action and service learning

You can join an existing thread or start your own discussion in the Open Forum area.

How

World Wide Web

Where

www.mightymedia.com/talk/working.htm

Set Me Free

The Internet is the perfect teacher's aide. It doesn't eat much, costs very little, and contains more information than a hundred Libraries of Congress. So whether you teach in a huge metropolitan high school or a one-room rural schoolhouse, the Internet is available to help make information stored around the world accessible to anyone with a computer and a modem.

And with the Free University of Berlin FTP site, you can access a huge assortment of education-related files stored in Germany, including information on physics, mathematics, chemistry, meteorology, geography, computer science, and medicine.

In addition, you'll find educational and not-so-educational games, puzzles, pictures, and utilities for DOS, Windows, OS/2, and the Mac. All work and no play....

How

FTP

Where

ftp.fu-berlin.de

Go To

pub/mac (for Mac users)
pub/pc/msdos (for DOS users)

pub/pc/os2 (for OS/2 users)

pub/pc/win3 (for Windows users)

 If you're on the U.S. side of the Atlantic, this site might move a little slowly, so try to access it during non-peak hours.

That's Not My Department

Whether the U.S. Government's trying to solve the healthcare problem or take over a small country, you can bet the result will be overblown, over budget, and probably not work quite as it was intended. So, I didn't expect much from the Department of Education Gopher site, but I was wrong. This site offers a *huge* collection of shareware and freeware for the Mac, PC, Amiga, and other computers.

How many items constitutes "huge"? Tons. In other words, I don't know. But I do know that you'll run out of disk space long before you even make a dent at this site. (I lost count at around 600 shareware and freeware programs.) While this site is occasionally difficult to get into, be patient and keep trying—preferably in the off-peak hours. The results are well worth it.

How

Gopher

Where

gopher.ed.gov

Go To

Educational Software

Download

Too many to list. Be sure to read the Directory of Contents file here to find out what's available.

 If you're accessing the Internet using a Web browser, don't forget to key in the prefixes *http://* for Web sites, *gopher://* for Gopher sites, and *ftp://* for—you guessed it—FTP sites.

World Wide Web U.

Some of the most memorable events of my college days were those times when I was exposed to students and teachers from different cultures and countries. I had a Spanish teacher from China, an English teacher from France, and a French teacher from Minneapolis. Talk about diversity! I mean, I'd never even *met* anybody from Minneapolis before.

Here's a site that manages to capture a bit of that diversity. You'll find links to hundreds of universities and colleges around the world, including information about the campuses, programs offered, maps, information on different departments, where to write, and much more. There's even a link to St. Mary's College of—you guessed it—Minnesota.

How

World Wide Web

Where

www.mit.edu:8001/people/cdemello/univ.html

CAUSE and Effect

One of the great by-products of the computer revolution is that information that used to take days or even weeks to access is now available instantly. Nowhere is this technology growing faster than in our schools—and it's not just students who are taking advantage of computer technology. Librarians, deans, teachers, and professors are experimenting with the information resources available electronically.

All this makes for a more efficient faculty, right? Sounds good, but, unfortunately, that ain't always the case. Fortunately, organizations like CAUSE are available to help educators learn to manage and use the information resources available to higher education. An international non-profit association, CAUSE is dedicated to enhancing higher education through the effective management and use of information resources.

With over 3,200 members on 1,200 campuses throughout the United States, Canada, and Mexico, CAUSE is promoting more effective planning, management, and evaluation of technology and other information resources in colleges and universities.

Find out more about CAUSE at its Gopher site, including its membership directory, upcoming events, publications, and its resource library.

How

Gopher

Where

cause-gopher.Colorado.EDU

AskERIC and You Shall Receive

When it comes to surfing the Internet, many educators no doubt feel they'll never catch up with their students—and that's just the elementary-school teachers. When it comes to high-school kids, teachers have never stood a chance. Well, maybe help has finally arrived.

The Educational Resources Information Center (ERIC), a federally funded national information system, is helping to level the playing field. AskERIC provides a variety of services and products to educators on a wide range of education-related issues.

If you don't know the answer, you can always AskERIC.

Designed to be used by teachers of all grade levels, AskERIC provides a wealth of information and search utilities, including complete lesson plans, help for rural schools, environmental education, international studies, and much more.

How

World Wide Web

Where

ericir.syr.edu

Learning to Learn Online

Contrary to what Sister Agnes might have had me believe when I attended St. Joseph's Parochial Reformatory as a kid, learning doesn't have to consist of getting rapped on the knuckles every time you mess up your multiplication tables. It can even be fun. So tell the good Sister to put down the ruler—better yet, ask her nicely—then log on to this Gopher site to get great educational software for the PC.

Who knows, maybe after Sister Agnes sees how much fun learning can be, you'll get her to change her whole teaching philosophy. On the other hand, you probably don't have a prayer.

How

Gopher

Where

gopher.archive.umich.edu

Go To

For DOS software, go to:

Merit Software Archives

MSDOS

Educational

For Windows software, go to:

Merit Software Archives

> MSDOS
> Windows
> Educational

Seek and You Shall Find

Unless you've got the entire *Encyclopedia Britannica* memorized, the beginning of any school project has always meant long hours in the library conducting research. Nothing's changed, except that now much of that research can be done online. The Info Zone Web site shows students how to break down the seemingly overwhelming task of research into manageable steps. You'll learn how to brainstorm, locate and access resources, organize data, and much more.

You'll also find valuable links to other sites on the Internet that will help you gather the information you need to do the best work possible, regardless of the type of research project you're doing.

How

World Wide Web

Where

www.mbnet.mb.ca/~mstimson

Special Kids, Special Needs

Technology in Special Education is a comprehensive monthly newsletter published by DREAMMS for Kids, a non-profit organization comprised of members who've combined their knowledge of computers with their love and dedication to helping with the special needs of handicapped children.

This newsletter includes articles on technology, adaptive software and hardware, the Department of Education, upcoming conferences, and hot special-education product announcements. The following instructions will land a complimentary issue at your door via snail mail.

How

Email

Where

DREAMMS@aol.com

Message

Please send me a complimentary issue of *Technology in Special Education*.
(Be sure to include your postal address)

Search Me

All kidding aside, the Internet, and particularly the Web, have some extremely valuable education sites available to students. And one of the best is the Boulder Valley School District's (BSVD) Research Sources for Students Web page.

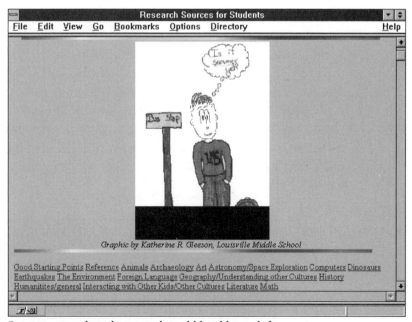

Bet you never thought research could be this much fun.

Combining an easy-to-use format with hundreds of valuable, educational, interesting, and fun links, BVSD has created a research site that will have students and teachers coming back again and again.

How

World Wide Web

Where

bvsd.k12.co.us/docs/research.html

The Homework Page

In my first six years of school, I had a principal who neither believed in homework nor allowed teachers to assign any. While I don't know if the man was ever officially sainted, you can bet that there were a lot of kids praying for him to stay healthy.

But what a shock when I started junior high, where homework was not only assigned, but I was sure that teachers got together before school to see who could assign the most homework with the shortest deadline. But with the Internet, students can now fight back.

The home page is a collection of Internet links that helps kids research school projects, learn math, download online books, and much more. Organized by categories as diverse as Arts, Engineering, Environment, Government, and Health, the Homework Page also includes special fun links for kids, Generation X (whatever *that* is), and "Other Interesting Collections."

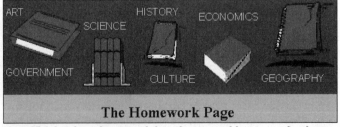

The official "I-hate-homework-but-there's-nothing-I-can-do-about-it-so-I-might-as-well-make-the-best-of-it" page.

How

World Wide Web

Where

www.tpoint.net/~jewels/homework.html

Where to Find Way More Goodies

Both *Arts* and *Books and Literature* provide extensive information and software that's educational for individuals of all ages. The *Arts* chapter includes several online exhibits that provide a great way to introduce children to fine art. But even with pains taken to include sites that include only G- and PG-rated art, the works of some artists might be disturbing to small children. Be sure you preview before you let your kids view.

In the *Family and Home* chapter, be sure to check out SAFE-T-CHILD Online, which shows kids how to protect themselves in a fun, easy, and non-fearful way. The *History* chapter includes several Web sites that introduce U.S. and world history to kids in a fun way. Kids love to explore, and the historical Web links they'll find at many of these sites will encourage them to discover on their own.

The *Kid Stuff* chapter tells you how to download games for kids available from the Educational Software archives at gopher.ed.gov.

The *Science and Nature* chapter provides lots of ways for kids of all ages to learn and have fun at the same time. Be sure to check out the Student Solar Information Network mailing list. This chapter also explains how to access *Science*, *Discover*, and *Earth & Sky* magazines online. There are also several sites and programs for learning about space and astronomy.

For free updates to this book via FTP or the Web, go to: coriolis.com

It doesn't much matter whom one marries for one is sure to find the following morning that it was someone else.

Samuel Rogers

Family and Home

Alms for the Financially Challenged

My philosophy has always been, if you can't afford it, charge it, which has made me about as popular in shopping malls and restaurants as I am *unpopular* with collection agencies and banks. What's everybody so upset about? It's not like I'm using real money or anything.

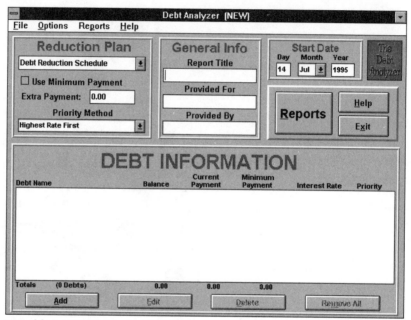

Your ticket out of debtor's prison.

If you've fallen into the same trap and can't get out, here's a shareware program that might help spring you. Debt Analyzer for Windows can save you hundreds of dollars in interest by helping you reduce and eliminate debt. This program analyzes your debt and creates reduction and consolidation schedules to help you prioritize your bills and accelerate your payments. And if you like the shareware version, you can even charge the registration fee....

How

FTP

Where

ftp.csusm.edu

Go To

pub/winworld/finance

Download

debtw200.zip (318 K)

Help Is in the Mail

Parenting by mail: There's not a parent today who wouldn't find this idea occasionally appealing. While most of us can't raise our kids from a distance—with the possible exception of boarding school—you can get long-distance help through Internet mailing lists. Here's a sampling of some of the more popular ones:

PARENT-L is a forum for discussing issues related to breastfeeding and the care of nursing babies, with subjects such as life with a nursing toddler, nursing during pregnancy, tandem nursing (for *real* thrillseekers), societal attitudes toward breastfeeding, and weaning.

How

Email

Where

listproc@helix.net

Message

subscribe PARENT-L *Your Name*

FREE (Fathers' Rights & Equality Exchange) is a nonprofit organization whose members believe that both fathers and mothers should share equally in the parenting and support of their children.

Where

free-join@vix.com

Message

Include your name, address, telephone number, and email address (be sure to state whether it's okay to share your email address with other FREE members)

Gifted Toddler discusses topics related to very young children who are gifted or potentially gifted. You'll have to subscribe to find out more.

Where

majordomo@eskimo.com

Message

subscribe gtot-l

Twins provides an open forum for the discussion of issues relating to twins and any other multiple births, including research, parenting, and issues for adult twins.

Where

owner-twins@mit.edu

Subject

Twins Subscription
Add a brief note asking to be added to the list

Child-Free is for people who choose, or have been forced to remain, child-free, and provides valuable insights and ideas about the effects of remaining childless as a lifestyle choice.

Where

majordomo@lunch.engr.sgi.com

Message

subscribe child-free

CACI (Children Accessing Controversial Information) is for parents who want their children to be able to explore the Internet, but are concerned about them accessing undesirable material. CACI members do not advocate censorship. Instead, they are interested in discussing other solutions.

Where

caci-request@cygnus.com

Message

subscribe

Stranger Danger

Child safety always comes first at SAFE-T-CHILD Online.

Contrary to what you may have read or heard, about the safest place your child could be these days is in front of the computer. Stranger things have happened, but I've yet to hear of a single child lured away from their keyboard and into a car by a stranger offering candy.

But since the rest of the world can't be as safe as cyberspace, here's a Web site to help you make things as safe as possible. SAFE-T-CHILD, a leader in child security, is now on the Internet with SAFE-T-CHILD Online.

SAFE-T-CHILD Online shows kids how to protect themselves in a fun, easy, and nonfearful way. Some of the services currently offered, free of charge, include:

- The interactive Rate Your Child's Street Smarts, which allows parents to quickly diagnose strong and weak areas of their child's personal safety knowledge
- Excerpts from *Not My Child! 30 Simple Ways To Help Prevent Your Child From Becoming Lost, Missing, Abducted, or Abused*, written by SAFE-T-CHILD founder and president, Jan Wagner

How
World Wide Web

Where
yellodino.safe-t-child.com

Stop the Abuse

Each year, child abuse becomes more of a concern to parents and society in general. While even one case of child abuse is too many, the estimated

numbers of sexually and physically abused children each year is staggering. That's why Internet sites like the National Data Archive on Child Abuse and Neglect are so important.

Part of the Family Life Development Center, the National Data Archive on Child Abuse and Neglect Gopher site includes current newsletters, information on subscribing to the Child Maltreatment mailing list, and loads of links to other child abuse and neglect-related sites on the Net.

How

Gopher

Where

gopher.fldc.cornell.edu

Essential Software

If your house or business is burglarized or destroyed, the last thing you want to think about is listing everything that needs to be replaced on an insurance form. That's where Essential Home Inventory can help.

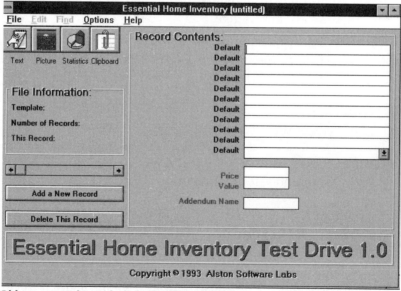

Did you remember to include the kitchen sink?

Essential Home Inventory is an easy-to-use shareware program to help you "intelligently" manage your personal and household inventory. Both flexible and fast, Essential Home Inventory is perfect for not only cataloging and managing your household and business items, but also for generating insurance reports and estate plans.

How
FTP

Where
ftp.csusm.edu

Go To
pub/winworld/database

Download
ehi10.zip (104 K)

Once you've created an inventory list, be sure to store it someplace where it'll be safe in case your home or business is destroyed.

How Do I Love Thee?

Love letters: your spouse loves to get them—preferably from you—though spouses aren't always that particular. Unfortunately, anyone who's ever tried to write one knows that they usually come off sounding like bad limericks. What's a would-be romantic to do?

Some of the automatically generated love letters at this site would even make Roxanne blush.

The Cyrano Server might be just the outlet for your expression of emotion. You provide the adjectives, nouns, and adverbs that best describe your mate, and Cyrano does the rest. The result: Steamy, surreal—even desperate (I could have written *that* one)—love letters and poems.

Too much of a good thing? No problem; this site also includes a Dear John generator to help you dump your worn-out love electronically.

How

World Wide Web

Where

www.nando.net/toys/cyrano.html

Who's the Sap in the Family Tree?

How far back can you trace your family tree? If you're like most people, you'd be hard-pressed to name a great-grandparent. If you're looking for help tracing your family's history, the Genealogy Gopher at the University of Michigan can help.

You'll find lots of software, links to genealogy literature and groups, and much more. Maybe now you'll be able to figure out which relative was responsible for introducing insanity into the family tree.

How

Gopher

Where

gopher.archive.umich.edu

Go To

Merit Software Archives

MSDOS Archive (Merit Network, USA)

Genealogy

Don't forget that the Big Three online services—America Online, CompuServe, and Prodigy—all provide Internet access, including access to the World Wide Web. To access the Web, log on to your service, then enter:

AOL—Keyword Web from the Go To menu
CompuServe—Go Web
Prodigy—Jump Web

Rate Your Mate

C'mon, we've all done it—whether we want to admit it or not. You know, those little quizzes in magazines that ask you embarrassing personal questions about your spouse so you can find out what they're *really* like. But then, if you can answer all the questions, you must already know, so what are you wasting your time for?

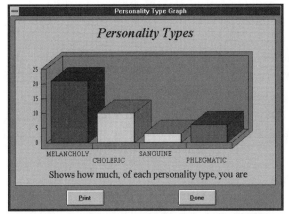

Now you're getting personal with Personality Profile.

But if you just can't resist, here's a program that will save you the cost of the latest *Cosmo*. Personality Profile quizzes you on your (or your better half's) strengths and weaknesses, then spits out a comprehensive personality profile. (Be prepared for a large dose of reality.) To add to the insult, you can display your personality as a graph or print the results.

How

FTP

Where

ftp.csusm.edu

Go To

pub/winworld/educate

Download

profile.zip (582 K)

Stick to It

You've probably heard it said that if you want to hide something from your kids, you should put it under the soap. By the same token, if you want to be sure your kids don't miss it, you should stick it on the refrigerator. These days, that's likely to be just as true if you stick it on the computer.

Now you can turn your Windows screen into the electronic equivalent of your refrigerator door with the WillNotes sticky

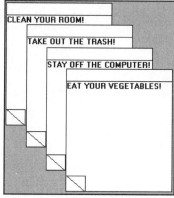
Just some friendly reminders for the kids courtesy of Mom, Dad, and WillNotes.

notes system. These virtual Post-Its are easy to use and impossible to miss. Now your kids won't be able to say they didn't see it.

How

FTP

Where

gatekeeper.dec.com

Go To

pub/micro/msdos/win3/desktop

Download

wnotes21.zip (104 K)

If you're accessing the Internet using a Web browser, don't forget to key in the prefixes *http://* for Web sites, *gopher://* for Gopher sites, and *ftp://* for—you guessed it—FTP sites.

Bringing Up Baby

There are about as many different philosophies on childcare as there are children, and the only thing everybody agrees on is that nobody knows it all—with the possible exception of my mother, who raised me perfectly. For the rest of you, the Department of Health and Human Services' Maternal and Child Health Bureau is placing loads of information on the Internet about caring for children, especially children with special health-care needs.

Some of the topics covered here include:

- Adolescence
- Child health
- Disabilities
- Infants
- Nutrition

You'll also find book reviews and free newsletters you can download or order.

How

Gopher

Where

mchnet.ichp.ufl.edu

Who's Watching the Kids?

Most parents surfing the Internet can easily see the benefits their children get from going online. Still, with all the media hype these days about the "dangers" of cyberspace, some parents are hesitant to let their kids explore the Internet at all.

But now with CYBERsitter, parents can monitor where their children are surfing or even make selected areas off limits. This easy-to-use program

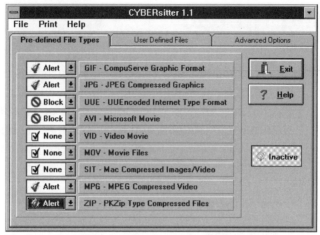

Finally, a babysitter who won't eat everything in the house.

lets you block certain areas of your computer from unwanted eyes or alerts you when they're accessed, including games, personal files, pictures, and more. You can even set it to notify you if your computer has been booted.

How

FTP

Where

solidoak.com

Go To

pub/solidoak

Download

cybersit.zip (277 K)

Designer Software

When it comes to decorating, my tastes lean toward what I like to call "contemporary college dormitory:" a couple of blacklight posters, a bean bag chair, and an old door resting atop some concrete blocks, and I'm ready to entertain. It may not match *your* tastes, but classics like this never go out of style, and it's guaranteed to fit into anybody's budget.

If you choose to ignore my design advice and you think it's time to try something new, try Design-A-Room before you buy a single piece of furniture. Design-A-Room turns your computer into a virtual interior design center by letting you experiment with different decorating ideas, using furniture, walls, and room fixture icons that you paste onto your screen. While it doesn't contain any bean bags or concrete blocks, it does let you move the furniture around without hurting your back. When you're satisfied with the room, you can save and print your work.

How

FTP

Where

gatekeeper.dec.com

Go To

pub/micro/msdos/win3/misc

Download

design11.zip (431 K)

Child Find Online

Every parent shares the nightmare of losing a child. But more and more people are harnessing the power of the Internet to help find those who are missing. Child Find Canada Online is one such site. Child Find posts descriptions and pictures of missing children, along with information about when they disappeared, where they were last seen, and who to contact if you have any information.

You'll also find an online version of the booklet *Child Safety on the Information Highway* by syndicated columnist Larry Magid. This easy-to-read guide helps put the issue of protecting your children online into perspective with an informative discussion of the benefits, risks, and rules of having your kids exploring cyberspace. It also explores parents' responsibilities for protecting their children.

How

World Wide Web

Where

www.discribe.ca

Living in the Past

Genealogy has never been more popular, and the same holds true for home computing. Here's a program that perfectly blends these two hot hobbies. PARENTS, a shareware genealogy program for Windows, helps make collecting and organizing your family tree easier. It helps you gather, store, and view information about all of your ancestors and relatives. You can enter and store vital statistics such as names, births, deaths, marriages, and more.

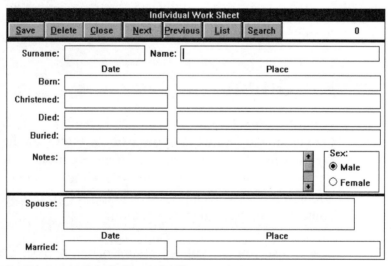

Use the Internet to climb your family tree.

Once the information has been entered, organizing it is a breeze. You can even print detailed information about any of your ancestors, as well as print your entire ancestral tree.

How

FTP

Where

gatekeeper.dec.com

Go To

pub/micro/msdos/win3/misc

Download

parwn306.zip (95 K)

Family Matters

Remember that strongbox your Grandfather gave you years ago? You know, the one gathering dust in the attic—the one with all the old letters, photographs and portraits, and other family documents that trace back a few hundred years. You don't want *your* grandkids to have to sort through that mess, do you?

I didn't think so. If you've got a Macintosh running System 7, you can catalog and organize your family history with the help of Heritage, a powerful but easy to use genealogy program. Heritage has no limit on the number of family members you can enter information for, although you are limited to 40 members until you pay the $15 shareware registration fee.

To use Heritage, start the program and then click on File|New. Enter the name of your family to create a new database. Then, when the blank database screen appears, click on Edit|New Person and enter the name and other information for a family member. A text editor window lets you enter plenty of biographical information for each family member, and you can even attach a photograph or drawing to each person's record.

Heritage has great documentation and includes a sample database of the Tudor family to help you understand how to use the program.

How

FTP

Where

micros.hensa.ac.uk

Go To

micros

mac

finder

m

m032

Download

m032heritage-215.hqx

If you have a Web browser, you can visit the author's Web site to get information about the availablility of the latest release of Heritage, as well as information about ongoing beta tests. The Web address is: www.eskimo.com/~grandine/heritage.html.

Where to Find Way More Goodies

The *Health and Nutrition* chapter also provides a wealth of material for keeping your family safe and healthy. If you're new in town, you'll especially find the physician referral service to be useful for locating family physicians. There's even a Web site that dispenses medical advice for minor emergencies, including burns, choking, and poisoning.

And when you're ready to take the family on vacation, be sure to browse the *Travel* chapter. You'll find lots of information on vacation planning, and you'll even find out some ways to keep the kids quiet and happy during those long car or plane trips.

For free updates to this book via FTP or the Web, go to: coriolis.com

Way More! FREE $TUFF

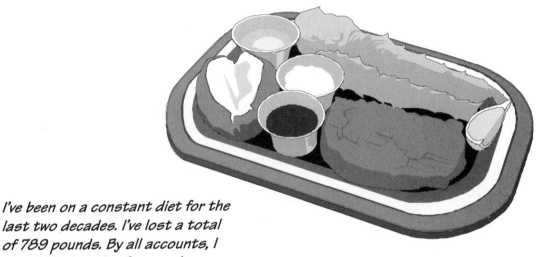

I've been on a constant diet for the last two decades. I've lost a total of 789 pounds. By all accounts, I should be hanging from a charm bracelet.

Erma Bombeck

Food and Cooking

Now That's Italian!

You don't have to go to Italy to find the best in Italian cooking, just go to Mama's. At Mama's *cucina* (that's *kitchen*, I think—I'm about as Italian as a Big Mac), you'll learn how to cook Italian, speak Italian, maybe even win a trip to Italy.

This site includes dozens of recipes—from *primi piatti* (appetizers) to *secondi piatti* (main dishes). If you'd rather not have to deal with the subtitles, you can learn some Italian phrases stored here as AIFF, WAV, and AU audio files.

And if you're not too late, Mama will even send you 3,225 lire worth of coupons to help you save on Ragú products (stop panting—that's around $2.20 American). And after dinner, Mama will even read you a 12th century Italian folk tale via AIFF, WAV, or AU. *Mangia bene*, eh?!

How

World Wide Web

Where

www.eat.com

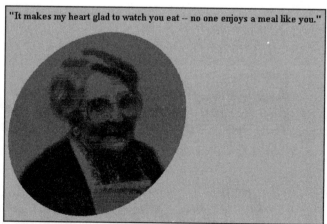

Come visit Mama's cucina at Ragú Net.

Now You're Cookin'

Look in the pantry of any of the best chefs and, along with a shelf full of cookbooks, you're bound to find a pile of recipes ripped from the back of cake boxes, handwritten on old envelopes, and cut out of old magazines. Sure, they can make a soufflé rise, but when it comes to organization, many cooks can't stand the heat.

Recipe Maker and Cookbook Manager are two Windows programs that can help. These applications make weekly grocery shopping, meal planning, and recipe organization a breeze. You can plan meals by the week, then generate a shopping list in minutes. With these shareware programs, you can recall your favorite recipes instantly, so you can spend more time cooking the perfect meal and less time looking for it.

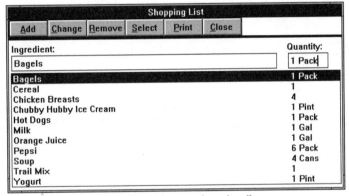

Let Recipe Maker help you with your shopping lists, too.

How
FTP

Where
ftp.csusm.edu

Go To
pub/winworld/database

Download
cbook110.zip (415 K)

rcpwin20.zip (74 K)

Suds by Mail

There's nothing like the taste of something homemade, and that's true for your beer, too. What was once considered the domain of bootleggers and moonshiners is now in the mainstream. These days, you're likely to find executives, managers—even writers (I took a blue ribbon at the Arizona State Fair, thank you very much)—dabbling in home brewing.

Here's a mailing list that will introduce you to thousands of brewers around the world. You'll find lots of help on getting started, recipe ideas, competitions you can enter, and much more.

How

Email

Where

homebrew-request@hpfcmi.fc.hp.com

Message

subscribe

While this list is mainly intended for discussing beer brewing, you'll also find information on making cider, mead, wine, or any other fermented—but not distilled—beverage. Beginners are welcome, as well as experienced brewers.

Eat Your Vegetables

Fruits and vegetables don't grow on trees—uh, if you know what I mean—so maybe it's time we start appreciating them just a little more. And that's just what you'll find at this Gopher site: lots of appreciation and respect for your fruits and veggies. You'll also find plenty of expert advice on growing the little buggers, including:

• An ecological approach to gardening
• Fact sheets on grapes and grape growing
• Current information on grape insect pests
• Tree fruit disease key

- Tree fruit news
- Vegetable insects and diseases
- Vegetable variety recommendations

How

Gopher

Where

gopher.cce.cornell.edu

Go To

Fruit and vegetable production and management

Mastering Your Meals

When I ask my wife what's for dinner and she says "reservations," I know it's my turn to cook. And, while I like to cook as much as the next guy (translation: hot dogs microwaved for 30 seconds taste better than ones right out of the fridge, though either is preferable to starving), I'm somewhat imagination-challenged when it comes to planning a menu. Meal-Master to the rescue.

Meal-Master is a menu-driven database system especially designed to manage recipes. With Meal-Master, you can store, update, and print your recipes in a variety of formats, and you can even search for recipes by title, category, and ingredient.

Surf to this Web site to find out more, then click on *Software* to download a shareware version of Meal-Master. You'll even find hundreds of recipes and cooking ideas stored here by clicking on *Recipes*.

How

World Wide Web

Where

www.primenet.com/~wilson/mm/mealmast.html

Download

MM802.EXE (209 K)

Shop Till You Drop

Show me someone who truly enjoys grocery shopping and I'll show you someone who gets giddy at the thought of getting their driver's license renewed. The shopping itself isn't so bad, but it's a pain trying to figure out what you need. There are enough things to worry about in this world without wondering whether you're out of milk.

With Grocery Consumer, tedium takes a holiday. This program lets you enter your menus, then generates a grocery list for you. Fill in the odds and ends and then it's off to the A & P.

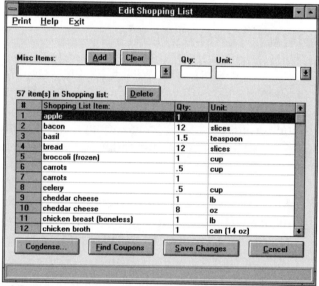

While it doesn't necessarily make the job fun, Grocery Consumer makes shopping at least easier.

How
FTP

Where
ftp.csusm.edu

Go To
pub/winworld/pim

Download

gc218.zip (218 K)

I had a little trouble getting this shareware to cooperate with me when I first downloaded it. It kept insisting that my 60-day evaluation period had expired, even though the program hadn't been on my computer even six *minutes*. I finally had to set my computer's calendar back a few months to get it to stop nagging me and start working right.

All Things Herbivorous

Every family seems to have at least one vegetarian, just like every family seems to have one member who by most accounts is certifiably cuckoo. Among my clan, the vegetarian is my oldest sister—the jury's still out on which of us is the crazy one.

If your tastes run toward bulgur wheat muffins, sunflower-seed casseroles, and carrot-juice shakes, you'll appreciate this mailing list devoted to the rabbit-food crowd. All aspects of vegetarianism are discussed here, including lifestyle, health, and recipes.

How

Email

Where

veggie-request@maths.bath.ac.uk

Message

subscribe veggie-request *Your Name*

Free Beer (Software)!

Brewing your own beer is less of a science than it is an art form. Especially for beginners, homebrewing is often difficult, and when you throw in the fact that most brewers down a couple on the side while cooking up a batch, it's no mystery why the final product is often less than tasty.

If you're thinking of dabbling in this popular hobby, be sure to download a copy of Brewhaha. This homebrewing freeware program is for those who enjoy making their own beer from scratch. And with Brewhaha, it's never been easier.

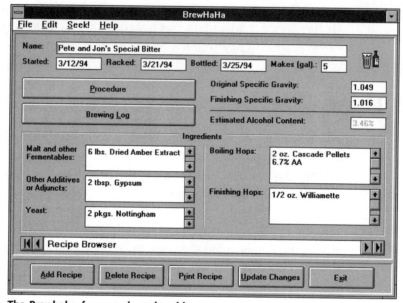

The Brewhaha freeware is no laughing matter.

You'll find several recipes and a brewing log to help you keep track of the intricacies of brewing. You can also add your own recipes, modify existing ones, and search for recipes you've already stored.

How

FTP

Where

gatekeeper.dec.com

Go To

pub/micro/msdos/win3/misc

Download

brewhaha.zip (456 K)

Nutritious and Delicious

If you think the nutritional pyramid was an ancient Egyptian health-food restaurant, run—don't walk—to the Food and Nutrition Information Center (FNIC) Gopher site. Part of the Department of Agriculture's National Agricultural Library, the FNIC provides information for anyone interested in proper nutrition.

You'll find food and nutrition software, reference assistance, bibliographies and reference lists for nutrition publications, lots of links to other health- and nutrition-related Gophers, and much more.

How

Gopher

Where

gopher.nalusda.gov

Go To

NAL Information Centers/Food and Nutrition Information Center

The Recipe for Success

It's late, you're hungry, and all that's in the fridge is a package of Tofu, some carrots you could tie into square knots, and something that looks like it used to be cheese. Sounds like you've got the makings of a *meal!* If you're not sure just what kind of meal these are the makings for, not to worry; the Internet's here to help spark your imagination—as well as your appetite.

From the common to the exotic, here's a recipe archive containing hundreds of ideas for whatever kind of mood your taste buds are in. Looking for Americana mainstream? Try the hamburger pie and apple crisp. If you'd prefer a late-night version of the food of the gods, go for the ambrosia and black forest pie. Not planning on going back to sleep? Pop *Forrest Gump* into the VCR and then go for the chicken gumbo. You'll find recipes for Tofu balls, carrot pudding, cheese grits, and more than 500 others. *Bon appetit.*

How

FTP

Where

gatekeeper.dec.com

Go To

pub/recipes

Download

Way too many to list

Where to Find Way More Goodies

The *Women's Health Hot Line* newsletter includes many articles on healthy cooking. You'll find the newsletter mentioned in the *Health and Nutrition* chapter, which also tells you where to find The Nutrition Expert Web site, sponsored by a group of registered dietitians providing online nutrition help across the Net. And if you still feel like you're feeding yourself just a little *too* well, you might want to download Diet Disk, a program written by a weight control counselor who lost 100 pounds. It too is mentioned in *Health and Nutrition*.

For a bit of just-plain fun, you might want to check out the Coca-Cola Web site, which provides information on everything you've ever wanted to know about this favorite soft drink and its history. The Coca-Cola Web site is mentioned in the *History* chapter.

Finally, if you can't get enough recipes, here's a great Web site devoted to nothing but great culinary creations: http://nearnet.gnn.com/wic/cook.04.html.

For free updates to this book via FTP or the Web, go to: coriolis.com

Way More!
FREE $TUFF

Is that really what they believe on the planet you're from?

Calvin, from Calvin and Hobbes, after listening to his dad espouse the virtues of being a good sport and that losing is a part of life.

Games

FREE $TUFF from the Internet

The Name of the Game Is Fun

Show me someone who says they bought their PC to balance their checkbook and I'll show you someone who needs to be forced—kicking and screaming—to check out this FTP site.

With more than 400 games for PC users to sink their bytes into, this site isn't the largest cache of computer games on the Net—but then it does contain more games than any one person will download in a lifetime. I dare you to prove me wrong. Here's a peek at what's waiting for you:

- **Entombed** Escape the ancient tomb
- **F-18 No Fly Zone** Keep the enemy away from where they don't belong
- **TC Space Fighter** 3D space game of fighting ships
- **FishHatchery** Buy and sell fish, hire workers, run the place
- **Frustration** Puzzle game
- **New Solitaire for Windows** The name says it all

Tom Cruise couldn't have asked for a better flight simulator.

How

FTP

Where

uiarchive.cso.uiuc.edu

Go To

pub/systems/pc/cica/games

The Domain for Games

The Internet—and particularly the Web—is an exercise in excessiveness. Anything that can be converted to bits and bytes is being put online, and most Web page creators follow the caveat of the more the better. Ah, gluttony.

The Games Domain is no exception. In addition to lots of game-related FAQs, you'll find thousands of links to PC, Mac, and Amiga games from around the world. Each link includes information about the game, its creators, and the site it's stored at. At last count, there were 766 links for Amigas, 62 for Macs, and a whopping 1,553 for the PC crowd. This is definitely the site for all others to try to equal.

How

World Wide Web

Where

wcl-rs.bham.ac.uk/GamesDomain/directd/directd.html

Not for Blockheads

After a hard day of destroying galaxies or blowing space aliens back to whatever dimension they oozed from, you'll want to check your testosterone at the door and unwind with something a little more cerebral. Amado, a creative logic puzzle, is not only challenging and stimulating, you don't have to kill anything when you play it—and it won't harm the ozone, either.

Sort of a cross between Tetris and Othello, Amado challenges you to match your scrambled blocks with the pattern selected by your computer in the fewest possible moves and the shortest amount of time. Sounds easy? So did the Rubik's cube, and I eventually ran over mine in the driveway (intentionally).

If you're *really* the intellectual type, there are also a lot of great cross-word-generating programs available at this site, like:

- crossw1.zip
- crossw2.zip
- cwcreate.zip
- cwpower.zip
- cwpro43.zip

Read the Directory of Contents for more info about these programs.

How

Gopher

Where

gopher.ed.gov

Go To

Educational Software
IBM Computers and Compatibles

Download

amado.zip (50 K)

If the files stored here do not include the .ZIP extension, simply add it before you download and it will unzip successfully.

Know When to Hold 'Em

Maybe the odds are against you at the blackjack table, but that doesn't mean you can't shave them a little. Combine your luck with a little strategy and you're guaranteed to win, or at least increase your chances of walking out with your shirt still on.

Professional gambler Thomas Gallagher created this handy blackjack crib sheet to help novices play like the pros. This pocket-size card gives you invaluable strategies, based on what you're dealt and what the dealer's showing. Card combinations are printed on an easy-to-read chart that takes the guesswork out of gambling. But be sure to keep cab fare in your shoe, just in case.

How
Email

Where
G71115@aol.com

Message
Please send me your BLACKJACK BASIC STRATEGY CARD, which I read about in WAY MORE FREE $TUFF FROM THE INTERNET. (Be sure to include your snail mail address.)

All Work and No Play...

I haven't been in an arcade in years, and have little desire to change my ways. But it won't be long before my kids are hounding me to take them, so I guess I'd better start saving my quarters. Until they (the kids, not the quarters) wear me down, maybe I can placate them with some of the games available here.

You'll find hundreds of Windows games (and many are freeware, which will save you countless quarters right there). A small sampling:

- **Anti-Ballistic Missile** A Windows version of that old Atari standby
- **Battles In A Distant Desert** Meet interesting people and kill them
- **Battles on Distant Planets** Meet interesting aliens and kill them, too
- **CornerStone** Sort of a Rubik's Cube with an attitude
- **Yacht-Z** An online version for the pre-MTV crowd

How

FTP

Where

ftp.csusm.edu

Go To

pub/winworld/games

Download

abm_cmd.zip (31 K)

bdd191.zip (131 K)

bdp191.zip (142 K)

cstone10.zip (73 K)

ytz26.zip (53 K)

 If you have trouble accessing this site, try its mirror at gatekeeper.dec.com in the directory pub/micro/msdos/win3/games. You can also find these games at ftp.cica.indiana.edu in pub/pc/win3/games. If *that* doesn't work, it's time to switch Internet providers.

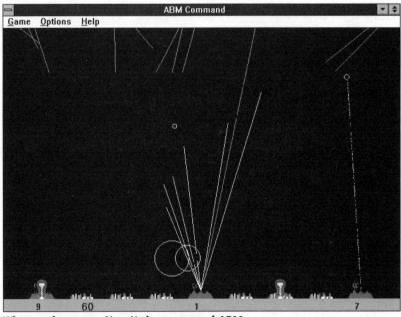

Whoops, there goes New York, courtesy of ABM.

I'm Game

Whether your gaming tastes run from solitaire to networked duels with dozens of players or, Navy warfare to Air Force battles in the sky, EINet's Gaming Resource Web page has dozens of games here to accommodate you.

This Web site offers the latest in fast-moving virtual reality, with bass-pounding soundtracks to match. You'll find Sonic-like side-scrollers, Dungeons & Dragons-type role-playing, and sophisticated edge-of-your-seat flight simulators.

Be sure to check out the links to the top five PC and Mac games as voted by Internauts who have surfed here, and be sure to vote for *your* favorites. The listings here change frequently, but you're guaranteed to always find the best in computer games. Some examples:

PC
- **Doom!** A game-related Web site would hardly be complete without a copy of this brutal-yet-gory immersion into virtual reality.
- **Raptor: Call of the Shadows** High-tech, vertical-scrolling flight simulator. You supply the airsick bag.
- **Rise of the Triad** As realistic as it is violent, this one's highly rated by top game 'zines.

Macintosh
- **Hornet** A realistic simulation of the U.S. Navy's F/A-18 Hornet. This demo doesn't let you mix it up in air-to-air combat, but it'll give you a good feel for the game.
- **Marathon** Described as "Doom for the Mac," this demo is touted as being even better than the PC version.
- **Blood Bath** This playable demo of the arcade game of the same name provides lots of action, suspense, and gore from a first-person perspective. Get them before they get you.

How
World Wide Web

Where

coyote.einet.net:8000/galaxy/Leisure-and-Recreation/Games/
chris-loggins/Gaming.html

Take the Stick

Sure, you can play a lot of your Windows games without a joystick, but
how realistic is that flight simulator when you've got to type *F* to turn
left and *J* to turn right? And did *A* stand for *Accelerate* or *Altitude*?

With WinStick, you can leave the keyboard to the word processor. This
application lets you program all your Windows games to run with a joystick. Now, blasting your online opponents will be more realistic than
ever, which will probably destine an entire generation of videophiles
into therapy. Don't say I didn't warn you.

How

FTP

Where

gatekeeper.dec.com

Go To

pub/micro/msdos/win3/desktop

Download

winstick.zip (49 K)

Be sure to read the readme.txt file *before* you load this program to avoid
locking up your system (like I did).

Video Game Nostalgia

Sure, the Free University of Berlin FTP site is packed with information
on physics, mathematics, chemistry, meteorology, geography, and computer science, but isn't it really known for its games? Apparently not—at
least not until now. And I'm sure their system administrators will be just
tickled that I steered you across the Atlantic to clog their bandwidth.

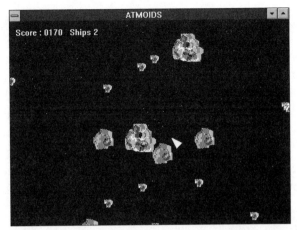

This space-age shoot-'em-up is just one of dozens of games you can download from Free University of Berlin.

They'll get over it, and you'll find lots of tried-and-true arcade-style games here, including a couple variations on Pong (the Mother of all other video games), Tetris, Tai Pei, chess, and checkers. If you're looking for cybergore, this definitely ain't the place, but if you want to have some non-violent fun in front of your computer, this site fits the bill. Also, most of these games are pretty small, so downloading them from Germany doesn't have to be an all-day job.

How
FTP

Where
FTP.FU-Berlin.DE

Go To
pub/pc/win3/games

Download
Too many to list. Explore a little and see what you come up with. Also, be sure to read the index.games file for descriptions of the programs stored here.

Don't forget that many Internet addresses are case-sensitive, so be sure to type them *exactly* as shown.

Couldn't You Gopher a Good Game 'Bout Now?

Gopher may not be the first choice for finding games on the Net, but for millions of Web-deprived users out there, it's their only choice. The maintainers of this Gopher site saw a need and filled it in a big way. The result: more than a thousand games for your video pleasure, including more than 700 for the Mac and 250 for PC users.

Be warned that there's a lack of documentation here, so finding any particular game is a battle in itself—but then again, no one's keeping score.

How

Gopher

Where

gopher.archive.umich.edu

Go To

Macintosh

Game

Go To

MSDOS

Games

Hot Dog, What a Site!

Coming from the era of Pong and Pac-Man, to say I'm just a little intimidated by some of the computer games available these days is an understatement. If Earth is ever attacked by mutant aliens, however, I can only hope there's a six-year-old kid on hand to blast them out of the sky. In the meantime, The Happy Puppy Web site will remain the training ground for future protectors of the universe.

Truly a lesson in overkill, Happy Puppy includes more than 100 of the most highly rated games for PCs. Some of them are monster downloads, but if you like shoot 'em ups, this site is definitely hard to beat. Since

Happy Puppy is continually updated, it's impossible to guarantee what's available at any given time, but here's a small sampling of what I found at press time:

- **3-Point Basketball** Sports simulator
- **Aladdin** Disney action demo
- **Battle Bugs** Buglife war simulator
- **Dark Forces** Space action
- **Day Of The Tentacle** Adventure from LucasArts
- **Epic Pinball** Action game
- **Wolfenstein 3D** 3-dimensional shoot-em-up
- **X-Wing** Space action

How

World Wide Web

Where

happypuppy.com/games/link/index.html

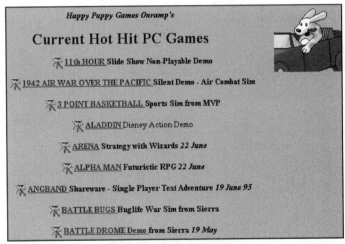

Fetch your favorite games from Happy Puppy.

If you have any trouble accessing this Web site, you might have better luck at its mirror at power.net/pup/games/link.

Pick a Card, Any Card

If you're a Mac user and into card games, you'll love the more than 50 programs available at this site. Hearts, poker, pinochle, blackjack, Chinese poker (whatever *that* is), even strip poker are all well represented here. In fact, you can download several different versions of blackjack or poker, depending on the way you like to play. Most of these programs have good to excellent graphics, and some have native Power Mac versions available. And best of all, the computer never deals from the bottom of the deck.

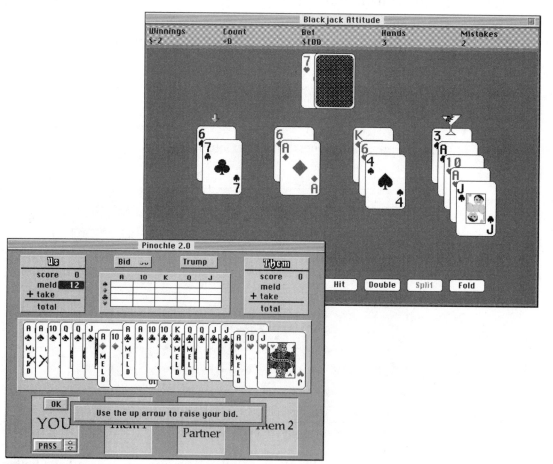

Whether you want to practice for your next trip to Vegas or your next try at beating Uncle Bob at pinochle, you'll probably find your card game of choice at this site.

136

How

FTP

Where

coombs.anu.edu.au

Go To

pub

macintosh

Download

Too numerous to list.

Destruction, Mac Style

Feeling a little downtrodden today? Angry at the boss, perhaps? Well, put yourself back on top of the world with Bolo, a game that *sounds* tame but is anything but. Bolo is a multi-player tank game for Macintosh users. You and the other players fight for control of a hypothetical island by building bunkers, gun emplacements, mine fields, roads, bridges, and just about any structure to help beat each other into submission, to achieve total territorial control.

Bolo supports up to 16 users playing simultaneously. You can play on a local network, or you can play directly across the Internet. The perfect way to make friends on the Internet and turn them into enemies the same day.

How

FTP

Where

bolo.stanford.edu

Go To

Public

Download

Bolo0.99.6.cpt

Where to Find Way More Stuff

The *Humor* chapter provides several diversions that aren't quite your run-of-the-mill computer games, but they're still fun. For instance, the Joker program displays a joke on command, and there are other programs that display rats, roaches, and other vermin on your screen. There's even an automated complaint-letter generator for those times when you really want to let somebody know you're mad.

The *Kid Stuff* chapter tells you how to download games for kids available from the Educational Software archives at gopher.ed.gov, and the *Language and Linguistics* chapter points you to the Jive Web server, where you can translate ordinary sentences into Jive, Cockney, or New York accents.

The *Movies and Television* chapter tells you where to find The TV Theme Songs Web page, which includes fun audio files from hundreds of TV shows—from the '50s to today. And finally, the *Sports and Leisure* chapter includes several software programs for games and other recreational activities, including kite building, golfing, baseball, and more.

For free updates to this book via FTP or the Web, go to: coriolis.com

Way More! FREE $TUFF

I saw a person wearing a T-shirt that said
"Question Authority", so I said to him,
"Who are *you* to tell *me* what to do?"

Marshall Deutsch

Government
and Politics

A Feather in Your Cap Web

I think it was Betty Crocker who said, "If you're satisfied with the food, then don't look in the kitchen." Then again, maybe it was Aunt Jemima. In any case, what's true when it comes to food is also true when it comes to government: Maybe it's better not to know what goes into it. But if you think you can stomach it, here's a Web site that shows you what's cooking on Capitol Hill.

With Cap Web, you can peek into some of the goings on in Washington, D.C. Just point and click to get information about your senators or representatives, including what committees they're assigned to, when they were elected, when their current terms are up, and where to send them email.

And if you slept through high-school civics, here's your chance to catch up with valuable information about the Executive and Judicial branches. There are even links to the Library of Congress, an interactive search utility for tracking down pending legislation, and much more.

How

World Wide Web

Where

policy.net/capweb/congress.html

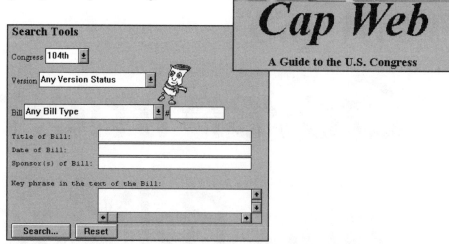

Cap Web teaches you about government the fun—as opposed to the hard—way.

Polling Away from the Pack

Whether it's time to elect a president or a new dog catcher, one of the most important—yet underappreciated—perks of democracy is the right to vote. Of course, that same democracy also gives you the right *not* to vote, a right exercised all-too-frequently by a vast majority of Americans.

If you're one of the apathetic, maybe this Gopher site at the University of Michigan will help spark your political interests. You'll find an extensive archive of national election data, as well as information about congressional races around the country, individual candidates, and several state races, with the promise of more to come.

Woodward and Bernstein types who wonder where money spent by their representatives is coming from can download Federal Election Commission quarterly summaries of contributions made to congressional candidates.

How
Gopher

Where
una.hh.lib.umich.edu

Go To
socsci
Political Science
Elections
United States

Drawn and Quartered

The *Congressional Quarterly* was founded in 1945 under the pretense that "only an informed public could forge a true democracy." Fifty years later, with television, radio, and newspaper coverage of the candidates at an all-time high, you'd think the public would be more informed than ever. If that's true, though, then how do you account for the Ross Perot supporters that are still out there?

Anyway, now you can get *CQ*'s unbiased reporting of Congress and national politics over the Internet. The *CQ* Gopher allows Internauts to explore current and archived files, including:

- Lead stories of the current *CQ Weekly Report*, "the most respected weekly publication on Congress"
- Current weekly news briefs from *The CQ Researcher*
- Status of appropriation bills and other major legislation
- Current catalogs from *CQ* Books and *CQ* Press
- Current schedules of *CQ*'s professional education seminars

How
Gopher

Where
gopher.cqalert.com

If you're accessing the Internet using a Web browser, don't forget to key in the prefixes *http://* for Web sites, *gopher://* for Gopher sites, and *ftp://* for—you guessed it—FTP sites.

Democrats Among Us

Yep, it's that time again, when everybody who's anybody (and then some) is running for office. That means having your favorite television programs interrupted by "paid political announcements," your phone ringing incessantly by campaign workers, and talk around the water cooler escalating into shouting matches over who's the better candidate. But wait, there's more: Election politics have now come to the Net.

One of the more extensive sites is the Democratic Party Activists home page. These digital Democrats are organizing cyberspace for the '96 elections with platform information, links to other Democrat-related sites, and lots of information on federal, state, and local government.

You'll also find software to download like Precinct Walker for Windows, which helps manage precincts, recruit volunteers, raise funds, identify potential voters, process absentee ballot requests, and more.

How

World Wide Web

Where

www.webcom.com/~digitals/

Democracy in action.

Party Time, Republican Style

If, after listening to Rush Limbaugh for three hours each day, you still haven't overdosed on conservativism, here's a Web site that might put you over the top. In addition to free online subscriptions to *DeMOCKracy* and *C-NEWS*, the Berkeley College Republicans Web site offers an extensive multimedia archive of QuickTime movies and GIFs of GOP favorites, direct fax links to Pete Wilson and Rush Limbaugh, an email

gateway to members of Congress, and membership in the Jesse Helms fan club (just kidding about that last one).

You can also download a copy of RightQuotes, a freeware program for the Mac that displays a Conservative or Libertarian quote every time you boot.

How

World Wide Web

Where

www.berkeleyic.com/conservative

A Grand Old Page for the Grand Old Party.

Have a Nice Day Anyway

That's one small check for man, and one giant debt for mankind.

Happy thoughts abound on the Internet, but don't look for them here. Instead, get ready for a sobering political and environmental reality check. The Clock of Doom freeware program isn't a clock in the usual sense. Instead, it displays not-too-pleasant data on government spending, waste, and general mayhem. Updated every second, your Clock of Doom can be set to display:

• How much the U.S. military spends

• How many acres of forest are destroyed

• The growth of the U.S. federal budget deficit

• The barrels of oil being used by automobiles

Had enough? You can modify the Clock of Doom to be a little less gloomy by displaying things like how many aluminum cans are recycled or how many mountain bikes are sold every second. Ahh, now isn't that better?

How

FTP

Where

ftp.csusm.edu

Go To

pub/winworld/clock

Download

cod100.zip (32 K)

 While Clock of Doom is freeware, there is a $10 registration fee if—according to the documentation—you voted for George Bush or Ronald Reagan, support indiscriminate logging of old-growth forests, or spell potato with an "e." Hmm. I wonder where *this* programmer's politics lie?

Politics by Mail

Nothing heats up an argument like politics—except maybe throwing religion or the New Coke/Coke Classic debate into the mix. If, however, you prefer to do your debating through your keyboard (a much safer way to go), here are several mailing lists:

C-News

A moderated list providing news, views, and information for conservatives. This one's all news and no discussion.

How

Email

Where

majordomo@world.std.com

Message

subscribe c-news

Dem-Net-Digest

For U.S. democrats interested in the policies and platforms of their party. Non-Democrats are warned that this list is not for inter-party debates.

Where

dem-net-digest-request@webcom.com

Message

subscribe

Fairness

This list serves as a government watchdog to monitor issues of "fairness" with respect to the American government. You'll get White House press releases, articles from papers and journals, and informed opinions on issues of interest.

Where

listproc@mainstream.com

Message

HELP

Firearms Politics

This unmoderated list for firearms rights activists is a forum for the free discussion of tactics, techniques, and issues related to the right to bear arms, without the anti-gun rhetoric.

Where

majordomo@world.std.com

Message

subscribe fap

Liberal Democrat Party

This list is for members and supporters of the liberal democrat party in the United Kingdom.

Where

majordomo@dircon.co.uk

Message

info LIBDEM-L

LiberNet

LiberNet is a mailing list that discusses issues related to libertarians.

Where

libernet-request@dartmouth.edu

Message

subscribe

Patriots

This list is devoted to the discussion of "claiming, exercising, and defending rights in America, past, present, and future." (Talk about your broad topics.)

Where

listserv@kaiwan.com

Message

subscribe patriots

Not Just for Political Scientists

Did you know that political action committees (PACs) are responsible for as much as 25 percent of all funds spent in elections for Congress? With over 3,500 PACs representing the interests of Big Business, it's no wonder these organizations have the ear of Big Government. Time for a

Science and politics do mix.

little grassroots revolution, I say. And here's a great place to arm yourself—with information, that is.

The Political Scientist's Guide is an interactive pointer to political and legal resources available on the Net. With links to an incredible collection of government-related data, this guide lets you access state, federal, and international information, and even lets you add information and links you've found on your own.

How

World Wide Web

Where

www.trincoll.edu/pols/home.html

SPAN-ing the Net

I read an article recently that said a television cable company was having trouble getting subscribers to pay up. So the company reprogrammed the deadbeats' connections to show nothing but C-SPAN on all 75 stations. Talk about cruel and unusual punishment.

Created over 13 years ago to provide gavel-to-gavel coverage of the House of Representatives, C-SPAN—though often on the boring side—has in fact provided millions of citizens and political junkies with a glimpse into how the workings of U.S. government, well, work.

Now with its own Gopher site, C-SPAN provides Internauts with current program schedules, reports and articles, an archive of historic documents and speeches, and much more. Teachers using C-SPAN in the classroom (presumably as a substitute for corporal punishment) will want to check out the link to lesson plans and teaching tips.

How

Gopher

Where

c-span.org:70/1

Trading Peanuts for Peace

When General MacArthur said that old soldiers never die, they just fade away, he could have added that the same is true for presidents. If it weren't for charity golf events, you'd hardly ever see one. The exception, of course, is Jimmy Carter, who you're more likely to see resolving international conflicts than hitting balls down the fairway.

And now you can find the former president on the Internet, along with The Carter Center Web site, his Atlanta-based think tank dedicated to ending world conflict, disease, hunger, and poverty. And that's just before breakfast. Access this site to learn more about the Carter Center and how you can get involved.

How

World Wide Web

Where

www.emory.edu/CARTER_CENTER/homepage.htm

Not a Shred of Evidence

You don't need that file any more, so simply delete it and it's gone, right? Not exactly. You actually haven't deleted *anything*; you've simply told your computer that the space is available for use in storing other files. This system works great if you have to undelete something, but it really stinks if you're trying to get rid of sensitive or confidential data.

Short of removing your hard drive and whacking it with a hammer, there's no guarantee that what you delete today won't somehow end up in somebody else's hands tomorrow. Unless, of course, you *terminate* it. The Terminator file deletion utility is like an electronic shredder that makes recovering deleted documents virtually impossible. Rumor has it that this is the same program Ollie North uses for all his electronic document shredding needs. Not only does it slice, dice, frappe, and shred your

FREE $TUFF from the Internet

documents, it also makes julienne fries. By the way, this is a Windows
program; sorry, but it's not available for Mac users.

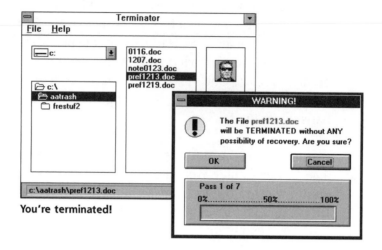

You're terminated!

How
FTP

Where
gatekeeper.dec.com

Go To
pub/micro/msdos/win3/desktop

Download
term20.zip (37 K)

The documentation included with Terminator beats the point into the
ground that once you delete a file with this program, it's gone for good.
And they ain't kidding. Use this one with caution.

A Week in Washington

Personally, I get my news mainly from Oprah, Phil, Sally Jesse, the
Weekly World News, and whatever I overhear in the supermarket pro-
duce aisle. But if you're like most people, you get your news from television, supplemented with an occasional glance at the local paper or a

national magazine. So what about all the news these traditional media don't report? A lot of important stories are slipping through the cracks.

Washington Weekly, an online news 'zine devoted to bringing unbiased political reporting to the Net, is your cyber-alternative to the traditional media. You'll get both sides of the hottest issues inside the Beltway, as well as in-depth analyses and opinions.

You'll also find an extensive collection of speeches by Newt Gingrich and President Clinton, as well as detailed portraits of all 1996 presidential candidates.

How
Gopher

Where
dolphin.gulf.net

If you aren't Web-deprived, be sure to check out the *Washington Weekly* Web site at www.federal.com.

Don't Be a Fuss Budget

If you think making a family budget is hard, try making one for every family in America. Here's an online "game" that lets you play congressperson with taxpayer money. Simply start slashing to cut the federal deficit and balance the budget.

If you lean to the left, you can increase spending in areas that you feel need beefing up. Sorry, but printing more money isn't allowed. Sound easy? Wait till you see the havoc created by your cuts. Talk about chaos theory.

How
World Wide Web

Where
garnet.berkeley.edu:3333/budget/budget.html

Government for Sale

Looking for a good plasma arc furnace? Maybe some slightly used metallurgical grade fluorspar? Kyanite? Regardless of what you're buying, there's a good chance the U.S. government is selling it.

The FinanceNet Gopher site provides daily listings of government assets for sale, including aircraft parts, office furniture, communications and lab equipment, automated data processing equipment, and more. You'll even find entire buildings for sale, though no monuments (yet).

How

Gopher

Where

pula.financenet.gov

Go To

Government Asset Sales

Federal

Commerce Business Daily Government Sales Listings

You can also receive a copy of the current daily listing automatically via Internet email by sending a blank email message to cbd@financenet.gov.

Democracy Comes to the Net

As a rule, when I see anything containing the word "committee," my knee-jerk reaction is to turn and dive as quickly as possible behind the nearest potted plant. It's nice to come across the occasional exception. This time, the exception is the Democratic National Committee (DNC) Web site.

This is a great site for less conservative Internauts to access DNC publications and press releases, audio and video clips, links to other Democratic Internet sites, and much more.

The Democratic National Commitee home page

How

World Wide Web

Where

www.democrats.org

It's Okay, I'm Insured

After the recent savings-and-loan fire sale, it would be a major under-statement to say that the public's confidence in American banking is "shaken." "Beaten to a pulp" is more like it. In fact, more than a few people didn't sleep soundly until they started using their money for mattress stuffing. Here's a Gopher site that may help alleviate your fears.

The Federal Deposit Insurance Corporation (FDIC) is the independent deposit insurance agency created by Congress to boost public confidence in our banks. You'll find information on institutions insured by the FDIC, regulations governing which deposits are insured, consumer-oriented publications, and lots of statistics. There is also lots of online help on how you can buy FDIC-held assets.

How

Gopher

Where

gopher.fdic.gov

Gopher Goes to Washington

Did you know that Fred Grandy, Gopher from TV's *The Love Boat*, went on to further fame as a member of the House of Representatives? Alas, his second gig got canceled, too, although he did serve six years (in Congress, not prison). Not a bad run when you consider *The Love Boat* lasted nine years and Congress isn't nearly as entertaining.

Now with the U.S. House of Representatives' Gopher service (no relation), you can access the latest legislative information as well as information about members, committees, organizations of the House, and other U.S. government information resources. You'll find:

- Email addresses
- Leadership information
- Schedules
- Visitor information

How
Gopher

Where
gopher.house.gov

Safety First

The Occupational Safety and Health Administration (OSHA to those who prefer alphabet soup) works to ensure the safety of workers throughout the country. Its mission, "to save lives, prevent injuries and illnesses, and to protect the health of America's workers," is just as important today as it was when it was formed 25 years ago.

At the OSHA Gopher site, you'll find information on OSHA's past, present, and future, including regulations, manuals, corporate violations and settlements, and more. There are also statistics showing the decline in on-the-job injuries and deaths as a result of OSHA regulations.

How

Gopher

Where

gabby.osha-slc.gov

Where to Find Way More Goodies

The Department of Health and Human Services' Maternal and Child Health Bureau is placing loads of information on the Internet about caring for children, especially children with special health-care needs. See the *Family and Home* chapter for more information.

The gopher.well.sf.ca.us site provides links to several government agencies, including the Bureau of Labor Statistics, the Consumer Product Safety Commission, the Small Business Administration, the Social Security Administration, and the Department of Commerce.

The *History* chapter includes several sights that help provide some insight into the shaping of politics and political history in the U.S. and the world. And, of course, the *International* chapter includes several sites that deal with international politics and issues.

The www.fac.org Web site, mentioned in the *Law* chapter, is devoted to First Amendment issues. As you probably already know, politics have come to the Internet, thanks to several recent concerns regarding censorship on the Net. *NetWatchers* magazine is devoted to keeping tabs on legal issues affecting cyberspace. See the *Law* chapter for more information. *Law* also lists several other sites that deal with governmental and political issues, such as the California Civil Rights Initiative (CCRI).

For free updates to this book via FTP or the Web, go to: coriolis.com

Way More! FREE $TUFF

The need of exercise is a modern superstition, invented by people who ate too much and had nothing to think about.

George Santayana

Health and Nutrition

Ooh, That Smarts

If you're looking for relief from that pain in the back (no, not you-know-who), it may be as simple—or as complicated, depending on your dedication—as doing a few exercises or losing a few pounds. Here are a couple of programs that can help:

- **Backache Relief Now!** This program helps you find relief from your aching back. You'll learn about spinal anatomy, arthritis, slipped discs, aging, sports for back pain sufferers, proper posture, therapies, exercises, and much more.

- **Diet Disk** Written by a weight control counselor who lost 100 pounds, this program will help you hit your goal weight the right way: safely and without fad diets.

As an added bonus, be sure to download a copy of Brainiac!, a state-of-the-art computerized neuroanatomy atlas that lets you point and click your way through the central nervous system (very cool).

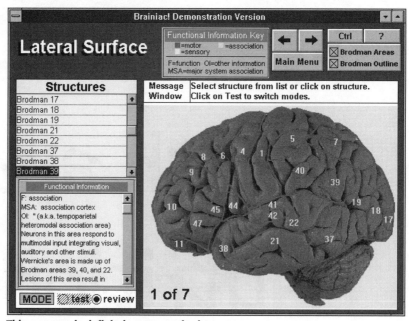

This program is definitely not a no-brainer.

How

FTP

Where

ftp.uci.edu

Go To

med-ed/msdos/education

Download

bkache56.zip (190 K)

diet.zip (112 K)

brainiac.zip (987 K)

Take Two Aspirin and Call Me in the Morning

Whether you're a pharmacist or a hypochondriac, you'll feel right at home at the PharmWeb Net site. In addition to tons of information about the pharmaceutical industry, PharmWeb brings you the latest in research, breakthroughs, and FDA approval.

You'll also find links to pharmacy-related universities, companies, organizations, mailing lists, newsgroups, and more.

How

World Wide Web

Where

www.mcc.ac.uk/pharmacy/

Just for the Health of It

Look around the desks of most hard-core Internauts (present company excepted, of course) and you're likely to find empty Coke cans, candy wrappers, and potato chip bags. When you're ready for some exercise beyond reaching for the Caps Lock key, make this Gopher site your first stop on the superhighway to fitness.

You'll find lots of health-related software, including programs that teach human anatomy and behavior modification, a nutrition and exercise tracker, a program to calculate your life expectancy, and much more.

How

Gopher

Where

gopher.ed.gov

Go To

Educational Software
IBM Computers and Compatibles

Download

anat1.zip (19 K)
anat2.zip (39 K)
b_mod_1.zip (209 K)
b_mod_2.zip (93 K)
cvrisk.zip (57 K)
diet.zip (113 K)
dip.zip (63 K)
lifex.zip (24 K)
whysmoke.zip (43 K)

If your files don't include the ZIP extension, rename the files when you download them and you won't have any trouble uncompressing them.

Remember, shareware is *not* freeware. Try it out, and if you like it, be sure to follow the developer's instructions on how to register the software.

It's HIP to Be Healthy

Health in Perspective (*HIP*) reports the latest news, research, and developments in medicine and nutrition in a way that is both entertaining and easy to understand. You'll find information on:

- The effects of yo-yo dieting
- The latest findings on the health consequences of smoking (it's worse than we thought)
- Preventing lower back pain

How
Email

Where
news-request@perspective.com

Message
send hip-sample

Untangling the Web of Drug Abuse

The Web of Addictions Web site provides a huge compilation of information about alcohol and drug addiction. You'll find links to other addiction-related sites on the Internet, telephone hot lines you can contact for help, and a dictionary of drug slang.

How
World Wide Web

Where
www.well.com/www/woa

What a tangled web we weave.

Ready and Able

For many people with physical disabilities, their greatest barrier lies in how other people perceive them. Whether it's climbing a stairway or climbing a mountain, with the right motivation and determination, disabled people are proving anything is possible.

And speaking of possibilities, now it's possible to access the archives of *Ability Network Magazine* online. You'll find current and back issues of articles, essays, and poems written by and for the disabled. Some recent articles include:

• The Disabled Child: Building a Healthy Self-Image
• Chronic Pain
• Disabled Musicians Get Together Without Leaving Home

How

Gopher

Where

gopher.nstn.ca

Go To

NSTN CyberMall - Internet Storefronts
Disability Services
Ability Network - Cross Disability Magazine

Your Cure Is in the Mail

Mailing lists, the backbone of the Internet, cover every topic you can imagine—and many you wouldn't dare to imagine. Here's a sampling of health-related lists you can subscribe to.

12 Step
Subscribers discuss and share their experiences with 12-step programs like Alcoholics Anonymous, Overeaters Anonymous, and Alanon.

How
Email

Where
listproc2@bgu.edu

Message
subscribe ODAAT@bgu.edu *your email address*

ADD Parents
This list is for parents of children who have Attention Deficit/Hyperactivity Disorder.

Where
add-parents-request@mv.mv.com.

Message
subscribe add-parents

Allergy Discussion
You'll find discussions on treatments, self-help, allergy support systems, and the effect of allergies on health and lifestyles.

Where
listserv@tamvm1.tamu.edu

Message
subscribe Allergy *Your Full Name*

AIDS
This moderated list covers the medical, political, and social issues of AIDS and HIV.

Where
listserv@rutvm1.rutgers.edu

Message
subscribe aids

Alternative Medicine
This is a discussion of issues related to alternative or complementary medical research, including new findings, methods, and announcements of upcoming conferences and seminars.

Where
majordomo@virginia.edu

Message
subscribe altmed-res *your_email_address*

Fat Free
Check here for information on extremely lowfat (less than 15 percent of calories from fat) vegetarian diets. You'll find recipes, testimonials, food news, anecdotes, jokes, and and all sorts of questions related to lowfat vegetarianism.

Where
fatfree-REQUEST@hustle.rahul.net

Message
ADD

Self-Esteem Self-Help
Find out how to raise self-esteem by learning the principles and associated actions that raise self-esteem.

Where
listserv@netcom.com

Message
subscribe self-esteem-self-help

Smoke-Free
An online support group for anyone recovering from addiction to cigarettes.

Where
listserv@ra.msstate.edu

Message

subscribe smoke-free *Your Name*

If your mailer adds an automatic signature, use the command "end" on the next line to prevent majordomo from reading your signature as a series of commands.

Is There a Doctor In the House?

Whether you're looking for a pediatrician in Pittsburgh, a dentist in Detroit, or a physician in Philadelphia, let MedSearch make your search easier. This physician referral service searches for doctors in your area according to location, specialty, types of insurance accepted, fees, and many other criteria you can specify.

The doctor is in—and online.

You'll find physicians, surgeons, and dentists, as well as many other health-care specialists listed here. Plus, many of the doctors also include email addresses so you can contact them for a free initial consultation.

How

World Wide Web

Where

www.medsearch.com/pro

Gooood Morning, Internauts!

Here's the perfect Net site for anybody whose synapses fire first thing in the morning like an engine in need of a tune-up. Kind of the online equivalent of a good cup of java, Good Morning Thinkers! is billed as a wake-up service for your brain.

Each Monday morning, this automated mailing list emails you a short, light-hearted message designed to wake you up, pump you up, and keep you up through the long week. Now if you can just keep your eyelids up long enough to read it...

How

Email

Where

Majordomo@ThinkSmart.com

Message

subscribe Wake-Up_Brain

Are You Gonna Eat That?

Though you'd never know it from some of the fad diets floating around, good nutrition doesn't have to mean boring, bland food. But don't go trading in your carrot sticks and cottage cheese for bread sticks and Cheez Whiz just yet. There's a little more to it than that.

Good nutrition means more than an apple a day.

The Nutrition Expert is a group of registered dietitians providing online nutrition help across the Net. You'll find information on weight loss, cholesterol, sports nutrition, and diabetes, with more information on the way.

If you need additional help, there's also a for-fee telephone consulting service to answer your questions. Plus, when you call you'll receive a free comprehensive, custom-designed nutrition package via snail mail to help you reach your nutrition goals.

How

World Wide Web

Where

www.alaska.net:80/~tne/

A Healthy Dose of Net Sources

HealthMATRIX is an international collaboration of physicians, health workers, medical librarians, and computer specialists who bring you the latest information available on medical research and care. This database of Internet health resources is in hypertext format to make subscribing to newsletters, mailing lists, and newsgroups as easy as pointing and clicking.

With HealthMATRIX, you'll find lots of information on medical resources available on the Net, including an extensive list of Gopher and FTP sites to download public domain software.

How

FTP

Where

oak.oakland.edu

Go To

pub3/simtel-win3/internet

Download

hmatrix.zip (272 K)

This Is Only a Test

If you have anxiety attacks just wondering whether you're neurotic, you probably answered your own question. If you're still not convinced, the Keirsey Temperament Sorter is the test for you.

This personality test works much like the Meyers-Briggs test, only you don't need a licensed professional to administer it. Simply click on the buttons that best match your behavior and your test will automatically be scored and evaluated.

Tests are scored on four different scales:

- Energizing: extrovert vs. introvert
- Attending: intuitive vs. sensing
- Deciding: feeling vs. thinking
- Living: judging vs. perceptive

Click on *About the Test*, then *alt.psychology.personality FAQ* to learn more about the meaning of these terms and the way they apply to your personality.

How

World Wide Web

Where

sunsite.unc.edu/jembin/mb.pl

Special Children, Special Needs

Spend a few minutes with a handicapped child, and your knees jerk feelings of pity will be quickly swept away by the limitless energy and exuberance displayed by these special kids. In many cases, the only people who think of them as "handicapped" are those who haven't spent any time around them.

The Maternal & Child Health Network (MCH-Net) Gopher provides information about caring for children with special health-care needs. You'll find book reviews and journals, information on wheelchair training and HIV, links to other disability-related Gopher sites, and lots of other great resources.

How
Gopher

Where
mchnet.ichp.ufl.edu

Here's to Your Health

If you're serious about getting healthy, the first step is probably to turn that computer off, then drop and give me twenty. Naah, too obvious. The first step is to learn everything there is to know about health and exercise from the comfort of your own La-Z-Boy. Now we're talking.

This site has a miscellany of health-related Windows software, including a program to help disabled Windows users, an exercise log book, and a heart-attack simulator. You'll find:

- **Windows Access** Aid for individuals with disabilities who want to use Windows.
- **Code Red!** A cardiac arrest clinical simulation.
- **RunTrak** A logbook for runners.

How
FTP

Where
gatekeeper.dec.com

Go To
pub/micro/msdos/win3/misc

Download
accp.exe (195 K)
codered.zip (661 K)
runtrk11.zip (71 K)

Better Safe than Sorry

The Consumer Product Safety Commission (CPSC) was created as a government watchdog to protect the public against unreasonable risks of injuries and deaths associated with consumer products. With jurisdiction over nearly 15,000 products, including coffee makers, toys, and lawn mowers, the CPSC certainly has its work cut out for it.

At the CPSC Gopher site, you'll find information on how to get press releases and bulletins on unsafe products through the Internet, a toll-free hot line, "fax on demand," and lots of other consumer-safety freebies. There's also information on how you can report unsafe products to the CPSC.

How
Gopher

Where
cpsc.gov

Go To
CPSC Publications

Not for Women Only

While once the exclusive domain of the male species, the local gym these days is just as likely to include as many women getting in shape as men. And on the Internet, you'll find the number of sites related to women's health growing every day, too. Case in point: the *Women's Health Hot Line* newsletter.

While directed primarily toward women, this online newsletter provides information on a wide range of health-related issues, including:

- Heart disease in women
- Healthy cooking
- Skin cancer

How

World Wide Web

Where

www.soft-design.com/softinfo/womens-health.html

Be sure to look for the ELECTRONIC health freebie of the month available here.

Brain Drain

The Brain and Tissue Bank at the University of Maryland at Baltimore collects, stores, and distributes human brains and other tissue for research dedicated to the improved understanding, care, and treatment of developmental disorders.

You'll find a listing of brain disorders, tissue samples available to researchers, instructions on brain removal (don't try *this* at home), and lots of other cerebral information. If all this makes your brain hurt, there's also registry information for potential donors.

How

Gopher

Where

gopher.btbank.ab.umd.edu:1070

Okay, Cough It Up

Remember the recent Philip Morris recall of nearly one billion cigarettes because of possible contamination with a chemical used to clean the manufacturing equipment? Press releases by the cigarette maker said that anyone who accidentally smoked the tainted cigarettes would experience difficulty in breathing, watery eyes, and coughing. Hmm. That narrows it down to about every smoker I've ever met.

Action on Smoking and Health (ASH) is devoted solely to the problems of smoking and nonsmokers' rights. Anti-tobacco rhetoric runs rampant here, so smokers beware. You'll find "secret" tobacco industry documents, studies on the effects of second-hand smoke, and lots of links to anti-smoking and health-related Web sites.

Mind if I smoooooke?

How
World Wide Web

Where
ash.org/ash/

It's Better to Give

The Robert Wood Johnson Foundation (RWJF) Gopher provides information for anyone interested in learning more about the nation's largest private philanthropy devoted to health care, including its programs, projects, and proposals.

There's also lots of information about health care in the U.S., the full texts and excerpts of many of the foundation's publications, and funding information.

How
Gopher

Where
gopher.rwjf.org:4500

Accidents Happen

Parents know that, for their kids, every day brings a new bump, cut, or scratch. While most of these accidents can be taken care of with a Band-Aid and a cookie, more serious accidents *do* happen.

Here's a Web site that dispenses medical advice for all your minor emergencies. While none of it should be considered an alternative to real medical attention in serious cases, you'll find helpful information on many common maladies, including:

- Blistering, burns, and frostbite
- Breathing difficulty, choking, and fainting
- Bruising and puncture wounds
- Poisoning and bites
- Sprains and fractures

You'll also find lots of links to other online medical sources.

How

World Wide Web

Where

symnet.net/~afoster/safety/

Help for SIDS

The statistics are sobering: Each year, more children die of Sudden Infant Death Syndrome (SIDS) than cancer, heart disease, pneumonia, child abuse, AIDS, cystic fibrosis, and muscular dystrophy *combined*.

The SIDS Network Web site provides information about SIDS research, awareness programs, and how you can reduce the risk to your kids of this number-one killer of infants between the ages of one month and one year.

How

World Wide Web

Where

www.eskimo.com/~pageless/home/sidsnet

Where to Find Way More Goodies

The *Family and Home* chapter provides information on PARENT-L, a forum for discussing issues related to breastfeeding and the care of nursing babies, and also points you to the Department of Health and Human Services' maternal and Child Health Bureau, which is placing loads of information on the Internet about caring for children, especially children with special health-care needs.

The gopher.cce.cornell.edu Gopher site includes lots of information on raising and caring for vegetables, including ecological approaches to vegetable gardening. For more information, see the *Food and Cooking* chapter, which also tells you where to find information on vegetarianism. In addition, *Food and Cooking* points you to the Food and Nutrition Information Center (FNIC) Gopher site, which is part of the Department of Agriculture's National Agricultural Library.

Finally, the *Sports and Leisure* chapter includes a nice little training program (Macintosh) for runners, and tells you how to join the Better Bodies free email service, which is devoted to helping people stay fit and healthy.

For free updates to this book via FTP or the Web, go to: coriolis.com

Way More! FREE $TUFF

Nostalgia just ain't what it used to be.

Anonymous

History

History of the World, Part 1

You don't need H.G. Wells' time machine to get a glimpse of what life was like half a billion years ago. Now armchair travelers can go back in time with the University of California's Museum of Paleontology. Simply point and click your way across millions of years to learn about the fossils, facts, and fallacies of Earth's ancient history.

Whether you're interested in the age of dinosaurs, when man first walked the Earth, or the millions of years in between, this Web site has loads of information, pictures, and links.

Please, do not feed the dinosaurs.

How

World Wide Web

Where

ucmp1.berkeley.edu/timeform.html

176

History of the World, Part 2

While I wouldn't consider this site an in-depth study of world events, it *does* offer tons of interesting historical factoids on countries and continents throughout the world, including:

- Africa
- Asia
- Canada
- United States
- Europe

You'll also find a huge collection of GIFs and JPEGs of maps, flags, and landmarks from each country to download, as well as information on 19th- and 20th-century battles, wars, and conflicts, and an archive on Native American history.

How

FTP

Where

msstate.edu

Go To

docs/history

 Access the software subdirectory to download graphics viewers and unzipping programs, if you need them.

As American as Apple Pie

American history buffs and buffettes will want to check out this Gopher site with loads of programs for tracking and learning about historical events that helped shape the United States.

You'll get some great online lessons in American history, including a program that lets you read—and listen to—the Declaration of Independence.

Also, be sure to check out Timeline, a DOS program that provides an in-depth timeline of the Civil War, from the first shots at Fort Sumter to Lee's surrender at Appomattox. There's also lots of historical information on events leading up to the War between the States.

How

Gopher

Where

gopher.ed.gov

Go To

Educational Software
IBM Computers and Compatibles

Download

talk1776.zip (13 K)

timeline.zip (50 K)

Happy Birthday to You

Who do you share your birthday with? Find out by using the Encyclopedia Britannica's list of famous people's birthdays. Just click on your birthday and see what comes up. You'll get short biographies of the

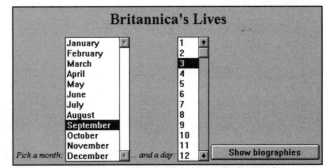

Make a wish, blow out the candles, then find out who shares your birthday.

famous and infamous alike—and if you're a subscriber to Britannica Online, the hyperlinks will take you to even more information about the people and events that share your birthday.

How

World Wide Web

Where

www.eb.com/calendar/calendar.html

Holocaust Research

While it's well documented that the Holocaust included the annihilation of more than 16 million people in extermination and concentration camps like Auschwitz, Treblinka, Buchenwald, and Dachau during World War II, there's a smattering of brain-impaired revisionists who actually reject the idea that these atrocities ever occurred.

The Holocaust Research List, a moderated digest devoted to Holocaust research, works to refute the claims of those looney-bins who deny the event. Due to limited space, subscriptions to the list are available by invitation only, and membership is limited to those who can provide research, editing, or writing skills to the project. Email the moderators for more information.

How

Email

Where

kmcvay@oneb.almanac.bc.ca

Subject

HLISTSUB

Things Go Better with Cyber Coke

Caffeine—it's the backbone of the Internet, or at least the backbone for most Internet addicts. And the number-one soft drink downed by Internauts is Coke. Since 1886, Doctor Pemberton's Pick-Me-Up (as it was originally known), has been perpetuating insomnia, rotting teeth, and firing synapses just a little bit faster in the brains of countless millions around the world—small prices to pay for that satisfying heart, nose, and throat rush.

The Real Thing on a real Web site.

And now the soft drink that helps fuel the Net is *on* the Net as well. At the Coca Cola Web site, you'll find loads of information about the Coca Cola Company, its history, and where it's headed in the 21st century. You'll also find some great graphics and audio files to download. Crass commercialism? Of course! But, then, how do you think they became the world's best-selling soft drink maker with the world's best-known trademark?

How

World Wide Web

Where

www.cocacola.com

Great Moments in History

How old was Paul Revere when he rode into the history books in 1775? Don't know? Don't care? Well, if that tidbit doesn't seem important to you, then, hey, you're not a *true history buff.* For bona fide trivia junkies and Jeopardy-contestant wannabes, morsels like this are essential information.

If you're a genuine factoid monger, you'll love Windows in Time, which you can use to sort and select information about historical people and

events, for new insights into old eras. You'll also get timelines and reports of historical events, like:

- The evolving conflict between Christians and Muslims
- The Renaissance
- The American and French revolutions
- The twentieth century

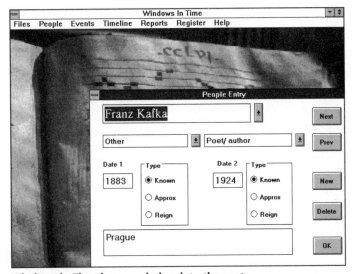

Windows in Time is your window into the past.

By the way, Paul was 40 when he started his ride, and was probably feeling close to 140 when he finished.

How

FTP

Where

ftp.csusm.edu

Go To

pub/winworld/educate

Download

wit.zip (160 K)

You're History

Who was born on this day? Who died? And more importantly, how many shopping days till Hanukkah? These are just a few of the questions answered when you access this Gopher site. You'll get daily highlights of historical events, as well as lots of almanac-like factoids like moon phases, times for sunrise and sunset, and more. Don't ask me why, but you'll even find some decent rock lyrics when you log on—not a bad bonus.

How
Gopher

Where
Niord.SHSU.edu

Go To
Daily Almanac (from UChicago)

Nagasaki Revisited

Fifty years after the atomic bombings of Japan, the words Hiroshima and Nagasaki evoke a myriad of emotions. While most people believe the bombings saved thousands of lives, others feel they were unnecessary. But often lost in the controversy are the tens of thousands who were killed by the blasts.

Yosuke Yamahata is making sure people remember. *The Nagasaki Journey* is a collection of photos taken by Yosuke in the days following the destruction of Nagasaki. You'll

A journey through post-apocalyptic Nagasaki.

182

also find recollections of the attack and its impact, written by people from both sides of the Pacific.

How

World Wide Web

Where

isaac.exploratorium.edu/nagasaki/mainn.html

Living in the Past

Almost everyone has tried to trace his or her family tree at some time. But what first seems like an entertaining afternoon project can quickly turn into an overwhelming chore of trying to organize dozens of dates, names, and locations. The result: a family tree that never quite takes root.

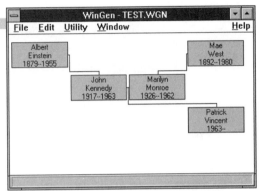

A sampling of the author's distinguished lineage.

Okay, it's true I've mentioned genealogy programs in the *Families* chapter. But there's more than one way to climb a tree, and WinGen makes keeping track of all the branches of your family tree easier than ever. Simply fill in the blanks and follow the prompts on your screen to create detailed histories of births, deaths, marriages, and chronologies of family events.

How

FTP

Where

ftp.csusm.edu

Go To

pub/winworld/pim

Download

wingen.zip (247 K)

America's Bloodiest War

Yankees vs. Rebels: the two flags of one nation.

While the American Civil War marked the freeing of African Americans in the United States, the abolition of slavery was actually considered a secondary issue at the time, with the North's overriding objective being to stop the South's secession and to preserve the Union. The bloody results speak for themselves: More U.S. soldiers died in the War Between the States than in all American wars *combined*.

You'll learn more about this pivotal time in American history at the U.S. Civil War Center's Web site. In addition to loads of Civil War- and Reconstruction-related archives, you'll find a wide assortment of Civil War Web links to indexes, letters, diaries, museums, discussion groups, newspapers, university archives, and more.

How

World Wide Web

Where

www.cwc.lsu.edu/civlink.htm

Don't forget that the Big Three online access services—America Online, CompuServe, and Prodigy—all provide Internet access, including the World Wide Web. To access the Web, log on to your service, then:

AOL—Keyword *Web* from the Go To menu
CompuServe—Go *Web*
Prodigy—Jump *Web*

A Day In the Life

Ever notice how some people hanging around the water cooler seem to know every important thing that *ever* happened on "this day in history?" Where in the world do these Cliff Claven wannabes get their information? They

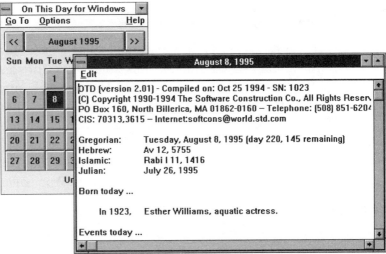

Anything exciting happen today?

probably owe their "keen insights" and historical knowledge to a program like On This Day for Windows, a shareware package that gives you the crème de jour, including:

- Gregorian, Hebrew, Islamic, and Julian dates
- Famous birth dates
- Great events
- Religious events

Now that their secret is out, you can match them fact for fact, or—better yet—reformat their hard drives.

How

FTP

Where

gatekeeper.dec.com

Go To

pub/micro/msdos/win3/desktop

Download

wotd_201.zip (188 K)

Your Gateway to the Past

If you're a student of history (and I mean genuinely *a student*, as in I've-got-to-get-a-good-grade-in-this-course-or-Mom-and-Dad-will-cut-me-off), then the Gateway to World History Web site just might be your ticket to adventurous learning. This academically oriented site provides links to document archives, online resources, search utilities, discussion lists, and many other resources useful for history research. You'll also find a list of history departments wired to the Net, general reference works, and links to other History-related Web pages.

How

World Wide Web

Where

neal.ctstateu.edu/history/world_history/world_history.html

When, in the Course of Human Events

A picture may be worth a thousand words, but the thousands of historical words stored at the Queens Borough Public Library Gopher site in New York are priceless. Here's a sampling of what's available online:

- Magna Carta
- Monroe Doctrine
- Emancipation Proclamation
- Gettysburg Address
- Martin Luther King's *I Have a Dream* speech
- Nelson Mandela's inauguration speech

How

Gopher

Where

vax.queens.lib.ny.us

Go To

Social Sciences/History

Historical Documents

Washington Surfed Here

Studying the past may be nothing new, but making all that information available on the Net is definitely an event of historic proportions. And here's a Web site that makes learning about the events of yesteryear as easy as pointing and clicking.

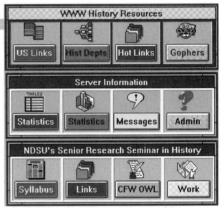

The History Resource Page provides a blast to the past.

You'll find a huge collection of historical topics covered here, as well as hundreds of links to history-related sites on the Net, including:

- The Smithsonian Institution
- The Library of Congress
- University history departments

How

World Wide Web

Where

134.129.87.200:80/jrhome.htm

If you're accessing the Internet using a Web browser, don't forget to key in the prefixes *http://* for Web sites, *gopher://* for Gopher sites, and *ftp://* for—you guessed it—FTP sites.

Where to Find Way More Goodies

Check out "The Treasure Chest of World Art" in the *Arts and Culture* chapter for hundreds of images from a variety of different civilizations and cultures. In the same chapter, be sure to check out the Toledo Museum of Art site for hundreds of paintings and images from some of history's greatest artists.

The *Books and Literature* chapter includes the Native American Literature mailing list, sites for finding classic works of literature online, and listings of former Nobel, Pulitzer, and other major prize winners.

The Info Zone Web site, mentioned in the *Education* chapter, provides information and tips to help students hone their research skills. And if you want to observe history in the making, be sure to browse the *Government and Politics* chapter, which includes lots of sites that deal with contemporary social and political issues.

If you're interested in Viking history and culture, be sure to go to the Viking Web site, the best place on the Net to access information about the culture of these Norsemen of old. For more information, see the *International* chapter.

For free updates to this book via FTP or the Web, go to: coriolis.com

Way More! FREE $TUFF

Always borrow money from a pessimist; they don't expect to be paid back.

Anonymous

Household
and
Family Finance

Internet, Take Me Shopping

Mail order shopping is now one of the hottest online interests, and sites like the Internet Catalog Mart are leading the way. You'll find more than 10,000 catalogs on over 800 topics here—all of which you can get for free. Simply select the catalogs you're interested in and fill out the electronic order form. Your request is automatically forwarded to the appropriate catalog houses, which will send their latest catalogs via snail mail. Here's a very small sampling of some of the categories you'll find:

- Appliances
- Autographs
- Auto-replica and conversion kits
- Bicycles and accessories
- Clothing
- Furniture
- Jewelry
- Skateboards
- Toys
- Woodworking

This list doesn't even scratch the surface, but you get the idea.

If you can imagine it, there's a good chance you can order it from a catalog available at the Internet Catalog Mart.

How

World Wide Web

Where

catalog.savvy.com

A word of caution: Order these catalogs with care. If you overdo it, you'll need to rent a post office box to handle the mail avalanche. But if you love to shop and hate the mall, this site's for you.

Now You're Going Places

A few years back, a friend of mine left small-town Carson City, Nevada, for a job in big-city Los Angeles, with the promise of a high salary and year-round sunshine to match. What he got was a high cost of living and plenty of smog. In fact, what he paid in rent alone canceled out his increase in salary.

Here's a program that will help ensure you don't make the same mistake. Place to Place compares the cost of living in different U.S. cities. While the demo version is limited to ten cities (Anchorage, Hartford, Chicago, St. Louis, Lincoln, New York, Pittsburgh, Memphis, Seattle, and Cheyenne), the registered version includes info on 300 cities.

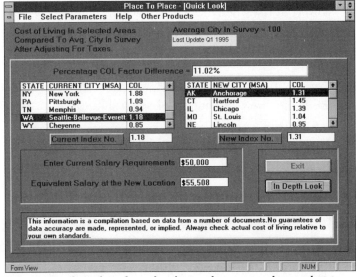

You can get there from here, but just make sure you know what to expect when you arrive.

Simply enter where you are and where you're going, as well as your current salary. Place to Place then gives you information on the difference in cost of living, how much you'd need to make for an equivalent salary, and more. It even provides addresses and phone numbers for chambers of commerce throughout the U.S.

How

FTP

Where

ftp.csusm.edu

Go To

pub/winworld/database

Download

ptp_demo.zip (1.7 MB)

Ask the Handyman

Does your idea of the perfect weekend involve repiping all the bathrooms? Or are you the ignore-it-and-it'll-go-away type who'd rather just rearrange the furniture to hide that gaping hole in the wall you made with your fist when the lampshade nearly ignited (again) after you screwed in the wrong type of bulb (again)? Regardless of your fix-it-up knowledge, the Handyman Hints mailing list is a must for anyone who owns a home.

Contributing Editor Glenn Haege, host of the syndicated radio show *Ask the Handyman* and author of several home-improvement how-to books, discusses:

• How your home works
• New products
• How to fix almost anything
• Workshop shortcuts
• How to choose the right contractor for the job
• How to replace a light bulb (okay, just kidding)

How

Email

Where

majordomo@cedar.cic.net

Message

subscribe handyman hints

Rate Your Rate

Dabblers in stocks wouldn't dare limit their portfolio's potential by buying shares in only local companies, so why would you want to limit your shopping for the best certificates of deposit rates to the banks just in your area?

With the Bank-CD Rate Scanner, you can expand your search for that elusive Holy Grail of CD rates beyond your local borders and quickly shop around the U.S. for the best deals. While you won't find fancy graphics at this Web site, you will find good information on the top CD rates from banks around the country. Just point and click to get direct access to the FDIC-insured suppliers listed here.

How

World Wide Web

Where

www.wimsey.com/~emandel/BankCD.html

Don't forget that the Big Three online access services—America Online, CompuServe, and Prodigy—all provide Internet access, including the World Wide Web. To access the Web, log on to your service, then:

AOL—Keyword *Web* from the Go To menu
CompuServe—Go *Web*
Prodigy—Jump *Web*

The Number You Have Dialed...

When speed dialers were introduced, they were supposed to be valuable business tools for contacting clients, as well as valuable safety tools for quickly calling help. Sounds good, but the only time I use mine is to call up my favorite radio station and to get hold of the Domino's Pizza Hot Line. In fact, I think I could have a pizza delivered faster than it would take me to figure out how to speed-dial the fire department.

But here's an easy-to-use shareware speed dialer with some features I haven't seen on any phone speed dialer. Quik Dialer, which works with your modem, lets you store hundreds of phone numbers in its online Rolodex, and you can even sort them by impor-

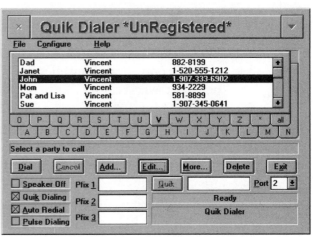

Isn't it time you called your mother?

tance. Plus, dialing is as easy as pointing and clicking, and it'll redial until you connect.

How

FTP

Where

ftp.csusm.edu

Go To

pub/winworld/dialer

Download

qdlr204.zip (212 K)

Consumer Publications

To a salesperson, there's nothing more terrifying than dealing with a well-informed customer. And with the Consumer Law Page Web site, you've got instant access to the latest consumer news and legal data. Once you access this site, simply click on *Brochures* to download over 100 helpful booklets, brochures, and articles on dozens of consumer-related issues, including:

- Automobiles
- Banking
- Credit
- Career/employment
- Funerals

If you manage to make it through this deluge of documents and are still hungry for more, click on *Articles* for excellent information on insurance, product liability, and many other consumer issues.

How

World Wide Web

Where

tsw.ingress.com:80/tsw/talf/txt/intro.html

Oh Give Me a Hoooome

When it comes to budgeting, I have a simple philosophy, which I borrowed from Roseanne: Pay anything marked "Final Notice" and throw the rest of the bills away. If you're looking for something a little more organized, maybe you should try Home Budget. This program lets you easily budget and manage your home finances and avoid the usual bill-payment headaches. Home Budget helps you:

- Track credit card spending
- Display charts and graphs
- Summarize, print, and view your finances

• Schedule auto payments

• Summarize your net worth

And after you've downloaded Home Budget, check out these other home finance programs located here:

MtgEdge A mortgage loan officer on software. This program prequalifies all borrowers, and gives complete closing costs.

QualifyR A home buyer's qualification program for home financing.

Home Budget - SAMPLE.TRN - [Account Book]						
File	Transaction	Account	Setup	Edit	View	Window Help

Add	Ctrl+A				From: Earliest	To: Latest
Delete	Del					
(Expense	Split			Clothing		
	Reconcile	Ctrl+R	Budget: 1440.00	Rec Bal: n/a		
	UnReconcile	Ctrl+U	Credit: 0.00	End Bal: 139.87		
Date	Find	Ctrl+F3	Account	Num	Debit	Credit	R	Balance

Date	Account	Num	Debit	Credit	R	Balance
01-Jan-94	BUDGET		0.00	180.00		180.00
13-Jan-94	Sort By... → Date		289.49	0.00		-109.49
01-Feb-94	Sort Ascending Debit amount		0.00	180.00		70.51
14-Feb-94	Shoes - Bata Credit amount		84.50	0.00		-13.99
01-Mar-94	Budget Allocation Account		0.00	180.00		166.01
04-Mar-94	Misc Clothes - WalMart	Visa	245.39	0.00		-79.38
01-Apr-94	Budget Allocation	BUDGET	0.00	180.00		100.62
05-Apr-94	Shirts - Jack Freeds	Visa	222.12	0.00		-121.50
07-Apr-94	Ties - Jack Freeds	Visa	49.40	0.00		-170.90
01-May-94	Budget Allocation	BUDGET	0.00	180.00		9.10
20-May-94	Jeans - Jeans R Us	Visa	59.94	0.00		-50.84
01-Jun-94	Budget Allocation	BUDGET	0.00	180.00		129.16
20-Jun-94	Suit - Zellers	Visa	99.99	0.00		29.17
01-Jul-94	Budget Allocation	BUDGET	0.00	180.00		209.17
20-Jul-94	Pants - Zmart	Visa	159.40	0.00		49.77
01-Aug-94	Budget Allocation	BUDGET	0.00	180.00		229.77
02-Aug-94	Misc clothes - WalMart	Visa	89.90	0.00		139.87

Sort Transactioins according to Credit amount | NUM

Home budgeting that won't cause you to pull your hair out.

How
FTP

Where
ftp.csusm.edu

Go To
pub/winworld/finance

Download

hb20.zip (212 K)

mtgedge.zip (47 K)

qualifyr.zip (148 K)

Hints for Home Owners

Owning a home is the American dream, but if you've bought one in a planned community, it could turn into an American nightmare of rules, regulations, and ridiculously rigid policies. The Home Owners Association mailing list is for homeowners, home associations, and residents in condos and townhouses who want to share advice, tips, and problems of living in planned communities. You'll also find help from other subscribers on how to make your community a more enjoyable place to live.

How

Email

Where

HOA-List-Request@Netcom.com

Message

help

Join the Club

If you've got an eye for a bargain, be sure to set your sights on the Consumer Information Network, where you'll find information on getting loads of freebies and cheapies for savvy shoppers.

Simply join any of the online clubs located here (membership is free) and you'll receive email once a month with information on new products, free product samples, electronic coupons, and lots of other special offers.

Currently, there are four clubs:

• **DialHealth** For anyone interested in health, fitness, diet, or nutrition

- **DialSoft** For users of home software, CD-ROMs, or online services
- **DialTravel** For anyone who travels
- **DialWealth** For anyone trying to save money and invest wisely

How

World Wide Web

Where

www.iis.com/clubs/

All-Consuming Knowledge

Once upon a time, it was thought that consumers could protect themselves against shoddy products and shady sellers through common sense, testing before purchase, and confronting the seller when dissatisfied, which no doubt led to the lynching of more than one snake-oil salesman at the hands of customers who felt taken.

Luckily, for buyers *and* sellers, there are now consumer rights organizations around the country that help buyers beware. At the Consumer Policy FTP site, you'll find lots of information on how to contact consumer protection offices around the U.S., where to write for helpful publications, and how to find other Net resources with more consumer information.

How

FTP

Where

consumer.policy.net

Go To

pub/..NCW/Consumer_Resources

That strange path (..NCW) isn't a typo. It's just this administrator's way of making sure you're paying attention.

Where Credit Is Due

Everybody makes mistakes, and getting a black mark on your credit can happen to anyone. But credit bureaus make mistakes, too, and often black marks can appear even when you haven't done anything wrong.

The Electronic Credit Repair Kit provides everything you need to help you repair your unfairly damaged credit. Just follow their suggestions to learn about:

- The Fair Credit Reporting Act
- Improving and repairing your credit report
- Getting free credit reports
- Requesting corrections

There are even sample letters you can use to write to credit agencies.

How

World Wide Web

Where

www.primenet.com/~kielsky/credit.html

Just for Fuss Budgets

Being on a budget is like being on a diet, and you *know* how well those work. The only difference is that, while diets help to slim down your waistline, budgets are designed to fatten up your wallet or pocketbook. Here's a program that will help put some weight back into your checking account.

Budget Manager helps you manage your household budget by creating categories of spending, income, and savings funds. You then assign your money to different funds (like food, telephone, and electricity) and Budget Manager makes sure you don't have more going out than is coming

in. When expenses exceed income, Budget Manager prompts you to pri-
oritize and cut expenses until they match your income. That will give
you a balanced budget. Now maybe you'll be able to afford that extra
piece of cheesecake.

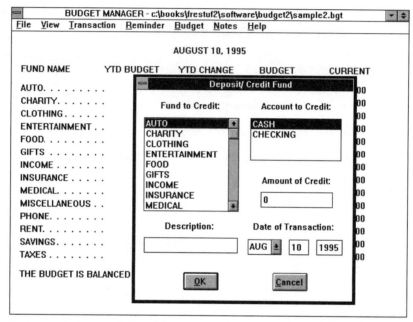

Once you start using Budget Manager, maybe you won't need that raise in
your allowance....Naaah!

How
FTP

Where
ftp.csusm.edu

Go To
pub/winworld/pim

Download
budget05.zip (117 K)

There's No Place Like Home

Nothing comes close to equaling the volume of red tape I had to cut through when I tried to land a student loan back in college—except for when I applied for a home loan a few years ago. In both cases, being whacked over the head with a two-by-four would have seemed a lot more pleasant than the bureaucracy I had to endure.

While this Web site won't help much with your student loan, it does provide top-rate information to anyone shopping for a home loan. The HomeOwners Finance Web site lets you compare your current loan with other loans available, find the best fixed and adjustable rates, and more.

There's also instant analysis of the latest trends in interest rates, a mortgage FAQ, help on refinancing, an online mortgage calculator, and a dictionary of real estate and mortgage terms.

How

World Wide Web

Where

www.internet-is.com/homeowners/index2.html

Graph Your Graft

If I were to create a graph of my financial history, it'd come out looking like the readout on a heart monitor whose signal just went flat. If you've been a little luckier in your finances than me, here's a program that lets you graph your fortune in all its glory. Seeing Your Money lets you create graphs of your financial data, and even lets you import data from programs like Managing Your Money, Quicken, or your favorite spreadsheets.

How

FTP

Where

gatekeeper.dec.com

Go To

pub/micro/msdos/win3/desktop

Download

sym.zip (482 K)

Now You're Getting Personal

Although exposing skeletons in your financial closet to thousands of others across the Internet may not be your idea of "personal" finance, it's actually a great way to get quick answers to your banking and budgeting questions.

The Personal Finance mailing list enables anyone with personal finance questions to network with people who have the answers. The mailing list is unmoderated and open.

How

Email

Where

majordomo@shore.net

Message

subscribe persfin-digest

Where to Find Way More Goodies

Before you decide to dress up your den with a traditional cuckoo clock, check out a few of the creations displayed at the deep-thought.biologie.uni-freiburg.de/~clock Web site, mentioned in the *Arts* chapter. These clocks definitely add a '90s twist to a centuries-old art form.

Turn to the *Travel* chapter for help figuring out how much vacation your family can afford this year. You'll find lots of information about air fares, bed and breakfast rates, and car rentals, as well as some great places to go.

For free updates to this book via FTP or the Web, go to: coriolis.com

Way More! FREE $TUFF

To be is to do.
Jean-Paul Sartre

To do is to be.
Albert Camus

Do be do be do.
Frank Sinatra

Humor

Just for Fun

The cable company just pulled the plug on your cable access. Serves you right for not paying your bill. But while you're getting things straightened out, there's no need to miss out on your favorite shows—if your favorite shows are on Comedy Central, that is.

At the Comedy Central Web site, you can get information about all your favorite Comedy Central shows, like:

- *Dr. Katz*
- *Absolutely Fabulous*
- *Kids In The Hall*
- *Mystery Science Theater 3000*
- *Politically Incorrect*

In addition to schedules, Emmy info, and even personal email analysis by Dr. Katz, you'll find tons of QuickTime and AVI film clips to download.

How

World Wide Web

Where

www.comcentral.com

Comedy Central and Dr. Katz: therapy for your funnybone on the Web.

Non-Profit Prophet

Are you destined for greatness? Will your programs run under Windows 95? And just where the heck did you put your car keys anyway? These and many of life's other mysteries are answered by the Usenet Oracle.

Sort of an online cross between a crystal ball and a Jay Leno monologue, the Usenet Oracle answers all questions posed to it. The answers aren't always what you'd expect, but what they lack in accuracy, they make up for in humor—and you can't beat the price (free, and worth every penny).

How
Email

Where
oracle@cs.indiana.edu

Subject
help

Did You Hear the One About...

If you think computer programmers don't have a sense of humor, here's a Windows utility that'll prove you wrong. Joker is a shareware program that supplies you with jokes on command—and then some.

You can set Joker to pop up a joke on your screen every hour, every other hour, or randomly throughout the day. Or, if you have time to kill, you can scroll through the hundreds of jokes stored in its database. And if your boss doesn't share your sense of humor, you don't have to let her in on the joke. Simply click the Hide button when you hear her coming.

How
FTP

Where
ftp.csusm.edu

Go To

pub/winworld/games

Download

joker12.zip (72 K)

Excuuuuse Me!

If "the dog ate my homework" is the best all-purpose excuse you can come up with, you'd better sit down, amateur, and see how the pros do it. The Evil Little Brother's Excuse Generator is just what you need to put some life into your worn-out excuses, apologies, and rationalizations.

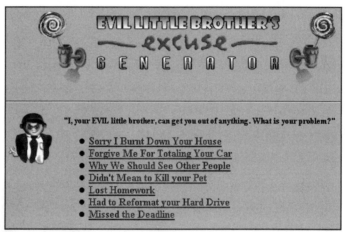

May I please be excused?

Simply input some basic information, like the name of an animal, power tool, body part, or kitchen utensil (don't ask—some things are better left unknown) and the perfect excuse for any occasion—including how you *really* lost your homework—will be generated automatically.

How

World Wide Web

Where

www.dtd.com/excuse

If you've got some time to kill after you've come up with the perfect excuse, click on *Back to Lab* and browse through some of the other links at Dr. Fellowbug's Laboratory of Fun & Horror. It tends to run a bit slowly, but it's worth the wait. This site's definitely *cool!*

Heard Any Good Ones Lately?

Some people take their computers just a little too seriously. With all of the crashes, disk errors, bad sectors, and lost files I've had to deal with, I think that if I didn't laugh I'd probably cry.

But here's a Gopher site that helps me lighten up just a little. In addition to lots of fun and games, you'll find computer-related jokes, stories, boners, groaners (lots of those), and more. There are also lots of puns and parodies to give your funny bone a humorous twist.

How

Gopher

Where

Alpha.CC.UToledo.edu

Go To

Entertainment

Jokes, Stories, And More

Don't forget that the Big Three online access services—America Online, CompuServe, and Prodigy—all provide Internet access, including the World Wide Web. To access the Web, log on to your service, then:

AOL—Keyword *Web* from the Go To menu
CompuServe—Go *Web*
Prodigy—Jump *Web*

Thanks for the Compliment (I Think)

Whether the medium is painting, literature, or film, surrealism has influenced every form of artistic expression, so why not the art of a good compliment? Now it has, if this Web site is any indication. Simply access this site for an automated surrealistic compliment.

The Surrealist Compliment Generator

Your laughter cascades into the eddies of my bathwater, and resounds warmly through my nasal cavities.

Reload this page to receive another extraditious compliment, or contrive one of your own devise...

The Surrealism Server, tellurite of Jardin Mécanisme.
lynn@pharmdec.wustl.edu

Complimentary compliments, compliments of the Surrealistic Compliment Generator.

Sort of a cross between Miss Manners and Timothy Leary, the Surrealistic Compliment Generator spews out compliments that are as flattering as they are bizarre.

How

World Wide Web

Where

pharmdec.wustl.edu/cgi-bin/jardin_scripts/SCG

Rats, Roaches, and Assorted Vermin

Every computer has bugs in it, but *rats?* Now that's a little more unusual, unless you've downloaded one of the programs stored at this site. Simply load 'em up and your screen—or better yet, the screen of some poor unsuspecting soul who doesn't have a heart condition—will be filled with roaches, worms, rats, and more. In fact, you'll find enough creepy crawlies here to make even Uncle Fester cringe. When you've had enough, just point and click to squish them on your screen. Ugh!

...nd you of those dorm-room

Here's a sampling of the programs available:

• Rats!
• Roaches Everywhere!
• Squish Bugs Game
• Worms

How

FTP

Where

ftp.csusm.edu

Go To

pub/winworld/games

Download

rats.zip (223 K)
roach.zip (16 K)
vermin.zip (50 K)
worm.zip (27 K)

Use Me and Abuse Me

Okay, take *this*: "You steal the cat's food, you ashtray smelling, silly-walking, earwax gargling, nostril-digging, heir of a direct mail lottery employee." *Whew*. Was that as good for you as it was for me?

If so, I've got to wonder about the people buying my books. I've also got to wonder about the people accessing the Abuse-A-Tron abuse generator. But if you're in need of a good verbal flogging, click the *Heap Abuse Upon Me* button, and brace yourself as the insults start to fly.

If you're a real glutton for punishment, just keep clicking for more insults. But then, like it says here, you should've been able to figure that out for yourself, camel lips.

How

World Wide Web

Where

www.xe.com/loyalty/abuse.html

Humor that's Long Overdue

When I think of some of the more humorous places to spend an evening, libraries do *not* immediately come to mind. In fact, I'd say they fall just below laundromats on my list of all-time fun hangouts. Boy, I hate it when I'm wrong. After checking out this site, I actually moved libraries *above* laundromats.

In addition to bumper stickers, light bulb jokes, and an assortment of other funny things, this site has a shelf-ful of library-related humor. You'll find books and magazines with library humor, library rules, funny quotations related to libraries, and more. Almost makes you want to become a librarian.

How

Gopher

Where

SNYMORVA.CS.SNYMOR.EDU

Go To

Library Services
Library Humor

The Cat's Out of the Bag

Think of a subject, any subject, and it's a sure bet you'll find something at the Cathouse FTP site that pokes fun at it. Don't believe me? Here's a *small* sampling of what's available:

- British humor
- Death
- Murphy's Law
- Political correctness
- Humorous quotes
- Sports
- Standup comedians

You'll also find lots of fun facts about your favorite humor writers, including Dave Barry and Douglas Adams. (Well, okay, you'll find lots of fun facts about *my* favorite humor writers.)

How

FTP

Where

ftp.cathouse.org

Go To

pub/cathouse/humor

Don't forget that many Internet addresses are case-sensitive, so be sure to type them *exactly* as shown.

Economy–Sized Humor

Why did God create economists? In order to make weather forecasters look good. If you liked that one, A) you're not an economist, B) you're not a weather forecaster, and C) you'll love the Economist Joke Page on the Web.

For reasons known only to the lunatics who manage this site, hundreds of jokes, riddles, and stories that poke fun at economists are stored here.

How

World Wide Web

Where

www.etla.fi/pkm/joke.html

Surely You Jest

Sure, the Internet isn't all fun and games, but you'd never know it from this Gopher site. Here's a perfect example of what happens when someone with a good sense of humor and too much time on their hands is let loose in cyberspace.

All joking aside, this huge archive of humor-related material includes lists of acronyms (now you'll know what IBM *really* stands for), answering machine messages we'd like to hear, graffiti we'd like to see, and letters we wish we'd written.

How

Gopher

Where

prism.nmt.edu

Go To

Schlake's Humor Archives

 Be warned that some of the jokes stored here are tasteless and offensive—kind of like my cooking.

Whaddaya Complainin' For?

There's nothing like putting pen to paper and taking out your aggressions on some poor public figure whose only crime is that he wants to put a freeway through your backyard. But who's got the time? Finally, *you* do. Grad student Scott Pakin has elevated whining to an automated art form with the Automated Complaint-Letter Generator.

Just enter some basic info like the complainee's name and how long you want to rake him over the coals (up to 10 paragraphs, but give the guy a break), and instantly you're provided with the perfect prose for your problem.

How

World Wide Web

Where

www-csag.cs.uiuc.edu/individual/pakin/complaint

 Remember, you heard about this little gem here first, so give *me* a break and send your letters somewhere else.

Where to Find Way More Goodies

For more laughs, read "Sign Here" in the *Art* chapter (hey, art can be funny). For something a little more cerebral—but just a little—surf over to the Tagline Archive Web site at www.brandonu.ca/~ennsnr/Tags, detailed in *Books and Literature*.

For laughs of another kind, try the *Movies and Television* chapter, which provides links to TV theme songs, great comedies around the world, and the Schoolhouse Rock Web site.

For free updates for this book via FTP or the Web, go to: coriolis.com

Way More! FREE $TUFF

I think there is an international market for maybe five computers.

Thomas Watson, Chairman of IBM, 1943

International

Out of Africa

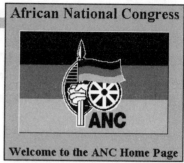

African National Congress

Welcome to the ANC Home Page

Goodbye apartheid,
hello democracy.

The African National Congress (ANC), majority party in South Africa's Government of National Unity, is keeping the international community up to date on its progress of bringing democracy to the Dark Continent.

At the ANC Web site, Internauts can get updates on South Africa's local elections, information and links to Net resources throughout Africa, email and phone numbers for contacting the ANC, and much more.

How

World Wide Web

Where

www.anc.org.za

News from the Motherland

For the thousands of Croatians who have fled their country's "civil" war, here's a mailing list that provides welcome news from the homeland. Run by volunteers who are literally dodging bullets to keep the Net community informed, this list keeps subscribers up to date on the latest developments in Croatia.

There are actually two news distributors available here: one in English and one in Croatian (with occasional articles in other South Slavic languages).

How

Email

Where

listproc@carnet.hr

Message

subscribe croatian-news *Your Name* (English version)

—or—

subscribe hrvatski-vjesnik *Your Name* (Croatian version)

Se Habla Español

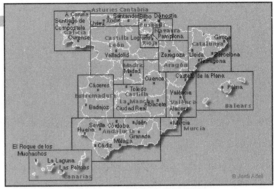

Spanish resources for Spanish speakers.

Ethnocentric Americans often forget the "World Wide" part of the Web and think of it as a U.S. national—as opposed to international—pastime. But sites like the Spain Internet Resources Web page help to remind us that, while the Net may have been created in the U.S. along with the first popular Web browsers, the Internet and World Wide Web are truly international phenomena.

This site provides a huge cache of information on Gopher, Web, and FTP servers throughout Spain. The majority of these sites are in Spanish, although many include English versions as well. In addition, you'll find:

- General info about Spain
- Travel and holidays in Spain
- A searchable database of Spanish email addresses

How

World Wide Web

Where

www.uji.es/spain_www.html

Don't forget that many Internet addresses are case-sensitive, so be sure to type them *exactly* as shown.

Hey Boys and Girls, What Time Is It?

It's always happy hour somewhere, and with WorldClock, you'll always know the location. The Daylight Position Map is a clock that displays a map of the world showing which areas are currently illuminated by the sun and which areas are dark (like you need a computer program to tell you that). It also displays your current local time, as well as Greenwich Mean Time.

Also while you're here, be sure to download a copy of the WorldTime International Clock for Windows, which lets you customize and show the time of day in up to six cities around the world at the same, um, time.

How

FTP

Where

ftp.csusm.edu

Go To

pub/winworld/clock

Download

world21.zip (60 K)

wtm21d.zip (83 K)

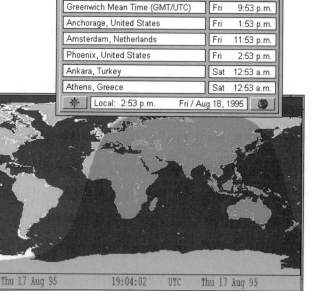

Too much time on my hands.

That Worldly Mac

The WorldTime International Clock that I just described is a Windows-only utility, but Mac users don't need to feel left out. A worldwide clock has long been available for Mac users, and it's built right into System 7. If you haven't discovered this one yet, give it a try. Just open the Map control panel and set your current location. Then, you can click on any point on the map and it will give you the time at that location along with its distance from you in miles.

How

I just told you.

Where

On your own Mac, silly—and think of all the download time you're saving.

Multiplying Like Rabbits

0 0 5 7 5 6 7 2 3 5 1 0

Haven't these people ever heard of family planning?

You think the Net's crowded now, just wait a few years and you'll really learn the meaning of the words *en masse*. In case you don't hear it, that distant rumbling is the population explosion, with shock waves being felt in all corners of the world. While currently at the 5.7 billion mark (plus or minus a few hundred million), the earth's population is predicted to nearly double by the year 2050. At that rate, they'll have to start burying us standing up.

Now you can keep track of each addition to the earth's bustling baggage. The WorldPOPClock—which uses the latest data on fertility rates, child mortality, and disease—is updated every 30 seconds with the latest estimates of world population growth.

How

World Wide Web

Where

sunsite.unc.edu/lunarbin/worldpop

International Alphabet S.O.U.P.

Do you find it impossible to distinguish between INTELSAT and INTERPOL, BAD and BADEA, or ECOSOC and ECOWAS? Believe me, you're not alone. But here's a site that makes it easy to keep track of the hundreds of seemingly random letters that make up the acronyms of dozens of international organizations.

From the Arab Bank for Economic Development in Africa (ABEDA) to the Zangger Committee (ZC), this site provides the key to cracking the acronym codes of over 180 different groups.

How

Gopher

Where

hoshi.cic.sfu.ca

Go To

David See-Chai Lam Centre for International Communication
1994 CIA World Fact Book
All Countries
Appendix.B

Link Up to LatinoLink

What do Raul Julia, Tony Orlando, and Roberto Clemente have in common? Yes, all three are dead—though Tony Orlando is making a comeback—but that's not quite what I had in mind. I was thinking more along the lines of their Puerto Rican heritage. But then, if you're hooked up to LatinoLink, you would've already known that.

This weekly Web publication for Latinos in the U.S. and Puerto Rico provides a wealth of information, stories, and photos of famous Puerto Ricans, Latino art, and its culture.

News | Commentary | Life | Business | Job Bank | Travel | Entertainment | Art | Archive | Feedback

All you want to know about this Commonwealth island of the West Indies.

Written by Latino journalists from the U.S. and Puerto Rico, LatinoLink also includes a free job bank, links to Latino travel and entertainment sites, and much more.

How

World Wide Web

Where

www.latinolink.com

Right on the Deutsch Mark

When news of Germany's reunification was first reported in 1990, it was mailing lists like this one that kept German expatriates abreast of historical developments like the crumbling of the Berlin Wall. While the everyday news sent out on this list pales by comparison, subscribers still get daily summaries of stories and events making news in Germany.

How

Email

Where

listserv@vm.gmd.de

Message

sub germnews *Your Name*

Plunder and Pillage for Fun and Profit

When you think about it, the Vikings of old had the art of world trade down pat: trade what you have for what you want, then go steal back what you had in the first place. Okay, so you can complain about the immorality of it all day, but you can't deny that the technique worked just fine (at least for the Vikings) for hundreds of years.

Velkommen to The Viking Network, the best place on the Net to access information about the history and culture of these Norsemen of old. Available in both English and Scandinavian, this site provides the facts and puts to rest the myths surrounding these medieval Scandinavian sea warriors. At The Viking Network, you'll get a fascinating and accurate glimpse into the people and events that helped shaped the history of Eastern Europe.

Hey, Hagar, where are the horns?

How

World Wide Web

Where

odin.nls.no/viking/vnethome.htm

If you're using Netscape (versions 1.0 and higher) to browse the Web, you can save yourself some keystrokes by skipping the *http://* prefix. Netscape assumes that if there's no prefix, you're accessing the Web.

Raise the Flag

The only thing I know *less* about than geometry is world geography. And when it comes to matching flags with their countries, I'd be hard-pressed to identify anything more than the Stars and Stripes—and that's on a lucid day.

But here's a program that could actually make learning the flags of the world (gasp!) *fun*. WorldFlag includes bitmaps and icons of just about every national flag in the world. And in addition to dressing up your documents with these colorful symbols, with just a few clicks of your mouse you can dress up your Program Manager by changing your existing Windows icons to flag icons. Not only will you learn the different flags, but your Windows desktop will start to look like the United Nations.

How

FTP

Where

gatekeeper.dec.com

Go To

pub/micro/msdos/win3/icons

Download

wrldflag.zip (81 K)

At the risk of sounding too technical, here's how to change an existing icon to a flag icon:

1. In the Program Manager window, click once on the icon you want to change to select it.
2. Select File|Properties to display the Program Item Properties window, then click on the Change Icon button.
3. In the File Name box of the Change Icon window, enter the path to wrldflag.dll (for instance, c:\software\flags\wrldflag.dll), and click on OK.
4. Select the flag you want and click on OK. Click on OK again to close the Program Item Properties window.

(All you Mac people out there quit smirking and be quiet!)

The Web's Goodwill Ambassador

Being an ambassador in Washington, D.C. is no picnic, you know. Grueling schedules made up of cocktail parties, nights at the theater, and presiding over supermarket openings leaves very little time for fun and games. But that doesn't mean the rest of us can't enjoy a brief respite from our daily grinds to surf through the information available at The Electronic Embassy.

From Afghanistan to Zimbabwe, you'll find information on over 170 embassies located around the Beltway of Washington, D.C., including addresses, phone numbers, and email addresses. Plus, many of the embassies are putting up Web sites of their own, with links to information about their countries, including maps, political reports, and even weather and tourism information.

How

World Wide Web

Where

www.embassy.org

This Just In...

When small-town events become international headlines, much of the story's local angle is stripped away. But here's a Gopher site that gives you a personal peek at local stories that get picked up around the world, many of which are in their native languages.

Here's a sampling of the countries whose news you can access here:

- Brazil
- Denmark
- France
- Holland
- Iceland

- Israel
- Italy
- Japan
- Korea
- United States
- Poland and other Eastern European countries

How

Gopher

Where

gopher.nstn.ca

Go To

NSTN CYBRARY - The Internet Public Library

Internet READING Room (News, Magazines, Books)

Daily News - Free Internet Sources

Hong Kong Web

Planning to visit Hong Kong someday? You better make it sooner instead of later. This British colony is slated to revert to Chinese control in 1997, and who knows what'll happen then. In the meantime, the business of business is booming in this international financial center, including its brisk tourism and textile markets.

Hong Kong Online provides valuable information on the tourism and commerce of Hong Kong. You'll also find lots of government-related data, as well as historical and cultural facts that show you the "real" Hong Kong.

How

World Wide Web

Where

www.hk.super.net/~webzone/hongkong.html

225

Where to Find Way More Goodies

The U.S. is one of the few exceptions, but for the rest of the international community, the metric system is the way to go. Check out the *Computers* chapter for some great conversion software.

You don't have to go to Italy to learn Italian, you just need to flip to the *Food and Cooking* chapter for audio files of Italian phrases. For even more foreign language programs, check out *Language and Linguistics*.

For up-to-the-minute international news, including the latest on business, sports, health, and entertainment, try the "CNN on the WWW" section of *Movies and Television*.

Finally, what could be more international than flying the friendly skies? Turn to the *Travel* chapter for lots of information for globetrotters.

For free updates to this book via FTP or the Web, go to: coriolis.com

On the Internet,
nobody knows
you're a dog.

An anonymous—
but wired—canine

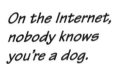

Internet

Resources

227

The Missing Link

Originally created as a site to categorize and search out the richest resources on the Web, NETLiNkS has evolved into a great starting point for newbies to learn the essentials of surfing and surviving in cyberspace.

Link up to NETLiNkS to find some of the coolest sites and sounds on the Web.

At NETLiNkS, Net newcomers and veterans alike will find loads of great Web links, including a daily dose of the best sites and resources available. If you're just getting your feet wet in cyberspace, click on the Newbie Help Link for lots of information on where to go, what to do, and how to do it. More experienced users can go straight to the Hot List for the latest and greatest on the Web. There's also a unique listing of Canadian resources, as well as links for African Americans.

How

World Wide Web

Where

www.interlog.com/~csteele/netlinks.html

If you're accessing the Internet using a Web browser, don't forget to key in the prefixes *http://* for Web sites, *gopher://* for Gopher sites, and *ftp://* for—you guessed it—FTP sites.

Thou Shalt Not Flame

One of the Internet's strongest appeals is also what makes it so controversial. For the most part, cyberspace is a free-for-all, with anyone saying, displaying, or downloading anything they want. While this creates a sense of freedom for most of us, it's always a small minority that create the most noise and threaten to ruin it for everyone.

That's why the Internet Society created the Internet Code of Conduct. This document should be required reading for anyone who ventures into cyberspace. In addition, the site contains a number of other valuable documents for anyone who wants to use the Internet to its full potential. Here's a partial listing of documents you can download:

- Ethics and the Internet
- Site Security Handbook
- Guidelines for Management of IP Address Space
- Domain Name System Structure and Delegation
- The Internet Standards Process
- Guidelines for Conduct On and Use of Internet
- NAS Report on Rights and Responsibilities in Networked Communities

How

World Wide Web

Where

www.isoc.org

SIFT and You Shall Find

Regardless of what's happening in the world, you can bet it's being talked about on the Net. Somewhere. The problem is finding it. With thousands of mailing lists and more than 10 thousand newsgroups on the Net, it's a pretty good bet that the information you're looking for has slipped through the cracks.

But with SIFT, you don't have to go to the information—the information you're looking for comes to you. The SIFT service lets you set up a personal profile for searching Usenet newsgroups. Simply enter the specific words or phrases you're looking for (like Windows 95, Mexico, or Springsteen—the more specific the better) and SIFT finds messages posted to newsgroups that match, then automatically emails them to you each day.

How

Email

Where

netnews@db.stanford.edu

Message

help

The Incomplete Guide to the Internet

When cyberspace stops growing, maybe somebody will create a complete guide of where to go, what to do, and how to do it on the Net. Don't hold your breath, though—the ride's just starting and there's no end in sight.

But here's a site with links to over 90 Internet how-to guides, lists, and other resources useful to Internet trainers or anyone else interested in learning more about the Net. This site includes links to:

- Internet guides
- Resources lists
- FTP archives
- Gopher sites
- Usenet newsgroups
- Mailing lists
- Search engines

Is this site complete? Of course not—but in cyberspace, what is?

How

World Wide Web

Where

www.brandonu.ca/~ennsnr/Resources/

Wizard of the Web

On the Web, it's better to look good than to feel good, and with Web Wizard, you'll always look *mahvelous* (at least your Web pages will). Web Wizard helps you to create great-looking Web pages in just a few minutes.

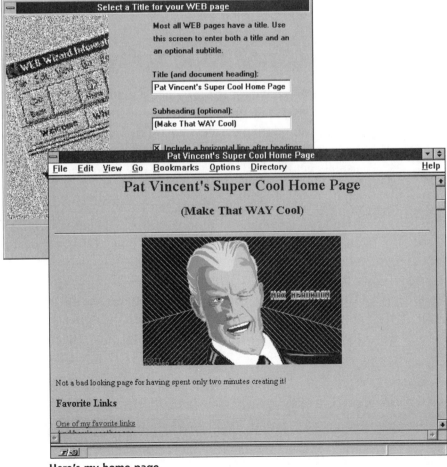

Here's my home page.

Simply point and click, and your home pages will be the envy of your cyberneighborhood, complete with artwork, graphics, and links to your favorite sites.

How

FTP

Where

ftp.csusm.edu

Go To

pub/winworld/html_edit

Download

webwiz16.zip (170 K)

How Do You Spell Mac Software? H-E-N-S-A

The HENSA database in the United Kingdom has one of the most extensive collections of Macintosh Internet utilities available. This site is restricted to U.K. users during business hours, but fortunately, U.K. business hours are the wee hours of the morning in the U.S. (and many other places), so you can usually get into HENSA during the day from the U.S.

Unfortunately, the indexing system at this site is just plain weird, so it's tough to find what you're looking for. To help you out, I've gone ahead and picked through the pile to find some of the best of the best Internet-related stuff for Mac users.

To use the HENSA database, click on Finder Software, and then click on the "Package Code" icon. From there, just click on the code range (for instance, a100-a200) that includes the file you want. I've included the file numbers in parentheses below. Here's a laundry list of goodies to look for:

Cpt2sit (file I457)
This one's an oldie, but it's still a classic. One of the most popular formats for compressing files stored on the Internet is CPT (Compact Pro).

But more Mac users have StuffIt than Compact Pro or any other compression-uncompression utility. If you've got the commercial version of StuffIt (version 3.5 or higher), you can uncompress CPT files easily. But the shareware version of StuffIt (3.0) doesn't handle CPT files. If you only have StuffIt 3.0, you'll want to download Cpt2sit ,which converts CPT files to SIT archives so that you can uncompress them with StuffIt.

CLIP2GIF (file a103)

This versatile little graphics utility quickly converts PICT and GIF files. You can convert PICT images to either GIF or JPEG format, and you can convert GIFs to PICT or JPEG format. CLIP2GIF is especially useful if you have Macintosh PICT images that you want to post to the Internet or incorporate into your own Web pages.

DAVE (file a148)

Ready to create your own Web pages, but don't want to learn HTML? Ask DAVE to give you a hand. DAVE can convert PageMaker files directly into HTML format. So if you're handy with PageMaker, as so many Mac users are, you can design your Web pages directly in PageMaker and then have DAVE convert them into HTML files that can be viewed with a Web browser.

HTML PRO (file a128)

With this program, you can create and modify HTML files even if you know very little about HTML. HTML PRO's menus include many common HTML formatting tags, so you can format your text documents into Web pages often by simply pointing and clicking. You can also display Web pages side-by-side with their HTML source code to help you learn what various HTML tags do and how they work.

MAC FTP LIST (file n061)

This one isn't a program, it's a text file of FTP sites on the Internet that either specialize in or feature Macintosh software. If you want to do your own snooping for Macintosh software, you'll definitely want to download this file. I suggest you print it and keep it in a binder for handy reference.

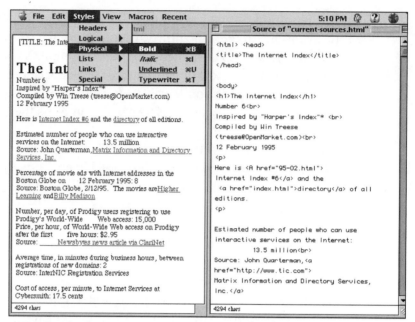

HTML Pro for the Mac provides an easy and painless way to use HTML while you're learning it.

RTF to HTML (file m182)

This program creates HTML files from text files coded in Rich Text Format (RTF). You might not realize it, but almost all word processors can save files in this common format. So you could, for instance, create an attractive Microsoft Word or a WordPerfect document, save it as an RTF file, then use the RTF to HTML option to convert the RTF tags into HTML tags. This is a great way to create Web pages simply by using your word processor.

How

World Wide Web

Where

micros.hensa.ac.uk/micros/mac.html

Legends in Their Own Minds

In every society, there are the famous and the infamous, and the Internet is no different. The Net.Legends FAQ points you to some of the most notorious Internauts ever to surf cyberspace.

Some are the good guys, while others wear the black hats, but all are interesting to read about and may even help you understand just how quirky, bizarre, and diverse the Internet's evolution has been.

With Net.Legends, you'll find out who's behind those annoying MAKE MONEY FAST messages posted to your favorite newsgroup (too bad they don't include a home telephone for *that* guy), who maintains the Usenet FAQs, and much more.

How

World Wide Web

Where

www.shadow.net/~proub/net.legends

A Scouting Outing

What's new? Careful when you ask that on the Net, because somebody's liable to answer you. Each week, the Internet boasts thousands of new sites and sounds, and keeping up with the avalanche is impossible. But if you ask what's *good*, that's a different question. That's when you need the *Scout Report*.

The Scout Report—a weekly publication covering the Web, FTP, Gopher, and more—assists Internauts in their ongoing quest to know what's new *and* good in cyberspace Simply subscribe, and once a week you'll get email detailing the best of the best of the latest of the most current of the newest Net stuff, uh, if you know what I mean.

How

Email

Where

scout-report-request@dsmail.internic.net

Message

subscribe

Mind Your Own Business

Three words nobody will ever use to describe the Internet: *inactive*, *stagnant*, and *unchanging*. I know they're all synonyms, but face it, one word just doesn't drive home the point. And with the Net's constant state of flux, how can any mere mortal hope to track all of the information available out there? The answer is...you can't. But now with the URL-Minder, you don't have to.

Simply register your favorite Web and Gopher sites with the URL-Minder, and you'll be notified by email every time they're updated or change locations. In addition, you can even have URL-Minder perform searches with your favorite Internet search engine, then notify you whenever the results change. Now you can spend your online time (and money) surfing where no Internaut has gone before, rather than constantly checking sites you've already visited just to see what's changed.

How

World Wide Web

Where

www.netmind.com/URL-minder/URL-minder.html

Don't forget that the Big Three online access services—America Online, CompuServe, and Prodigy—all provide Internet access, including the World Wide Web. To access the Web, log on to your service, then:

AOL—Keyword *Web* from the Go To menu
CompuServe—Go *Web*
Prodigy—Jump *Web*

Get Thee to a Users Group

Hey, you've been sitting in front of that computer long enough. What you need is a rest, a little time out of the house—something to get your mind away from cyberspace for a while. Nowhere to go? No problem. I'll bet there's an Internet users group meeting somewhere near you.

Here's a listing of Internet-related users groups around the world that hold real-life, face-to-face meetings about the happenings of cyberspace. This list is maintained online at the Rocky Mountain Internet Users Group (RMIUG—that's pronounced RMIUG—the U is silent) domain in Colorado. Now isn't that a nice change of pace?

How

Gopher

Where

gopher.rmiug.org

Go To

Rocky Mountain Internet Users' Group

User Group List

You can also access this list by FTP at ftp.rmiug.org/rmiug, or the Web at www.rmiug.org/rmiug/usergroups.html.

That's the Fax, Jack!

If your computer has a modem, odds are these days it's also got a fax machine built into it, just waiting for you to abuse it. In fact, probably the only thing keeping you from faxing your congressman in Washington is the cost of making that long distance call.

Well, worry no more. With the Internet FAX Server, you can send faxes for free almost anywhere in the world—including Washington. While not quite every corner of the globe is covered yet, this service is spreading fast and already includes much of Great Britain, Australia, Canada, and the U.S.

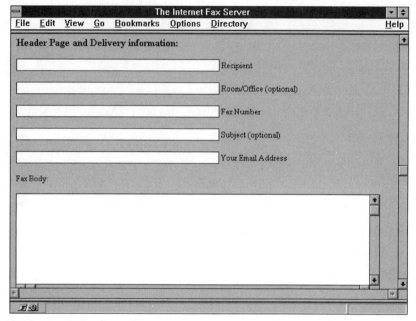

The fax speak for themselves.

How

World Wide Web

Where

town.hall.org/fax/faxsend-short.html

Outside the U.S., you'll have a better response using the European Web mirror at www.balliol.ox.ac.uk/fax/faxsend.html. Also, be sure to read the help documents here, including the information on how to fill out the fax form and what area codes are covered.

Just a Friendly E-Minder

If you're like me, you forget your appointments as soon as you make them. But if you're also like me, you check your email first thing every morning with that first cup of coffee. Finally, there's a service custom-made for us absent-minded-yet-obsessive Net addicts. E-Minder, a free reminder-by-email service sends the memory-challenged among us email reminders of special events, occasions, appointments, or anything else we've programmed it to prompt us.

Sort of a wake-up call service without the fancy hotel room to go with it, E-Minder lets you register the dates of occasions important to you. You can also specify how many days prior to the event you would like to receive your reminder, or even program it to remind you annually. When the date arrives, you're automatically sent a personalized email reminder. And you can register as many reminders as you like, for any occasion.

How
Email

Where
e-minder@netmind.com

Subject
e-minder help

Let's Get Graphic

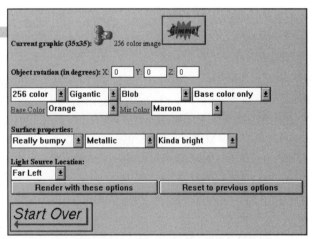

Sure, the Web is great because of its ease of use—I mean how hard can it be to point and click? But what really makes the Web—well, uh, the Web—is the graphics. And with the Interactive Graphics Renderer (IGR), jazzing up your Web pages with cool art has never been easier.

At IGR, you can quickly create graphics for your Web pages that are wild, wacky, and just a little weird—just like the Web.

This easy-to-use interface for designing customized graphics for your Web pages includes lots of objects, colors, sizes, and other options to help you create great-looking Web pages.

239

In addition, IGR includes a limitless supply of artwork for you to create and modify, and a simple interface for hassle-free downloading.

How

World Wide Web

Where

www.eece.ksu.edu/IGR

Once Upon a Time...

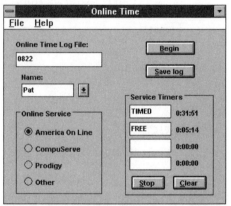

It's about time someone came up with an online timer.

Online Time Recorder makes it easy for you to keep track of the time you spend online. You can track per-minute charges, free time, extended usage, or any other time charges to help you stay within your service's monthly allowance, as well as to compare your service's monthly bill.

And with a built-in log file, Online Time Recorder will keep track of who's online, the date and time of each session, the amount of time spent in each section of the service, and the total time for each online session. You can even use it to record the time spent working on business projects to help you tally your billing.

How

FTP

Where

ftp.csusm.edu

Go To

pub/winworld/time

Download

oltime10.zip (42 K)

Harness the Web

With all this talk about the Web these days, it's easy for many of the Net's other tools to get forgotten in the hoopla. But a couple of years ago—light years in Net time—it was FTP, Gopher, and Archie that had the spotlight.

Now here's a site that brings these powerful—but sometimes overlooked—Net tools back to center stage. Just click on the links to access Net utilities like Archie, Gopher, and Telnet. Plus, there's lots of excellent information on creating your own home page and getting it published in cyberspace.

How

World Wide Web

Where

oeonline.com/~mrenick/util.html

Take a Bite out of TidBITS

This is the Web page for the well-written online newsletter *TidBITS*. The newsletter is devoted to providing insider information regarding Macintosh hardware, applications, and industry happenings, but it also provides extensive coverage of Internet issues and resources that are specific to Macintosh users. This is the essential source for the most up-to-date Mac info for all things online and off.

How

World Wide Web

Where

www.dartmouth.edu/pages/TidBITS/TidBITS.html

If you don't have a Web browser, you can still access TidBITS via their FTP site at ftp.tidbits.com. Go to the folder "pub," then go to the folder "info." Even if you do have Web access, you might want to visit this site.

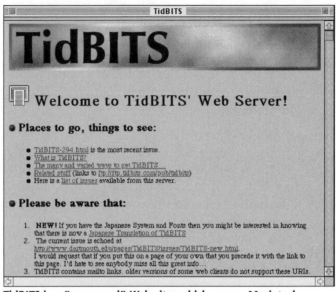

TidBITS is a "sponsored" Web site, which means Macintosh vendors pay for it, so you don't have to.

The editors of TidBITS include a separate folder ("select") that contains several excellent Internet-related utilitites for Mac users.

The Law of the (Cyber) Land

Talk about your hot topics. Here's a mailing list that combines the Internet, computers, and law into one comprehensive forum for discussion. You'll find in-depth analyses and hot debates on the still-gray legalities of free speech on the Net, copyright violations, pornography, and many other computer- and Net-related issues. Now if someone would just combine biking, brewing, and books into one mailing list, I'd never have to subscribe to another list again!

How

Email

Where

listserv@nervm.nerdc.ufl.edu

Message

subscribe cmplaw-l *Your Name*

Search Me

Woody Allen once said that in California, they don't throw their garbage away—they make it into TV shows. A lot of people would say the same thing when it comes to cyberspace. With its thousands and thousands of sites to choose from, the Internet is a browser's paradise. But finding the best—or even something remotely close to what you're looking for—is another thing altogether.

Here's a site that will help you find what you're looking for—or at least find something that will help you find what you're looking for. The Internet Sleuth links you to over 500 search engines and utilities on the Net. You can search by keyword, strings, alphabetically, or by nearly 40 different defined categories.

How

World Wide Web

Where

www.charm.net/~ibc.sleuth

Dear Dr. Internet...

You've read the manuals, you've called the support lines—heck, you've even swung a dead cat over your head at midnight—but you still haven't figured out this Net thing. Who ya gonna call? Dr. Internet, of course. Assuming you've been able to master email—or at least can limp your way through it—Dr. Internet could be the divine intervention you've been looking for.

Sort of a cross between Dear Abby, Click and Clack the Car Guys, and that know-it-all at the office water cooler, Dr. Internet (really a group of Project Gutenberg volunteers) answers general-interest questions about the Net each month from both newbies and Internet veterans.

How

Email

243

Where

internet@jg.cso.uiuc.edu

Message

Ask away. The doctor is in.

This Is a Test

That new browser you downloaded promises all the bells and most of the whistles available to make your Web surfing faster and a lot more fun. But you won't *really* know it's got everything it promises until you access the WWW Viewer Test Page.

This site acts as sort of a diagnostics tool for your browser. Just click the different buttons available to see if your browser will play QuickTime and MPEG videos, AU, AIF, and AIC sound files, and more.

How

World Wide Web

Where

www-dsed.llnl.gov/documents/WWWtest.html

Where to Find Way More Goodies

Internauts will want to check out the *Books and Literature* chapter to find out about the hundreds of Internet books on the market.

For a shot to the funny bone with an Internet twist, visit the Usenet Oracle, discussed in the *Humor* chapter. And before your kids start surfing cyberspace, turn to the *Kid Stuff* chapter for kid-tested and mother-approved Web sites suitable for the six- to ten-year-old crowd.

For free updates to this book via FTP or the Web, go to: coriolis.com

Way More! FREE $TUFF

You are only young once, but you can stay immature indefinitely.

Anonymous

Kid Stuff

Muppets...

As recognizable as Mickey Mouse—and maybe even Joe Camel—Kermit, Miss Piggy, Gonzo, and the rest of the Muppets are known throughout the world. And now you'll even find them in cyberspace.

It's time to get things started on the Muppet page tonight.

In addition to lots of information about Jim Henson Productions, you'll find a huge collection of episode guides for popular Henson projects, including *The Muppet Show*, *Fraggle Rock*, and *Sesame Street*.

This site also includes lots of other "Muppography," like movies featuring muppets, a comprehensive Muppet FAQ, and much more.

How

World Wide Web

Where

www.ncsa.uiuc.edu/VR/BS/Muppets/muppets.html

...And Puppets

Where do you think those Muppets got their start, anyway? Before Kermit and the gang got their big break, they made ends meet as finger puppets like the ones you'll find at the Hand Puppets Activity page.

Download Paper Puppets and Patterns.

Get Performance Tips from "The Professor"

Share ideas on making puppets from Scrap Materials.

Hot Link to other fun spots for kids!

Learn how to create your own puppets at the Hand Puppet Web site.

You'll find lots of downloadable patterns for creating your own puppets, as well as performance tips, ideas on making puppets from scraps around the house, and even information on hand shadows.

How

World Wide Web

Where

fox.nstn.ca/~puppets/activity.html

Mutant Mania

The Quad Squad, Heroes on the Halfshell, Radical Reptilians—call 'em what you want, but just don't call 'em late for a pizza feast! The Teenage Mutant Ninja Turtles are celebrating their tenth anniversary in 1996 with a year-long celebration that includes a new movie, live-action television, more cartoons, and personal appearances at a sewer near you.

One-quarter of America's favorite mutants.

While you're waiting for the fun to begin, whet your appetite with some of these TMNT bitmaps, which are free to download. Cowabunga!

How

FTP

Where

ftp.csusm.edu

Go To

pub/winworld/graphics

Download

turtle.zip (43 K)

If you have access to the Web, you can get more TMNT info—and even get email from your favorite hero on a halfshell—at www.wid.com/tmnt.

Join the Club

Regardless of your interests, in the vastness of cyberspace you can bet there are other Internauts who share them. And the Pen Pal Page can help you find them.

The Pen Pal Page connects kids around the world to discuss their cultures, likes, and dislikes. Simply fill out the online form with your name, user ID, age, and some other information, and the site's administrator will set you up with your own virtual cyberpal.

How

World Wide Web

Where

205.133.101.6/sfleming/tcm.htm

FYI

For the Web-deprived Internauts among you, here are a couple of mailing lists you can subscribe to and learn more about finding a pen pal on the Net:

- listserv@suvm.syr.edu with the message *subscribe K12Pals* Your Name
- pen-pals-request@mainstream.com with the message *subscribe*

And tell Mom and Dad it's time to upgrade.

How Much Is This Gonna Cost Me?

What's the value of a buck? About a dollar, I'd say. But if your kids aren't as money savvy as me, you'll want to get them a copy of Cash for Kids. This easy-to-use money tracker helps make it easier for kids to save money and spend it wisely—well, at least *wiser*.

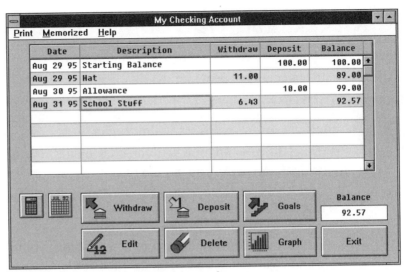

Financial planning can never start too early.

While it may look like a simple checkbook register, Cash for Kids is much more. Transactions are easily recorded and allowances can be deposited automatically. Kids can set future spending goals and easily graph their savings to show if they're saving enough. There's even an optional password security system so your kids can keep their records private. Before you know it, your kids will be giving *you* financial advice.

How

FTP

Where

gatekeeper.dec.com

Go To

pub/micro/msdos/win3/misc

Download

cfk.zip (77 K)

If you're accessing the Internet using a Web browser, don't forget to key in the prefixes *http://* for Web sites, *gopher://* for Gopher sites, and *ftp://* for—you guessed it—FTP sites.

Old MacDonald Had Some Sounds...

If your child is old enough to point a mouse, he or she will enjoy this little educational program. Kid's Clicks runs on any Color Mac that uses System 7.0 or higher. When you click on different parts of a picture, the program produces sounds related to where you click. The program includes one introductory module called "Farm Friends." If you click on the pig, the program oinks. If you click on the cow, the program moos. If you click on...well, you get the idea.

The program's author explains everything you need to create your own modules for your kids' enjoyment, and is asking for other users to submit their modules for public use. If you want to find out what other modules are available, you can contact the author at EricMLong@aol.com.

How

World Wide Web

Where

hyperarchive.lcs.mit.edu/HyperArchive/Abstracts/Recent-Summary.html

Download

Use the Search box, and type in "Kid Click." Then, click on the "Download" button to download the program.

Jurassic Internetting

Hundreds of millions of years ago—that's even before video games, kids—dinosaurs ruled the earth (not just Congress). While long since extinct, dinosaurs—or at least their bones—have made the greatest comeback in history and are now more popular than ever.

Here's a mailing list that discusses all aspects of these "terrible lizards." Volume on this list is light, ranging from a few messages to as many as a dozen a week. And don't worry; most participants aren't paleontologists, just dino-nuts, though some are extremely well versed.

How

Email

Where

listproc@lepomis.psych.upenn.edu

Message

subscribe dinosaur *Your Name*

Dear WinDiary...

Don't trust your most personal thoughts to a cheap thrift-store diary with a lock that any nine-year-old kid brother can pick. For your really important secrets, you need WinDiary. WinDiary is a combination calendar/ diary that replaces your Windows Calendar. With WinDiary, you can enter up to 758 characters in each daily entry for an entire year, and viewing past entries is as simple as clicking your mouse.

Plus, you can color code your entries according to their importance, and exporting your entries into your favorite word processor is a piece of cake.

How

FTP

Where

ftp.csusm.edu

Go To

pub/winworld/calendar

Download

windiary.zip (54 K)

Earn Your Merit Badge

During my brief tenure as a Boy Scout, I didn't get any further in the Scouting Handbook than to learn how to tie my sister to a tree. But those low-tech days are long gone. These days, Scouts are taking advantage of

Cyber-Scouting on the Web.

the high-tech information available in cyberspace to learn how to tie their sisters to trees. The more things change...

In addition to being courteous, brave, loyal, and truthful, the U.S. Scouting Service Project's Web site is a great starting point for finding loads of Scouting information on the Internet. You'll find information on Scouting units across the U.S. that have Web pages, interesting links related to Scouting, and lots of other resources for electronic Scouting.

How

World Wide Web

Where

www.HiWAAY.net/hyper/Scouts

Before you start sending me hate mail, I didn't forget about Web-surfing Girl Scouts out there. The site above is linked to the Official Girl Scouts of America Web site at www.HiWAAY.net/hyper/Scouts/gshp.html, which, unfortunately, was not working at press time. As a consolation, here's a Girl Scout mailing list you can subscribe to: Scout-Girls-Info@slic.cts.com.

Picture This

Considering that the Macintosh was designed to be a friendly, easy-to-use computer, it's always seemed strange to me that the Mac has never included a built-in drawing and painting program—as is the case with Windows. Fortunately, Craig Hickman's freeware version of Kid Pix is still circulating on the Internet.

This version only lets you draw in black and white, but it's still a powerful little program, and both kids and adults alike will enjoy spending hours at their Macs testing their artistic skills.

How
FTP

Where
ezinfo.ethz.ch

Go To
mac
education

Download
kidpix-10

You'll need to decode uncompress and this file using either StuffIt or Compact Pro.

What's Your Game?

Some of the most recent scientific studies indicate that children—and especially infants—know much more than the adults around them give them credit for. One study showed that infants as young as one year can grasp simple mathematics, have language skills much more advanced than ever imagined, and even have a rudimentary grasp of physics. Which only proves what I've known all along: Most of the drooling and whining is actually done by the parents.

Even though your little ones may not be ready for college just yet, here's a site that will help you start prepping them for the big day. You'll find educational games for kids as young as one year old, to help develop everything from their memories and language skills to helping to bring out the budding artist inside. Here are a few of the games and utilities available:

- Animated memory game
- Convert your monitor into an aquarium
- BabyGame for kids ages one and greater
- Computer coloring books
- A drawing program that lets kids make their own computer icons
- A word processor for kids that includes LARGE TYPE letters to make writing easier

How
Gopher

Where
gopher.ed.gov

Go To
Educational Software
IBM Computers and Compatibles

Download
amem.zip (226 K)
aquarium.zip (36 K)
babygame.zip (188 K)
colrbook.zip (121 K)
magic.zip (118 K)
makeicon.zip (17 K)
wpkids.zip (21 K)

The files here are compressed, but might not include the ZIP extension. Not to worry; simply rename the files with .ZIP tacked onto the end (for instance, wpkids.zip) and they'll unzip fine.

Once Upon a Time

Whether you've already been published, or are just getting started, the Children's Writing Resource Center is for you. You'll find lots of information on how to break into children's publishing, special reports on hot topics, the latest children's bestsellers, links to other great sites, the FAQs on writing for children, and much more.

How

World Wide Web

Where

www.mindspring.com/~cbi

You can also subscribe to the Notes from the Windowsill mailing list (kidsbooks-request@armory.com with the message *subscribe*) to get free reviews of children's books by email.

Comic Book Art and Artists

Available by Gopher or FTP, this site offers a huge collection of comic book art featuring downloadable pictures of all your favorite characters. And I do mean *huge*. You'll find hundreds of GIFs of your favorite heroes and heroines, as well as their nemeses. Here's a small sampling of what's available here:

- BlackWidow
- Tick
- Spawn
- Batman
- Captain America
- Magneto
- X-Men

Captain America is just one of the hundreds of characters you can download from this Gopher/FTP site.

Not to worry if your tastes run to less heroic characters. This site also includes plenty of *Bloom County*, *Outland*, *The Far Side*, and *Dilbert* art to occupy you. Plus, you'll find lots of info about the artists behind the artwork.

How

Gopher or FTP

Where

ftp.sunet.se

Go To

pub

comics

pictures

M-I-C-K-E-Y-M-O-U-S-E on the N-E-T

Who's the leader of the club that's great for you and me? I'll give you a hint: Besides being the world's largest rodent, his face is plastered on more toys, lunch boxes, and T-shirts than any other media icon—and the answer isn't Fabio.

If your next guess was Mickey Mouse, you're right on the money. And where there's Mickey, there's also Disney. On the Internet, you'll find tons of Disney-related sites, sounds, and mailing lists to get the latest information on Disney theme parks, upcoming projects, television cartoons, and more. Here's a sampling:

Walt Disney World
A comprehensive guide to Walt Disney World, including admissions, resorts, EPCOT Center, and Disney/MGM Studios. Subscribers receive this free online book four or five times a year, and it's a big one—about 235 K and growing.

How

Email

Where

toddm@twain.ucs.umass.edu

Message

subscribe WDW guide book mailing list

There's also a great Disney World Web site you can check out at www.travelweb.com/thisco/wdw/wdwhome/wdw.html.

Disney Comics

This mailing list comes all the way from Sweden, with discussions focused mainly on the Disney comics.

Where

disney-comics-request@minsk.docs.uu.se

Message

subscribe

Disney Afternoon Mailing List

This high-volume mailing list discusses *Disney Afternoon*, a series of animated television cartoons usually shown in a single two-hour block of sugar-induced afternoon mayhem. Cartoons discussed include *Darkwing Duck*, *Goof Troop*, *Bonkers*, *Aladdin*, and *Gargoyles*. Other related topics are also discussed, but the list maintainers stress that this is not a generic Disney discussion list. If you're looking for tips on visiting the Magic Kingdom, you won't find them here.

Where

ranger-list-request@taronga.com

Message

subscribe

A Day at Disneyland

This Web site has all the information you need to plan your trip to Anaheim, including operating schedules, directions, prices, and the Disneyland FAQ.

Where

www.best.com/~dijon/disney/parks/disneyland/

Euro Disney

Here's a Web site that includes information on Euro Disney's rocky history, hours, gate prices, hotel rates, special offers, and upcoming attractions.

Where

www.informatik.tu-muenchen.de/cgi-bin/nph-gateway/hphalle1/ ~schaffnr/etc/disney/

Tokyo Disneyland

Available in both Japanese and English, this site includes information on prices, hours, location, special discounts, and phone numbers to call for more help.

Where

www.toyo-eng.co.jp/NewHome/Messe/Useful-Info/Play/TDL/index-e.html

1 + 1 = Fun Squared (Sort of)

Personally, I have math homework to thank for making me the creative, imaginative person I am today, mainly because I constantly had to come up with better and better excuses to get out of actually doing it. But here's a program that could have made even *me* want to learn math— or at least it would have made it a little more palatable.

Master Math is a simple program aimed at helping elementary-school kids learn the basics. Kids select addition, subtraction, multiplication, or (yuk) division from the main menu, and are then quizzed flashcard-style. Their scores are then automatically tallied. There's even a game to play against your friends. But then, with friends like that, who needs math teachers?

How

FTP

Where

ftp.csusm.edu

Go To

pub/winworld/educate

Download

mmath194.zip (16 K)

It's the Ultimate

Calling this Web page The Ultimate Children's Internet Site might seem a bit presumptuous, but once you've checked it out, you won't think the claim is much of an exaggeration. You'll find over a hundred links to the best fun and educational sites on the Net for kids. Sorted by school grade, this site includes links to:

- Kids shareware
- Other lists for kids
- Links to other kids on the Web

Teachers and parents will also find a lot of valuable, fun, and educational stuff here. Happy learning!

How

World Wide Web

Where

www.vividus.com/~infov/ucis.html

As Simple as ABC

ABC123 helps preschool children learn to recognize numbers and letters by sight and sound. Just press a letter or number on your keyboard and you'll see it display on your screen while you hear it in either English or French.

Tested extensively by the creator's two-year-old, ABC123 is a proven and fun way for kids to learn their letters and numbers, er, their *lettres et numbres*.

How
FTP

Where
ftp.csusm.edu

Go To
pub/winworld/games

Download
abc123.zip (252 K)

Ho, Ho, Ho, on the Net, Net, Net

You better watch out, you better not cry, 'cause Santa Claus is online and watching. Cleverly disguised as a Windows screen saver, Santa's keeping a watch out for naughty cyberboys and girls. Here are some of the screen savers you can download:

• New Santa-saver with sound
• Scene of snow falling around a house
• Several winter and Christmas animated scenes

Jingle all the way with these Christmassy screen savers.

How

FTP

Where

gatekeeper.dec.com

Go To

pub/micro/msdos/win3/desktop

Download

santa3.zip (545 K)

santascr.zip (24 K)

ssxmas.zip (13 K)

xmassave.zip (8 K)

Kid-Safe Surfing Sites

Here's a list of kid-tested and mother-approved Web sites that are not only suitable for the six- to ten-year-old crowd, but kids may even find them more fun than afternoon television. (Heaven knows they're more educational.) These sites include pages full of fun projects and experiments created by school kids around the globe, software you can download, online stories you can see and hear, electronic encyclopedias, and much, much more.

How

World Wide Web

Where

www.pathfinder.com

www.kidscom.com

www.interport.net/kidsspace

www.cs.yale.edu/homes/sjl/froggy.html

ppc.westview.NYBE.North-York.ON.CA/WWW/wcss.html

mack.rt66.com/kidsclub/home.htm

www.ccnet.com/pegpoker/

www.klsc.com/children/

www.freenet.ufl.edu/~afn15301/drsuess.html

www.portal.com/~rkoster

I-site.on.ca/Isite/Education/Bk_report/

www.eden.com/~greg/cb/index.htm

www.ucalgary.ca/~darmstro/kid_links.html

longwood.cs.ucf.edu/~MidLink/

robot0.ge.uiuc.edu/~carlosp/color/

www.pd.astro.it/local-cgi-bin/kids.cgi/forms

www.safesurf.com/wave/sskwave.html

www.primenet.com/~sburr/index.html

ipl.sils.umich.edu/youth/StoryHour/

www.wln.com/~deltapac/ocean_od.html

gagme.wwa.com/~boba/kids.html

bingen.cs.csbsju.edu/~tnichol/forkids2.html

www.tpoint.net/~jewels/davesfun.html

www.webfeats.com/illusion/index.html

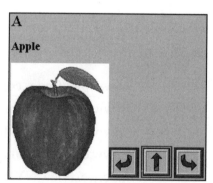

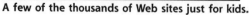
A few of the thousands of Web sites just for kids.

Animate Your Mouse

Animouse turns your Windows mouse cursor into fun, animated icons. Packed with over 80 creative and wild designs, Animouse adds a personal touch to your Windows desktop.

Here's a sampling of some of the cursors:

- Tropical fish
- Grandfather clock
- Marble that rolls when you move the mouse
- Crushed Macintosh
- Drill that spins when you press the mouse button

How

FTP

Where

gatekeeper.dec.com

Go To

pub/micro/msdos/win3/desktop

Download

animous5.zip (78 K)

Where to Find Way More Goodies

You're never too young to enjoy the Net, and here's proof: The Baby Art Gallery mentioned in the *Art* chapter includes high-contrast images designed to stimulate infants. Read more about it in the "Can You Say Monet? I Knew You Could" section. In the same chapter, you'll find an online coloring book and an art gallery created just for kids.

And if you're kids like to draw, they'll love creating online greeting cards at the Build-A-Card Web site. Look for it in *Books and Literature*, which also contains information on lots of electronic books kids can download.

And what do kids always want more of on their computers? Games, of course, and in the *Games* chapter, you'll find hundreds, even thousands, to download.

The next best thing to going to Disneyland is for Disneyland to come to you, and in the *Movies and Television* chapter, that's exactly what happens. Try the "Coming Soon to a Theater Near You" section for pictures and video clips of Disney movies, and information and previews about upcoming projects.

For free updates to this book via FTP or the Web, go to: coriolis.com

Way More! FREE $TUFF

What we've got here is failure
to communicate.

*Captain (Strother Martin),
Cool Hand Luke*

Language and Linguistics

Do You Speak Gopher?

So what if you don't know the World Wide Web from the Wide World of Sports. Just 'cause you're Web deprived doesn't mean you can't still access some great software. And here's a terrific Gopher site to prove it. You'll find dozens of programs to help you learn a foreign language, including:

- Arabic
- Chinese
- French
- Greek
- Hebrew
- Japanese
- Russian
- Vietnamese

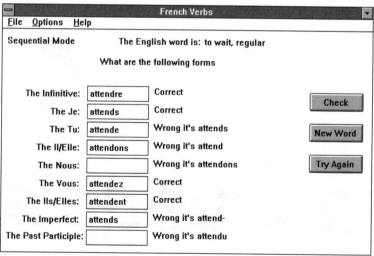

Pardon my French.

How

Gopher

Where

gopher.archive.umich.edu

Go To

Merit Software Archives

MS-DOS Archives

Foreign Lang

Language Links

Do you speak Spanish or Italian? Hey, who doesn't? French? Oui. But what about Russian, German, Dutch, or Portuguese? Um, well.... If not, check out the Foreign Languages for Travelers Web page. This site acts like your personal online interpreter, with many common—and not so common—languages covered here.

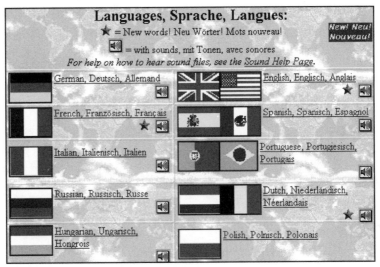

Watch your language—and hear it, too.

Designed to help itinerant globe trotters master the basics of a foreign language, Foreign Languages for Travelers provides words, phrases, and tutorials for over a dozen languages. You'll find lists of common words and phrases, along with their translations, sound files you can click on to hear the words, and a huge assortment of links to other language pages on the Web.

How

World Wide Web

Where

insti.physics.sunysb.edu/~mmartin/languages/languages.html

What's That Supposed to Mean?

While English is the overwhelming language of choice for Internauts, there are *thousands* of other great sites available on the Net in every imaginable language. So why surf a small pond when there's an ocean of Net sites waiting for you?

And the international flavor of the Net makes it a natural source for getting help learning a foreign language. Here are just a couple of great Windows language programs and tutorials that you can download by FTP:

- Ultimate Language Tutor v3.0 for Windows
- Flash card program for learning foreign languages

How

FTP

Where

ftp.csusm.edu

Go To

pub/winworld/educate

Download

4lang31.zip (84 K)

fwwin10b.zip (203 K)

Now You're Speaking My Language

The problem with traveling to other countries is that everyone speaks a foreign language. Until all those *foreigners* become a bit more considerate, here's a Gopher site that might make your travels just a little less, well, foreign.

You'll find dozens of DOS and Windows language programs to help you learn French, Hebrew, Latin, Italian, and more. Here's a small sample of what's available:

- **canton20.zip** Cantonese (Chinese) tutorial program
- **engtutr1.zip** English tutorial
- **french.zip** A beginning French program
- **german.zip** German verb and vocabulary quiz
- **hebrew.zip** Hebrew tutorial
- **japan.zip** Self-paced basic Japanese tutorial program
- **latin.zip** Basic Latin tutor

Be sure to read the Directory of Contents file to find more.

How

Gopher

Where

gopher.ed.gov

Go To

Educational Software
IBM Computers and Compatibles

I Can Kanji, Can You?

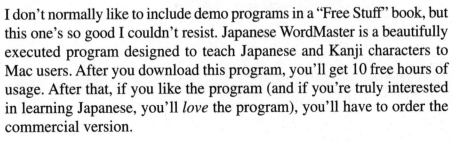

I don't normally like to include demo programs in a "Free Stuff" book, but this one's so good I couldn't resist. Japanese WordMaster is a beautifully executed program designed to teach Japanese and Kanji characters to Mac users. After you download this program, you'll get 10 free hours of usage. After that, if you like the program (and if you're truly interested in learning Japanese, you'll *love* the program), you'll have to order the commercial version.

Japanese WordMaster is an instructional designer's dream. It includes lots of fun graphics and exploits all of the multimedia capabilities of Macs (for instance, you can click on the sound button to hear the pronunciation of any Kanji character or word). The program includes a complete dictionary, and includes a game-like interface that lets you try your hand at identifying characters and words within a time limit that you can define. Learning Japanese has never been so much fun.

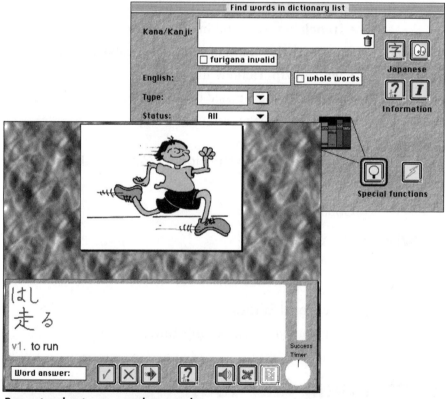

Run out and get your own demo version
of Japanese WordMaster off the Net.

How

FTP

Where

ftp.pht.com

Go To

pub

mac

application

Download

Japanese WordMaster.hqx (1.8 MB)

Pardon Me, but Your Vernacular Is Showing

"Hello, how are you? Welcome to the World Wide Web!"

A simple enough sentence, to be sure. But run it through the Jive Web editor and you're bound to get some interesting results. Just enter the text you want to modify and click on Submit for some wild, weird, and generally wacky results. Here's an example of the jargon I got back:

- **Cockney** ('Ullo, 'ow are you, roit? Welcome to the bloody World Wide Web!)
- **Jive** (Hello, how is ya'? Welcome t'de Wo'ld Wide Web. Right On!)
- **New York** (Hello, howahrya? Welcome tuh de Wawhld Wide Web! Okay?)

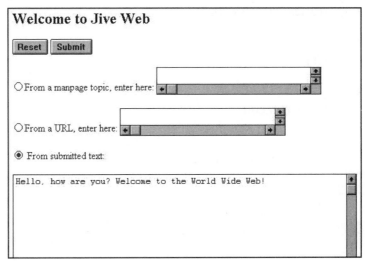

Just enter the bloody text 'n' let the Jive Editor do the flinkin' rest!

There's also Newspeak, Australian, German, Drawl, Finnish, and Valspeak (Hello, like, how are you? Welcome to thuh World Wide Web! Gag me with a SPOOOOON!). I couldn't have said it better myself.

How

World Wide Web

Where

luke.lcs.mit.edu/~philg/jiveweb.html

Latin: It's All Greek to Me

When it comes to learning a foreign language, Latin probably isn't the first or most exciting language on your list. It has also gained the reputation that it's gasping and wheezing its final breaths. But tell that to someone studying medicine or law.

Here's a simple program to help you learn the language of ancient Rome. It contains the text of the first book of *The Fables of Phaedrus*. Never heard of it? Neither have I, but I'm sure it's very popular among the scholarly crowd. And if you're studying Latin, you can't beat this program for online vocabulary help. In addition to all XXXI fables (that's 31— see, you're learning already), you'll also find helpful notes about the stories *ad nauseum*.

How

FTP

Where

ftp.csusm.edu

Go To

pub/winworld/educate

Download

phaedr1.zip (45 K)

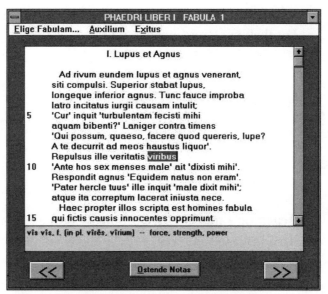

Latin, the language of theologists, philosophers, and fraternal organizations everywhere.

Caveat emptor (let the buyer beware): The interface to this program is written in Latin. Ah, but *dum spiro spero* (where there's life there's hope); to convert the interface to English, press F5. Also, if you need the definition of a Latin word, simply double-click on it.

The Language of Email

The Internet—especially the Web—is a technological marvel, with enough sound, pictures, and video to rival a Cecil B. De Mille production. But don't forget, it's still words that drive the Net—and that means email.

Here are just a few of the many mailing lists devoted to language and linguistics:

A Word a Day
This list introduces you to the "music and magic" of strange new words. (When somebody figures out exactly what *that* means, drop me a note.) Subscribers get an English vocabulary word and its definition by email

FREE $TUFF from the Internet

each day. Sometimes they're quirky, sometimes they're inspirational, but they're almost always fun.

How

Email

Where

wsmith@wordsmith.org

Subject

subscribe *Your Name*

Teaching English as a Second Language
This list is designed for anyone interested in learning more about teaching English around the world.

Where

listserv@cunyvm.cuny.edu

Message

subscribe TESL-L *Your Name*

Esperanto
This list is for people interested in the neutral international language Esperanto. Discussions about the language itself, the Esperanto movement, publications, and news are encouraged—and discussions *in* Esperanto are especially encouraged.

Where

esperanto-l-request@netcom.com

Message

subscribe

Don't forget that many Internet addresses are case-sensitive, so be sure to type them *exactly* as shown.

Stuttering

This list discusses stuttering research and support. Subscribers include researchers, speech-language pathologists, National Stuttering Project members, and, of course, people who stutter.

Where

listserv@vm.temple.edu

Message

sub stutt-l *Your Name*

Literature for Lexicographers

To paraphrase Francis Bacon, some words are to be tasted, others to be swallowed, and some to be chewed and digested. Francis would have loved this Gopher site, where you can belly up to the Net for an all-you-can eat smorgasbord of word-related shareware programs.

You'll find software to help build your vocabulary and impress your easily impressed friends. Here are just a few of the programs you can download:

- **THESAUR** An easy-to-use, menu-driven online thesaurus
- **THESAUR (non-resident version)** Another great shareware thesaurus
- **Word-A-Day** Build your vocabulary one word—and day—at a time

How

Gopher

Where

gopher.ed.gov

Go To

Educational Software
IBM Computers and Compatibles

Download

thesar36.zip (166 K)

thesar39.zip (147 K)

wordaday.zip (49 K)

Have You Heard the Word?

If you love words, but refuse to take them too seriously, here's a match made in heaven—or cyberspace anyway. *The Word Detective* is a bi-monthly newsletter covering the origins of words in a fun and light way.

The Word Detective Web page is piled high with word trivia and games.

Based on the syndicated newspaper column *Words, Wit and Wisdom* by Evan Morris, *The Word Detective* falls somewhere between the *Oxford English Dictionary* and a *Monty Python* sketch as it brings you fun factoids about the origins of words and their usage. Access this site to find out how you can get a free sample issue sent to you via snail mail.

How

World Wide Web

Where

www.escape.com/~words1

Sir Ilych, Can You Read Cyrillic?

This unique Web page provides you with everything you need to know to convert your Macintosh to a Russian-language system. You can transform your keyboard into the Cyrillic alphabet, add Cyrillic fonts to your system, and you can even create a Russian Internet connection interface or a Russian version of System 7. This site isn't a tutorial in Russian, but if you already know Russian and want your Mac to understand it too, this site's definitely for you.

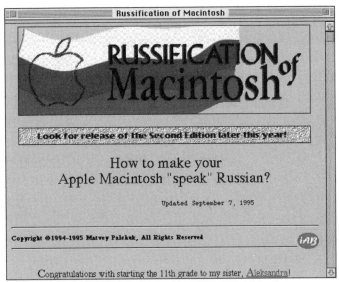

Is your Mac in need of a cold boot? Well, send it to Siberia.

How

World Wide Web

Where

http://www.pitt.edu:81/~mapst57/rus/system.html

Have Translator, Will Travel

If English is your first language, you'll love this site. You'll find tons of software that makes learning a second language easier than ever—assuming it was easy in the first place. In addition to the basics, (French, Italian, Spanish), aspiring bilingualists will find dictionaries and translator software for Brazilian Portuguese, Serbian Cyrillic, Danish, Polish, Russian, and more. Here's a sampling of the online dictionaries and translators available here:

- English-Danish-English
- English-Croatian-English
- English-German-English
- English-Norwegian-English
- English-Serbian Latin-English

277

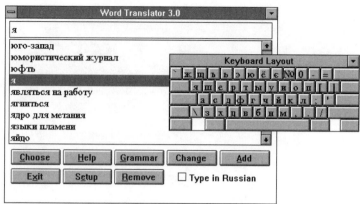

A Tsar is born with this Russian translator software.

How

FTP

Where

gatekeeper.dec.com

Go To

pub/micro/msdos/win3/misc

Download

wt4w3abp.zip (654 K)

wt4w3ade.zip (651 K)

wt4w3ace.zip (792 K)

wt4w3afe.zip (634 K)

wt4w3age.zip (653 K)

wt4w30ne.zip (664 K)

wt4w3ape.zip (783 K)

wt4w3are.zip (819 K)

wt4w3asc.zip (807 K)

wt4w3asl.zip (796 K)

wt4w3ase.zip (628 K)

Be sure to read the INDEX file for information about the different programs available to download.

Communication Breakdown

The Internet is a great place to find hundreds of valuable resources on communication disorders and disabilities—if you know where to look. But here's a document whose researchers have already done the work for you.

You'll find over *400* Internet resources for students and professionals involved in the fields of speech-language pathology, audiology, speech science, communication disabilities, and more. At over 145 K (that's roughly 80 pages of text, folks), this is one of the most comprehensive listings of these Net resources you'll find online.

How

Gopher

Where

gopher.lib.umich.edu

Go To

What's New and Featured Resources

Clearinghouse for Subject-Oriented Internet Resource Guides

List of All Clearinghouse Guides

Communication Disorders and Sciences; J. Kuster

You can also access this information by FTP at una.hh.lib.umich.edu/inetdirsstacks/commdis:kuster.

Many Languages, One World

The Human-Languages Page is devoted to bringing together information about the languages of the world—and I mean *all* languages of the world. While it hasn't quite achieved that goal yet, don't write it off. You'll find a truly amazing collection of world-spanning language resources listed here, ranging from dictionaries to language tutorials to spoken samples of languages.

In addition to information and links to language pages as diverse as Aborigine, Afrikaan, Estonian, Gaelic, Klingon (really), and Vietnamese, you'll find an impressive collection of multilingual resources, books and literature archives, linguistics labs and institutions on the Net, and many other linguistics resources. This is definitely a page you'll want to add to your list of favorite sites.

How

World Wide Web

Where

www.willamette.edu/~tjones/Language-Page.html

Sign Here, Please

Okay, you can sign the alphabet, but mastering the next step of sign language can prove to be a bit more difficult. And while with other languages you can pop a tape into your car stereo and practice during rush hour, this is generally not a good idea with sign language.

But here's a program that'll leave you speechless. This easy-to-use program for Windows teaches you the basics of American Sign Language (ASL). Just type in a word or sentence and this nifty program signs it back to you. You can even minimize the program to an icon, then drag and drop a text file from the File Manager onto it, and it'll sign the filename.

How

FTP

Where

ftp.csusm.edu

Go To

pub/winworld/educate

Download

signing.zip (496 K)

If you're interested in learning more about sign language, check out the SLLING-L mailing list. Formerly ASL-LING, SLLING-L discusses sign-language linguistics. Discussions of deaf culture, education, medical advancements in the studies of deafness, and so on are discouraged, except as they relate to sign linguistics. Send email to listserv@yalevm.ycc.yale.edu with the message *subscribe*.

Direct Me to the Nearest Foreign Language

Knowledge is power—or so say the old Saturday-morning Schoolhouse Rock commercials—and Knowledge Computing is leading the way in bringing the power of PCs to the world through its innovative multilingual software.

The Multilingual PC Directory is the definitive guide to multilingual and foreign language products for IBM PCs and compatibles. It includes details of nearly 400 foreign-language products available in over 70 countries from over a thousand manufacturers, publishers, and affiliates. If you want to word process in Portuguese, do spreadsheets in Spanish, or create graphics in Greek, The Multilingual PC Directory is definitely for you.

Available in hard copy, Windows Help format, or online, this source guide includes product and company profiles, computer requirements, and languages supported. Contact information is also covered, including addresses, telephone and fax numbers, and some email addresses.

How

World Wide Web

Where

www.knowledge.co.uk/xxx

If you're using Netscape (versions 1.0 and higher) to browse the Web, you can save yourself some keystrokes by skipping the *http://* prefix. Netscape assumes that if there's no prefix, you're accessing the Web.

Linguistics Links

Words, words, words. From their origins to the changing way they are pronounced, modified, and arranged to convey a message, words are a fascinating topic.

And if you love linguistics, you'll love this Gopher site. You'll find lots of shareware programs to assist in the study of language, including historical linguistics, pronunciations, etymology, semantics, and grammar.

How
Gopher

Where
gopher.archive.umich.edu

Go To
Merit Software Archives
MS-DOS Archives
Linguistics

Que Pasa in Cyberspace

What's happening on the Internet for Spanish speakers? Mucho, and this site is on its way to listing them all. The NetOpen Directory, an online listing of Web sites for Spanish speakers, is still in its infancy, but is growing fast.

You'll find links to Spanish Web sites in:

• Arte - Museos (Art - Museums)
• Instituciones Públicas (Public Institutions)
• Entidades Financieras (Banks)
• Ficheros (Files)
• Música (Music)
• Negocios (Business)

- Periódicos (Newspapers)
- Proveedores de Internet (Internet Providers)
- Universidades - Ciencia (Universities - Science)

How
World Wide Web

Where
www.indra.com/jewels/cybercom/netopen

Where to Find Way More Goodies

Anyone who loves word games will want to check out the "Not for Block-heads" section of the *Games* chapter for great software that helps you create your own crossword puzzles.

Also, when you're ready to try out a few of the foreign phrases you've learned, check out the *International* and *Travel* chapters for information about places to go and people to talk to around the world.

For free updates to this book via FTP or the Web, go to: coriolis.com

Way More! FREE $TUFF

A jury consists of twelve persons chosen to decide who has the better lawyer.

Robert Frost

Law

Life, Liberty, and the Pursuit of Free Speech

I'm sure you know never to yell fire in a crowded theater, but what about yelling movie in a crowded firehouse? One thing I *do* know, though, is that you're not going to find the answer at this Web site. But if you're looking for other cutting-edge information on First Amendment issues, The Freedom Forum First Amendment Center at Vanderbilt University is the place to go.

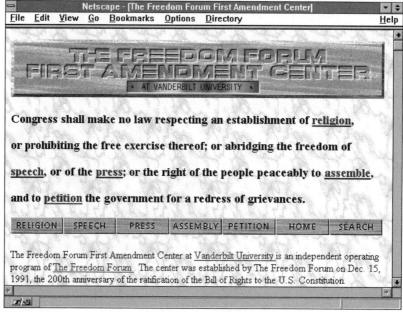

Freedom of speech hits the Net.

Established on December 15, 1991 (the 200th anniversary of the ratification of the U.S. Constitution's Bill of Rights, for those of you who slept through American History), The Freedom Forum is the online choice for debate on free expression and freedom of information issues. This site will give you a better understanding of First Amendment rights and values, including freedom of religion, free speech and press, and the right to petition the government and assemble peaceably.

You'll also find plenty of documents to download, including Supreme Court rulings, information about *Freedom Speaks*—the nation's only television show devoted exclusively to First Amendment issues—and much more. There are also lots of links to information about other First Amendment issues.

How

World Wide Web

Where

www.fac.org

Call-a-Lawyer...

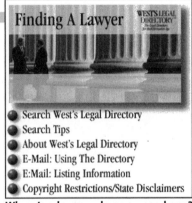

Where's a lawyer when you need one?

After reading my third John Grisham novel, I came to the conclusion that lawyers command about as much respect as journalists—which is to say they're somewhere between snakes and leeches on the food chain. But when you need one, who ya gonna call?

West's Legal Directory (WLD) can help you get all the information you need to select the lawyer who's best for you. You'll get information about law firms, government offices, corporate law offices, and lawyers throughout the United States and Canada. Maybe WLD will help lawyers get the respect they deserve. Now if they could just do the same for journalists.

How

World Wide Web

Where

www.westpub.com/WLDInfo/WLD.htm

...and Hire One, Too

Rumor has it that Janet Reno was surfing the Internet's online want ads one day looking for a cheap housekeeper when she came across this Department of Justice (DOJ) Gopher site, which lists current job openings in the

DOJ. While she never did find a housekeeper, the rest—as they say—is history.

You may not be lucky enough to find a listing for Attorney General (then again, the way things are looking for Janet these days, you might), but qualified applicants will still find some top-rated government jobs posted here. Here are a few recent listings:

• Executive Office for Immigration Review, Immigration Judge
• Immigration and Naturalization Service, Assistant District Counsel
• Presidential candidates—must have thick skin, short memory, and good sense of humor

Okay, I made that last one up, but keep checking this site and you're sure to find some great opportunities here.

How
Gopher

Where
justice2.usdoj.gov

Go To
Justice Department Attorney Job Listings

Check out some of the other links here for some pretty good DOJ and FBI information.

No Justice, No Net

Being the avid Internaut that I know you are, you're probably very interested in the laws and legislation that affect cyberspace and Net surfers. Rest assured that there's plenty of information out there, if you know where to look. For the most part, though, you'll be disappointed with outdated data, non-existent links, and less-than-newsworthy news (I know I was).

So let someone else do the dirty work for you. Lawyer Marshall K. Dyer has created *NetWatchers*, a monthly cyberzine covering the Internet, the law, and what happens when "unstoppable force" meets "immovable object."

NetWatchers features in-depth articles on the laws affecting the Internet and the online world, with lots of information and links covering the legal, ethical, and policy issues of cyberspace.

IN THIS ISSUE

- *NEWSBYTES:*
  ASSORTED NET HAPPENINGS

- MILITARY COURT RULES ON E-MAIL PRIVACY

- CPSR FILES BRIEF IN FOIA CASE

- BCFE ANNOUNCES IT'S "HEROES AND VILLAINS"

- DAVID LOUNDY ON RICO

Watching the Net so you don't have to.

How

World Wide Web

Where

www.ionet.net/~mdyer/front.shtml

Do You Copy?

When does a copy become a copyright violation? It depends on who you talk to, and unfortunately, that just might be a very expensive lawyer if somebody sues you for infringement.

Before that happens, check out the Copyright Clearance Center (CCC) to learn all you need to know about protecting yourself—and your publications—in cyberspace. CCC can help make sure you comply with the U.S. copyright law and show you how to collect payments for your own copyrighted material.

How

World Wide Web

Where

www.directory.net/copyright/

Access the free CCC demo catalogs to see how easy online copyright searching can be. You'll also find links to information on U.S. copyright law and lots more.

> Don't forget that the Big Three online access services—America Online, CompuServe, and Prodigy—all provide Internet access, including the World Wide Web. To access the Web, log on to your service, then:
>
> **AOL**—Keyword *Web* from the Go To menu
> **CompuServe**—Go *Web*
> **Prodigy**—Jump *Web*

Mail-Order Law

One thing Internauts never seem to get tired of discussing is their online rights and how they're continually violated by "Big Brother governments that fear the Internet *because they don't understand it!*"(Hey you! Get off the soapbox!) If you need to let off some steam, maybe venting through one of these mailing lists is the way to go. Here are several law-related discussion groups you can access:

Lawyers and the Internet
This mailing list enables lawyers, law students, legal assistants, law professors, and other legal eagles to discuss how to use the Internet in connection with the study, practice, and development of the law. It is not intended to allow persons to seek free legal advice, so don't even think about it.

Where

net-lawyers-request@webcom.com

Message

subscribe

Youth Rights

The Youth Rights mailing list discusses the rights of kids and teens. It's open to anyone regardless of age and focuses mainly on individual liberty, although a wide range of other topics are also discussed.

Where

listserv@sjuvm.bitnet

Message

sub y-rights *Your Name*

Animal Rights

This list acts as a public news wire for items relating to animal rights and welfare. This is not a discussion list, but instead focuses on news items, requests for information on events, or responses to requests for information.

Where

ar-news-request@cygnus.com

Message

subscribe

Academic Sexual Correctness

The Academic Sexual Correctness mailing list discusses and shares information regarding all aspects of university sexual control issues, including speech, censorship, harassment, student-professor fraternization, and so on. It's open to all academics and former academics, including students, professors, and staff.

Where

request@beach1.csulb.edu

Message

subscribe

Don't forget that many Internet addresses are case-sensitive, so be sure to type them *exactly* as shown.

Private Eye
This list is for private investigators or gumshoe wannabes.

Where

private-eye-request@netcom.com

Message

subscribe

Americans with Disabilities Act
Postings on this mailing list should relate to the Americans with Disabilities Act (ADA) and other disability-related legislation in the United States, as well as other countries.

Where

listserv@vm1.nodak.edu

Message

subscribe ada-law *Your Name*

Order in the Court

Maybe it's just my guilty conscience about all those overdue library books, but accessing this site is about as close to a federal court that I ever want to get. But if you've got nothing to hide, check out the U.S. Federal Court home page.

This site is a clearinghouse for information from and about the Judicial Branch of the U.S. government. In addition to information about how the federal courts operate, you'll find monthly newsletters of the federal courts, press releases, and ways to access federal court records online.

How

World Wide Web

Where

www.uscourts.gov

That's Affirmative

The California Civil Rights Initiative (CCRI) is the proposed California ballot proposition that would eliminate government affirmative action programs. This Web page shows you what CCRI is all about and what its backers hope to accomplish.

Whether you're in favor of affirmative action or opposed to it, check out the CCRI Web site.

You'll get an in-depth look at the history of CCRI, information about its supporters, and what the future holds for this grassroots initiative, which could have a wide-sweeping effect on the programs offered by federal and state governments. You'll get:

- The latest news concerning the CCRI campaign
- The facts about the initiative
- Information about the people behind CCRI
- A message from California Governor Pete Wilson
- Information about how you can help with CCRI
- The entire text of the proposition

How
World Wide Web

Where
www.cal-net.com/ccri

Calling All Cars

For over 60 years, *The FBI Law Enforcement Bulletin*, the most widely read law enforcement publication in the U.S., has provided important and practical information about fighting crime and tracking criminals. Now, this valuable monthly publication can be accessed on the Internet.

With articles on forensics, personnel management, criminal law, and more, *The Bulletin* features the latest information for today's law enforcement officers. Columns like *The Bulletin Reports* and *Police Practice* columns provide readers with the latest advances in police science and techniques. Some recent articles include:

- *Tactical Surveillance with a Twist*
- *Law Enforcement Communication Security*
- *On the Cutting Edge: Law Enforcement Technology*
- *On the Line: Email Responses*
- *Virtual Reality: The Future of Law Enforcement Training*
- *Police Practice: Developing an Identity Book*
- *Computer Crime Categories: How Techno-Criminals Operate*

How

Gopher

Where

justice2.usdoj.gov

Go To

Federal Bureau of Investigation

A Site Worth Patenting

Whether you're a full-time inventor or part-time tinkerer, you need to protect your rights to that better mousetrap you're building. And what if somebody's already thought of it?

Before you put the time and effort into inventing your invention, check out the Internet Multicasting Service's archives of the U.S. Patent and Trademark Office (USPTO). You'll find listings of all patents issued in the U.S. for 1994 and 1995, as well as some helpful utilities and documents for making your search a little easier. This service is not affiliated in any way with the USPTO.

How

World Wide Web

Where

town.hall.org/cgi-bin/srch-patent

If you'd like to get weekly mailings of all patents listed in the most recent issue of the *USPTO Patent Gazette*, send email to patents@world.std.com with the message *help*.

The Internet, Legally Speaking

Gray Cary Ware & Freidenrich is a full-service commercial law firm representing many of California's telecommunications, manufacturing, software, banking, and financial institutions. And now it's hanging its shingle in cyberspace.

And that's good for you, because the Gray Cary Ware & Freidenrich Web site includes lots of information about doing business on the Internet, protecting yourself legally in cyberspace, and other legal issues—and it won't cost you $200 dollars per hour. In addition, you'll find the full texts of the U.S. copyright, trademark, and patent laws, as well as links to many other legal resources on the Net.

How

World Wide Web

Where

www.gcwf.com

This Court Is Now In Session

In Greek mythology, Hermes was the messenger of the gods. Today, he's the messenger of the Supreme Court—definitely a demotion, but the hours are better and you can't beat the benefits. This site, part of Project Hermes, a highly successful experiment started in 1992 to make Supreme Court documents available to the public quickly and easily, distributes full-text Supreme Court opinions almost before the Justices' chairs are cold.

Perfect for anyone studying law, government, or general current events, Project Hermes includes court rulings, concurring and dissenting opinions, and many other court documents for anyone else who wants their legal information right from the source.

How
FTP

Where
ftp.cwru.edu

Go To
hermes

For help in navigating this site, be sure to review the README documents stored here.

That's Criminal!

If you're thinking of a career in law enforcement, but don't know where to start, keep this in mind: Many law enforcement agencies around the country are raising their educational standards from a high-school diploma to at least a two-year college degree. And don't even think about working at the federal level without a bachelor's degree.

The University of South Florida Department of Criminology provides information on graduate and undergraduate criminology programs and degrees available, as well as the latest innovations in law enforcement, corrections, and juvenile justice. You'll also find links to other great criminal justice Internet sites.

How

World Wide Web

Where

www.cas.usf.edu/criminology/index.html

The Law of the Land

When it comes to local laws and ordinances, common sense can go a long way toward helping you stay within the rules. But if you're planning to spend any time away from the homeland, you might want to check out this Web site first.

The Leiden University Faculty of Law Web page offers links to sites around the world that deal with international law and human rights. You'll find Web, FTP, and Gopher links to the United Nations, the European Union, and many other international organizations.

In addition, there are lots of links to law libraries, law-related lists and newsgroups, universities, research centers, environmental law sites, and the laws of other countries from Albania to Yugoslavia.

How

World Wide Web

Where

rulj287.leidenuniv.nl/lawlib/

Legal Eagle Dictionary

If you work for a law firm—or at least didn't miss a second of the O.J. Simpson trial—you might think you know the law pretty well, and you

might be right. But when it comes to spelling some of that legalese, you probably feel more like Beetle Bailey than F. Lee Bailey.

The *Legal Dictionary* comes to the rescue. This handy word-processing spell checker contains 75,000 bytes worth of legalese and Latin legal terms—enough to tongue tie the entire O.J. Dream Team, with Marcia Clark thrown in for good measure.

How

Gopher

Where

gopher.ed.gov

Go To

Educational Software

IBM Computers and Compatibles

Download

lawdict.zip (75 K)

Be sure to read the read.me file that comes with this program for instructions on how to load the dictionary.

This Is Only a Test

Are you:

- Interested in applying to law school, but not sure where to start?
- About to take the Law School Admissions Test (LSAT) and hoping to avoid the cost of high-priced preparation courses?
- Looking for a way to meet representatives from dozens of different law schools, all in one place?
- Concerned about whether you can afford law school in the first place?

If you answered yes to any of these questions, you're definitely not alone. The line forms to the right, and it's a long one.

But here's your shortcut to getting the help you need without the hassle: Law School Admission Council Online contains information on the LSAT, including a schedule of test dates, deadlines, and fees. In addition, you'll find out how to meet law school representatives, get LSAT preparation materials, and legal education books.

The first step to getting into law school.

You'll also get the facts on law school financial aid, plus you'll learn how to order informational materials online and free of charge, including:

- *Thinking About Law School: A Minority Guide*
- *LSAT/LSDAS Registration and Information Book (U.S. Edition)*
- *LSAT Registration and Information Book (Canadian Edition)*

How

World Wide Web

Where

www.lsac.org/list.htm

Legalese in Black and White

With O.J.'s lawyers tied up with more legal maneuvers (you know, book deals, movie rights, and speaking engagements), your calls to them for legal help may go unanswered. Not to worry, though: You've seen enough episodes of *L.A. Law* to know your way around the courtroom. Just fill out the forms and sign the necessary papers, and you'll be able to handle 90 percent of the legal hassles most people have to deal with.

This site includes dozens of online legal forms you can download. Here's a small sampling:

- Demand For Arbitration
- Demand For Mediation
- Stockholders' Agreement
- Articles of Incorporation
- Stock Purchase Agreement
- General Consent Agreement
- Independent Contractor Agreement
- General Power of Attorney
- Agreement Settling Boundary Line Dispute
- Authorization To Release Employment Information
- Product Licensing Contract
- Breach Of Contract Notice
- Formal Request For Credit Report
- Freedom of Information Act Request

How

World Wide Web

Where

www.gama.com/forms.htm

Be sure to read the legalese included at this site: "Nothing on this, or on any other hypertext linked page, constitutes legal advice. These forms are provided as a public service only and there is no warranty of any kind given, including warranties of fitness of purpose, suitability, or merchantability. Please consult an attorney in your jurisdiction regarding your particular problem or need. Mileage may vary; see dealer for details."

What a Terror

It used to be that terrorism was something you read about in the International section of your newspaper. My how times have changed. With the

Oklahoma City and World Trade Center bombings, and the Unabomber on the loose, the threat of terrorism has now reached Small Town America.

Drastic times call for drastic measures—like the Terrorism Watch Report mailing list. In addition to ads and information about counterterrorism products and services on the market, subscribers get the latest news about terrorism around the world—including inside the U.S.

How
Email

Where
BenVenzke@delphi.com

Message
Please subscribe me to the TWR P&S listserv

Libraries for Litigators

All law students know that, while they may have a bed to sleep in, their real home is the law library. Maybe the 'Lectric Law Library can help ease the strain. The 'Lectric Law Library helps you find and access the law-related information, products, and services you need.

With one of the most extensive private-sector collections of no-charge legal resources on the Net, the 'Lectric Law Library includes legal encyclopedias and dictionaries, legal software, case information and transcripts on the Simpson and Menendez trials and the Oklahoma City bombing, as well as legal forms, court rules, and, of course, legal jokes.

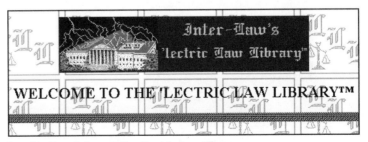

Practice 'lectric law at the 'Lectric Law Library.

How

World Wide Web

Where

www.inter-law.com

The Crime of the Century

Billed as the crime of the century, O.J. Simpson's murder trial has been as much of a media circus as it has been a showcase for the high-tech forensics used by modern police departments. And now all that criminal-science wizardry has reached an even higher plateau with this computer animation of the actual murder scene.

Using all of the crime scene and forensic evidence available, c|net central gives you a virtual re-enactment of the Nicole Brown Simpson/Ronald Goldman murders. Only the murderer knows exactly what happened that night, but this animation re-creates how expert witnesses believe the double murder was committed.

You'll find five different versions of the animation software you can download and view, including versions for Windows, Mac, and Unix systems, ranging from 1.6 MB to 5.7 MB. If you have a slower Net connection, you may want to choose a smaller version.

How

Web

Where

http://www.cnet.com/Central/Tv/Stories/Murder/index.html

While the animation here avoids showing anything gory, the nature of it is in itself somewhat disturbing and chilling. Parents may want to preview this to decide if it's suitable for their kids.

Where to Find Way More Goodies

Read about the legal smoke screens put up by cigarette manufacturers and the rights of nonsmokers in the *Health and Nutrition* chapter. Also, learn your legal rights as a consumer in the "Consumer Publications" section of *Household and Family Finance*, where you'll find over 100 helpful booklets, as well as the latest consumer news and legal data.

In the *Internet* chapter, learn how to subscribe to a mailing list that combines the Internet, computers, and law into one comprehensive forum for discussion.

For free updates to this book via FTP or the Web, go to: coriolis.com

Way More!
FREE $TUFF

I'm not an actor!
I'm a movie star!

Alan Swann (Peter O'Toole),
My Favorite Year

Movies and Television

Home Movies

The Internet is about making the most information available to as many people as possible. But then, information is in the eye of the beholder, isn't it? Sure, you can explore the Library of Congress and get quotes for your stock portfolio until your mouse pointer wilts from exhaustion, but that doesn't mean you can't have a little fun, too.

So put away the work for a few minutes, fire up your favorite movie viewer, and check out some of the MPEG videos available at this site. You'll find lots of movie clips covering loads of topics, including:

- Supermodels
- Animation
- Television
- Music

There's also a great MPEG FAQ to help you get the most from your viewing.

How

World Wide Web

Where

www.eeb.ele.tue.nl/mpeg/index.html

If The Netherlands seems like a long way to go for a night at the movies, try one of the mirrored sites shown here, including the U.S. at peace.wit.com/mpeg. Also, if you need an MPEG viewer for Windows, you can download one via FTP at oak.oakland.edu/SimTel/win3/video. The file name is mpegexe.zip. If you need an MPEG viewer for the Macintosh, you can download one at ftp.pht.com/pub/mac/_application. Download the file mpeg-mac-03.hqx (242 K).

Look at That View

Have you ever shown up at a theater and then discovered you've missed your movie because you got the starting time wrong? Of course, *I* would never do something like that, but I'm sure it's happened to somebody. (Actually, I recently went to the wrong *theater* and got stuck paying six bucks for something I wouldn't have bothered to rent.)

You'll feel the same kind of disappointment when you download megabytes of video footage off the Net only to discover you don't have the right kind of viewer to play it. Here's a site that'll help you avoid these kinds of bonehead mistakes made by a certain author. You can download viewers for the three most common video formats you'll come across on the Net: Video for Windows (AVI), QuickTime (MOV), and MPEG (MPG).

How

World Wide Web

Where

www.igc.net/viewers.html

Download

vmpeg12a.zip (150 K)

vfwrun.zip (467 K)

qtw11.zip (318 K)

All three of these viewers are Windows software. While QuickTime movies are actually intended to be viewed on the Mac, the same company that created the Mac version also created QuickTime for Windows so PC users wouldn't feel left out.

Television Trivia, or Is That Redundant?

There are worse things, I suppose, than watching endless hours of mindless television drivel—for instance, *reading* endless hours of mindless television drivel (or writing about it for that matter).

But for those who just can't get enough of the boob tube, here's a Gopher site to satisfy your craving. From *ALF* to *The Young Indiana Jones*, you'll find a huge assortment of episode guides for all your favorite shows. There's also lots of TV trivia, interviews, information on the creators and producers of some of the best—and worst—shows ever aired, and much more.

How
Gopher

Where
wiretap.spies.com

Go To
wiretap online library

mass media

television

Sci-fi junkies should check out the archive of episode guides for TV science fiction shows by FTPing to sflovers.rutgers.edu in the pub/sf-lovers/TV/EpisodeGuides subdirectory.

The Envelope Please

There are lots of other awards given in the motion-picture industry, but since 1927 none has matched the prestige of that small gold-plated Academy Award statue nicknamed Oscar.

And if Oscars were given out for Best Academy Award Web site, this one would earn the honor. The Official Interactive Guide to the Academy Awards includes information on all the nominees and winners, the Academy Awards show on television, Oscar trivia, and much more. There's even an Oscar game you can play online, as well as links to the Academy of Motion Picture Arts and Sciences.

How
World Wide Web

And the winner is...this Web site.

Where

visualize.pacopost.com

Most clips here are in the 2- to 4-megabyte range. So unless you're running on an ISDN or T1 line, you'll want to download these in the off hours.

TV and Movie Mailings

With millions of computer users now armed with multimedia-equipped hardware, the marriage of movies, television, and the Internet is a natural. And once it's on the Net, you can bet somebody's talking about it. Here are a few of the many mailing lists devoted to discussing TV, moviemaking, memorabilia, and more:

Late Show News

This mailing list is a weekly electronic newsletter full of facts and opinions on the late-night television talk show industry, including guest listings.

How

Email

Where

listproc@echonyc.com

Message

subscribe late-show-news *Your Name*

Filmmakers

The Filmmakers' mailing list deals with all aspects of motion picture production, with an emphasis on technical issues. Construction and design issues are stressed, especially for those working on tight budgets. And the subject here is film—not video.

Where

filmmakers-request@dhm.com

Message

subscribe

Movie Posters

This mailing list is for collectors of movie memorabilia, including posters, lobby cards, stills, or any movie-related collectible.

Where

listserv@listserv.american.edu

Message

subscribe mopo-l *Your Name*

What's On Tonite!

Get the TV listings for your area mailed to you automatically each day.

Where

circulation@paperboy.com

Message

subscribe *edition Your Name*
The *edition* entry indicates your time zone (Eastern, Central, Mountain, or Pacific). For instance, subscribe mountain Joe Smith

Actors Online

This mailing list is for working or aspiring actors and actresses in Nova Scotia's thriving film and television industry, as well as the performing arts as a whole. Though targeted at Nova Scotians, this mailing list should be of interest to others, too.

Where

majordomo@ccn.cs.dal.ca

Message

subscribe ns-actors

Comedy from the UK

If you're interested in humor with a British twist, check out this archive of TV situation comedies made in the UK. Stretching back to the 1960s, this site contains a huge collection of British shows, as well as information about the stars and the people behind the scenes. There's even a terrific search utility to help you track down information about your favorite stars.

How

Gopher

Where

info.mcc.ac.uk

Go To

Miscellaneous items

The definitive list of UK sitcoms

The Story of My Life

Everybody's got a story to tell, and if yours isn't as boring as most of 'em, here's a site where you can tell it. And who knows, if it's got the drama of *Airplane!*, the humor of *Silence of the Lambs*, or the suspense of *Ishtar*, Krost/Chapin Productions just might want to make it into a movie (hey, it's possible).

Follow the instructions at this Web site to find out how to send in your life story and, who knows, it might just be you they're talking about when they say "this movie is based on a true story." In Hollywood, stranger things have *definitely* happened.

How

World Wide Web

Where

www.lainet.com/~kcprods

TV Tunes

Just sit right back and you'll hear a tale, a tale of a *very* cool Web site. The TV Theme Songs Web page includes audio files from hundreds of TV shows from the '50s through today.

You'll find comedies, dramas, adventure, sci-fi, soaps, kids shows, and much more. Remember *The Banana Splits*? It's here. *The Courtship of Eddie's Father*? Got it. *The Bionic Woman*? Yep. You'll also get the Theme of the Week, a huge collection of audio players for Windows, DOS, Macs, and Unix, and lots of great links to many TV and sound-related sites around the Web.

How

World Wide Web

Where

ai.eecs.umich.edu/people/kennyp/sounds.html

Don't forget that the Big Three online access services—America Online, CompuServe, and Prodigy—all provide Internet access, including the World Wide Web. To access the Web, log on to your service, then:

AOL—Keyword *Web* from the Go To menu
CompuServe—Go *Web*
Prodigy—Jump *Web*

Read Any Good Movies Lately?

The next best thing to seeing your favorite movies is reading them—and I'm not talking about subtitles. I mean the actual scripts and screenplays from some of the greatest plots ever put on celluloid.

The Script Emporium Web site has scripts from cult classics like *Blade Runner*, *The Crow*, and *Dune*, as well as some of the best comedy, action, drama, and adventure films ever produced. Look for:

- *The Empire Strikes Back*
- *Batman Forever*
- *Die Hard*
- *Ferris Bueller's Day Off*
- *Monty Python and the Holy Grail*
- *The Lion King*

In addition, this site has some great links for anyone who's serious about getting started in screenwriting.

How

World Wide Web

Where

www.cs.tufts.edu/~katwell

Let Your Cable Be Your Guide

What's coming to your favorite cable channel? Find out with the 24-Hour Cable Movie Guide. You'll find listings for HBO, Cinemax, Encore, Showtime, American Movie Classics, and The Movie Channel, as well as all the TV networks. Plus, new schedules are posted two days in advance to give you plenty of time (hopefully) to figure out how to set your VCR up.

How

World Wide Web

Where

emporium.turnpike.net/W/wto/tvguide.html

This guide is for American TV and covers the various time zones.

Coming Soon to a Theater Near You

Disney's on a roll these days and my wallet's got the scars to prove it. Between the merchandising of hits like *Pocahontas*, *The Lion King*, and *Beauty and the Beast*, not to mention the ticket prices for more adult fare like *Crimson Tide* and *While You Were Sleeping*, sometimes I feel that I'm single-handedly responsible for Disney's steady climb in the stock market.

If you're not doing your part to make Disney's bottom line the envy of many third-world countries, here's a good place to start. You'll find information on the latest releases from Walt Disney's Buena Vista, Touchstone, and Hollywood Pictures, as well as pictures, audio clips, and movie trailers that you can download. This site's being updated constantly, so check back often for the latest look at what's coming.

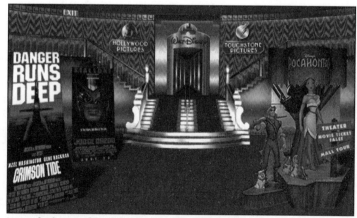

Now playing at this Web site: the best from Disney.

How

World Wide Web

Where

www.disney.com

Two Tickets, Please

In Hollywood, it's a fine line between box office boffo and box office *awful*, depending on how many millions of moviegoers are standing in line. And the way Hollywood accountants keep the books, who can tell if that movie grossing tens of millions of dollars its opening weekend will ever turn a profit?

But here's a site that only cares about the bottom line. The Weekend Box Office Report Web site simply reports the weekly winners in ticket sales. So, access this site to find out what the masses are watching. Do you think they know something you don't?

How

World Wide Web

Where

www.leonardo.net/aasen/topbox.html

Bring Down the School House

If you're like me, you were raised on a daily ration of situation comedies, afternoon game shows, and Saturday morning cartoons. And no Saturday would have been

WOW is right! This site has all the fun and laughs of its Saturday-morning counterpart.

complete without the pre-MTV video music of Schoolhouse Rock.

Now you can get the best of Schoolhouse Rock at the Schoolhouse Rock Web site. You'll find classics (yes, *classics*) from Grammar Rock, History Rock, Multiplication Rock, and Science Rock, including *Interjection* (WOW!), *Preamble*, and *Conjunction Junction*. You can download the audio files, the lyrics, and pictures, and there's even audio player software for you to download.

How

World Wide Web

Where

hera.life.uiuc.edu/rock.html

I Think I Cannes

When Frank Sinatra sang "If I can make it there, I'll make it anywhere," he could have been talking about Cannes. For nearly 50 years, up-and-comers in filmdom have rubbed egos with giants in the movie biz to compete for top honors at the Cannes Film Festival.

At the Film Scouts on the Riviera Web site, you'll get the latest information from the Cannes International Film Festival. You'll find reviews, information about award winners, the latest gossip, and much more.

You'll also get the lowdown on who's making deals with whom, interviews with stars and starmakers, and lots of titilating tidbits on Cannes infamous hotspots and nightlife.

How

World Wide Web

Where

www.interactive8.com/cannes/welcome/welcome.html

Don't forget that many Internet addresses are case-sensitive, so be sure to type them *exactly* as shown.

PICT a Movie, Any Movie

MovieMaker is a nice little program that allows you to convert a sequence of PICT files into a QuickTime video. This is an especially useful program if you're an animator, because you can create your individual animation cels in PICT files, and then use MovieMaker to organize them into a QuickTime movie.

How

FTP

Where

ftp.pht.com

Go To

pub

mac

application

Download

movie-maker-13.hqx (194 K)

CNN on the WWW

Around the clock, CNN provides television viewers with the latest news. And just like what you've come to expect from the world's most popular news source, CNN Online provides up-to-the-minute reports from around the world to the Internet.

U.S. NEWS	WORLD NEWS
BUSINESS	SPORTS
SHOWBIZ	POLITICS
WEATHER	TECHNOLOGY
FOOD & HEALTH	STYLE

| Contents | Search | Welcome Page | Help |

If it's happening in the world, it's happening on CNN Online.

You'll also find comprehensive business and technology reports, as well as sports, health, entertainment, and more. Plus you'll always find lots of great footage of today's top stories that you can download to watch again and again.

How

World Wide Web

Where

www.cnn.com

Quick! Get QuickTime for Free!

Until recently, Apple refused to distribute QuickTime 2.1 over the Net, and actually was charging users $10 to purchase the software, which never made sense to me since it comes free of charge with System 7.5. I guess this policy didn't make sense to Apple, either, because now you can download QuickTime 2.1 as well as the Movie Player for free. If you've got a Mac and you've been unable to view QuickTime movies, these utilities will end your video blues.

How

World Wide Web

Where

www.support.apple.com/pub/apple.sw.updates/US/Macintosh/
SystemSoftware/other_System_Software

Download

QuickTime 2.1.hqx   (1.5 MB)

MoviePlayer 2.1.hqx

QuickTime_for_Windows_2.0.3.exe

The QuickTime 2.1.hqx file includes the MoviePlayer.

Let's Put On a Show

Want the latest scoop on today's biggest stars? Of course you do! Who wouldn't want to read about people who have more fun, money, and excitement than all us mortals combined?

If it's happening in showbiz, it's happening at the Mr. Showbiz Web site.

And Mr. Showbiz is here to see that you don't miss a bit of it. A mix between Gene Siskel and Robin Leach, Mr. Showbiz brings you the latest movie gossip, news, gossip, reviews, gossip, previews, and—oh yeah—gossip.

And since there's more to life than movies, Mr. Showbiz provides you with a daily dose of TV-related info, too. There are plenty of Emmy updates, previews of upcoming shows, and the inside story on Garry Shandling's beauty secrets. That last one alone makes this site a must-read.

How

World Wide Web

Where

web3.starwave.com/showbiz

Heeere's Leno

Broadcast in 32 countries around the globe, *The Tonight Show with Jay Leno* is one of the most popular shows in the world. And with this great Web site, it's bound to become one of the most popular attractions in cyberspace as well.

The Leno Web page gives you highlights of last night's show, information on upcoming guests, video and audio clips, lots of photos, and much more. There's also information on how to get tickets to the show.

Highlights of the best moments from The Tonight Show are available on the Leno Web Page.

How

World Wide Web

Where

www.nbctonightshow.com

Hooray for Hollywood

Remember how much fun it used to be to hit the Saturday matinee for an all-you-can-watch marathon of low-budget movies fueled with multiple trips to the candy counter for a satisfying sugar rush? If not, then, hey, you never really had a childhood. My personal best was a 12-hour single-sitting marathon of all seven *Planet of the Apes* movies one afternoon in Anchorage, Alaska. And you probably thought Alaskans didn't have that kind of culture.

The Sony Web site may never match the nostalgia I feel for the old Fireweed Theater in Anchorage, but it makes up for it in high-tech wizardry that includes movie clips, pictures, interviews, contests, and software you can download. You'll also find sneak previews of coming attractions, Hollywood news, links to classic films, and much more.

Download your own sneak previews from the Sony Web site.

How

World Wide Web

Where

www.spe.sony.com/Pictures/SonyMovies/index.html

Play It Again, Sam

A lot has changed in a hundred years of film making, and the use of music is no exception. Once just a secondary part of a movie's production, soundtracks have become a big part of the success of many box office hits (can you say *Saturday Night Fever*?).

The Web Wide World of Film Music (no that's not a typo) is a huge collection of movie soundtracks, with links to magazines related to film music, audio clips, information about the composers of your favorite soundtracks, along with interviews, and, of course, music you can download. While probably not the prettiest Web page you'll come across, this site doesn't have to look good—as long as it sounds good.

How

World Wide Web

Where

web.syr.edu:80/~ebedgert/wwwfm.html

Raiders of the Lost Web Site

Indy's back! Everyone's favorite whip-cracking, globetrotting treasure hunter is now on the Net. At the Indiana Jones Web site, you can join forces with Dr. Jones to explore the treasures found at this site. You'll discover a

Just in the nick of time (like always), the Indiana Jones home page.

huge assortment of pictures, sounds, and movie clips, including a great shot of the opening scene of *Raiders of the Lost Ark*, where Indy is chased by a boulder.

There are also updates on upcoming Indy projects, including a new movie, fan clubs, theme-park rides related to Indiana Jones, theories about the Lost Ark of the Convenant, links to other Indy Net sites, and much more. This is definitely a thrill-a-minute Web page.

How

World Wide Web

Where

dialin.ind.net/~msjohnso

Where to Find Way More Goodies

For even more television programming, turn to the *Government* chapter for the latest C-SPAN coverage of the U.S. Congress, including program schedules, reports and articles, and an archive of historic documents and speeches.

You can also check out your favorite cable comedies in the *Humor* chapter, including links to:

- *Dr. Katz*
- *Absolutely Fabulous*
- *Kids In The Hall*
- *Mystery Science Theater 3000*
- *Politically Incorrect*

Before you try viewing video clips of your favorite movies or TV shows, make sure you've got your Web browser working right. Go to the *Internet* chapter to find out how to run your browser through a few diagnostics that'll let you know if you can play QuickTime, MPEG, and other videos.

For free updates to this book via FTP or the Web, go to: coriolis.com

Way More! FREE $TUFF

Opera is when a guy gets stabbed in the back and, instead of bleeding, he sings.

Ed Gardner

Music

Charge Me Up!

I didn't have time to tour with the Stones this year (just too darn busy with this book), so I promised "the guys" I'd at least help plug their new credit card. If you've tried and tried

The most famous tongue in the world is now accepted around the world.

and tried, but still can't get no satisfaction, maybe you need the Rolling Stones Mastercard. After all, what could be more satisfying than using a card that saves you money on purchases at hundreds of music stores, is accepted at more than 12 million locations around the world, has no annual fee for the first year, and has a competitively low interest rate?

Check out this site and tell 'em Mick, Keith, and the guys sent you over for your own Rolling Stones Mastercard.

How

World Wide Web

Where

www.its.com/rsopen.html

Direct Me to the Music

The International Computer Music Association (ICMA) Library is your starting point for finding music-related computer software on the Internet. This huge shareware and freeware directory of Mac and PC programs is perfect for anyone interested in using their computer for playing, composing, or reading music.

How

FTP

Where

dartmouth.edu

Go To

pub/ICMA-Library/catalog.txt

Music to Your Ears

I don't care how many thousands of dollars you pump into beefing up your state-of-the-art home stereo system, when it comes to raw power, nothing matches the energy you feel when you're packed into a standing-room-only arena watching your favorite band blasting away. And sometimes the music's pretty good, too.

Come see WILMA for the best information about live music around the world.

The Worldwide Internet Live Music Archive (WILMA) is your one-stop stomping ground for concert and band information. In addition to a huge collection of reviews and links to the world's hottest groups, WILMA has venue listings of thousands of clubs, theaters, concert halls, and stadiums around the world, as well as tour information and concert reviews of hundreds of bands.

How

World Wide Web

Where

underground.net:80/Wilma

If you're using Netscape (versions 1.0 and higher) to browse the Web, you can save yourself some keystrokes by skipping the *http://* prefix. Netscape assumes that if there's no prefix, you're accessing the Web.

325

Are Bagpipes Your Bag?

Did you know that bagpipes can be heard up to a mile away? That's good to know if your neighbor is thinking about taking up the instrument. So you'll either love me or hate me for including this site—there probably aren't many of you who fall in between. To some, the sound of bagpipes conjures up fond longings for the misty, sparry hills of Scotland. To others, the instrument sounds like an overweight oboe with a really bad attitude.

If you're a bagpipe aficionado, grab your kilt, then take the high road to this Gopher site.

You'll find a huge archive from the rec.music.makers.bagpipe newsgroup, sound files to download (but only if you *must*), and many other items of interest to lovers of Scotland's national instrument.

How

Gopher

Where

cs.dartmouth.edu

Go To

Bagpipe Archives

True gluttons for punishment—er, I mean true bagpipe lovers—will want to subscribe to the bagpipe mailing list at bagpipe-request@cs.dartmouth.edu with the message *subscribe*.

Music Manager

Your CD collection may be the envy of the free world, but its organization makes post-communist Russia's government look like a lesson in efficiency. What you need is your own music archivist.

The Music Librarian can help you with all your music media management. You key in the artists, albums, songs, and musical categories, and this easy-to-use database makes it a breeze to find just the right song for just the right occasion.

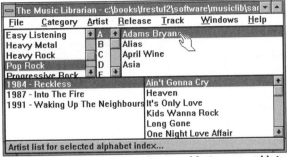

Put another dime in the jukebox, and let's start rockin'.

How
FTP

Where
ftp.csusm.edu

Go To
pub/winworld/database

Download
musiclib.zip (312 K)

Live, In Concert!

Want to stay on top of the latest music happenings, but just don't have time to hobnob with the Grammy crowd? Well, for over a decade, POLLSTAR has provided music industry insiders with concert tour schedules, box office results, industry directories, and music news.

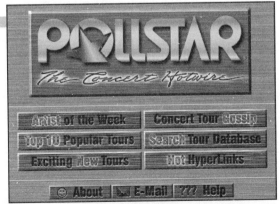

Try POLLSTAR for the latest concert news and reviews.

Now, Web surfers like yourself can access much of the same data, including concert schedules, information on upcoming tours, industry gossip and party chatter, information and interviews with feature artists, and links to lots of other great music sites.

How

World Wide Web

Where

www.pollstar.com

Man, That Tiny Elvis Is Huge!

Nearly 20 years later, The King is still as popular as ever, with hardly a week going by when you don't see his picture splashed across some grocery-store tabloid *(Elvis' Ghost Helped Me Lose 200 Pounds!)*. With his image displayed on everything from satin sheets to baseball caps, it's no big stretch to say that Tiny Elvis for Windows was a natural.

Inspired by the corny-yet-classic Tiny Elvis skits on NBC's *Saturday Night Live*, Tiny Elvis—decked out in The King's famous white jump suit and blue suede shoes—is a corny-but-classic Windows icon that lounges around your desktop. When you least expect it, he pops to his feet to comment on your "huge" icons, windows, cursors, and so on, then shows off a few quick trademark Vegas-style poses before sitting back down. If you want to see more of The King, and he hasn't been sighted in your town recently, this on-screen incarnation sure beats buying his postage stamps.

How

FTP

Where

gatekeeper.dec.com

Go To

pub/micro/msdos/win3/desktop

Download

tel101.zip (198 K)

 I wish I could include a picture of Tiny Elvis here, but he's just to, well, *tiny*.

The Sound of MacMusic

 If you have a Mac and you're into music or sound editing, this Web site is indispensible. The Mac Sound Utilities home page includes links to just about every sound and music utility ever created for the Mac. This site's especially useful for finding programs that can convert PC, Unix, and other sound formats to Mac sound formats. The MIDI Utilities link offers you dozens of applications for playing, editing, and converting MIDI files, but there are plenty of other links that are equally useful. Here's a quick sampling of files you can download:

- CD Players (several to choose from)
- Chroma 32
- File Player
- Harmonizer
- Mu-zak
- Player Pro
- Sound Hack
- Sound Effects
- Sound App
- SoundMachine
- Sound Shrinker
- Sound Track
- Sound Trecker
- Soundz

How

World Wide Web

Where

www.wavenet.com/~axgrindr/quimby4.html

329

Lotsa Music Links

If you're looking for a comprehensive source for sound clips, music archives, musicians, recording companies on the Web, musical newsgroups, and just about anything else that's music related, this is the place to visit.

This Web site is little-known because it bills itself with the relatively humble and misleading name "Sites with audio clips." But in truth, this page has the most comprehensive listing of links to everything on the Web that involves music, both for PC and Mac platforms.

How

World Wide Web

Where

www.eecs.nwu.edu/~jmyers/other-sounds.html

Musical Mailing Lists

Reading about music when you'd rather be listening to it is like looking at a picture of a cheeseburger when you'd rather be eating one. Still, regardless of the music you like—whether it's rock, grunge, blues, or heavy-metal-hip-hop-rockabilly-new-wave-folk-classic crossover blends—you can bet that on the Net there are thousands of people discussing it. Here's a small sampling of what's available:

Blues

This mailing list is for anyone who can't get enough of the blues.

How

Email

Where

listserv@brownvm.brown.edu

Message

subscribe blues-l *your name*

European Top 20 Chart
Subscribe to this list for a weekly listing of Europe's top twenty pop hits.

Where

eu20-request@a3.xs4all.nl

Message

subscribe eu20 *your_email_address (Your Name)*

Grunge
This high-traffic mailing list discusses all topics related to grunge rock, including concert reviews and recommendations, band tour dates, quotes, band gossip, insider information, and anything else you would typically find in a music magazine.

Where

listserv@ubvm.cc.buffalo.edu

Message

subscribe grunge-l *Your Name*

Lucky Town
Bruce Springsteen's the topic on the Lucky Town mailing list. If you like The Boss, you'll like the issues discussed here.

Where

luckytown-request@netcom.com

Message

subscribe luckytown

Monkees
This list discusses the TV show and musical group The Monkees.

Where

majordomo@primenet.com

Message

subscribe monkees-digest

Le Jazz on le Net

When you think jazz, you probably think New Orleans, Kansas City, St. Louis, or Chicago—and if this was the turn of the century, you'd be right on the money. But today's jazz is no longer a regional or even national phenomenon. Jazz has gone international, with a worldwide audience stretching to every corner of the world. And nowhere is this more prevalent than France.

Actually, France has a history of stealing away underappreciated jazz masters from the U.S.—Phil Woods, Dexter Gordon, and dozens more. France continues to show a strong appreciation for "America's Art Form," even while America has all but abandoned it. So, if you love jazz, check out the Jazz in France Web site, with information about the best in jazz from France. You'll find loads of information on upcoming events, including festivals, TV and radio programs, and music awards, as well as information on jazz magazines in France and where to buy recordings.

How
World Wide Web

Where
www.erb.com/cdeus/jazzfr.htm

Pump Up the Volume

From the Andrews Sisters to Frank Zappa, here's a Net site that brings you tons of information on your favorite recording artists. Ranging from classical to pop and folk, these archives include hundreds of discographies and thousands of lyrics.

Music lovers can also get concert information, press releases, games, a huge archive of pictures, audio samples, and much more. And if you really want to go for *Baroque*, check out the reviews and recommendations of the best classical recordings available.

How
FTP

Joliet Jake and Elwood Blues: The Blues Brothers.

Where

ftp.uwp.edu

Go To

pub/music

Peak hour connections are at a premium here, so if you have trouble getting in, try the mirror site at cs.uwp.edu or wait till the off-peak hours.

Rockin' the World

Forget about new wave, disco, pop, and rap—in the '70s it was rock that ruled the airwaves, and *Rock Around the World* was rock's radio show. Heard on more than 160 stations coast to coast in its prime, as well as on American Forces Radio & Television Services worldwide, *RATW* introduced America's youth to such groups as The Who, Fleetwood Mac, Elton John, Bob Seger, E.L.O., and many others.

At the *Rock Around the World* Web site, you'll find a great collection of audio recordings from interviews with many stars from the '70s, like Paul McCartney, John Lennon, Bob Dylan, Joe Cocker, and Eric Clapton.

And if you're too young to remember, check out the archive of today's biggest names, including Hole, Collective Soul, Chris Isaak, and Blues Traveler.

Post-Beatles Paul McCartney still rockin' in 1976—and today.

You'll find pictures to download, reviews, news and features, and lots of information about the music scenes in Australia, Austria, Canada, Denmark, Europe, Finland, France, Germany, Hong Kong, Ireland, Italy, Japan, The Netherlands, Norway, Portugal, Spain, UK, and—of course—America.

How

World Wide Web

Where

www.ratw.com

Dead Ahead to This Gopher Site

Jerry Garcia may be gone, but he won't be forgotten by his faithful Deadhead followers. And at the Grateful Dead Gopher site, you'll find a great collection of memorabilia for one of music's most enduring bands.

You'll find transcripts of Garcia interviews, lyrics to the band's songs, set lists, sound files to download, and much more.

Jerry's still belting 'em out in
cyberspace.

How

Gopher

Where

nemesis.Berkeley.EDU

 Here are some great Dead sites to check out by FTP:

- ftp.uwp.edu/pub/music/lists/gdeadstuff2
- ftp.apple.com/pub/gdeadstuff
- xanth.cs.odu.edu/pub/gdead

Music to My Ears

Your computer can be the most versatile tool in your music studio—
working overtime as an instrument, a jukebox, a composing tool, a label
printer, and much more. And at this site you'll find dozens of programs
to help online musicians squeeze the most music from their computers.
Here's a sampling of what's available:

- CD players and databases
- Guitar-teaching software
- WAV and AU players and converters
- Multimedia jukeboxes

- Piano keyboards for Windows
- Music composer software

How
FTP

Where
ftp.cdarchive.com

Go To
FTP_server/pub/win_util/13a

 Be sure to read the readme.txt file here for information about the programs you can download.

That's Life in the Big City

If you're looking for the latest news and gossip in African-American entertainment, the *Electronic Urban Report* (EUR) is the place to start. Created by RadioScope, a production of Bailey Broadcasting Services (the largest Black/Urban radio network in the U.S.) *EUR* is a free online newsletter packed with the latest happenings by today's hottest African-American entertainers.

You'll get the latest music buzz and showbiz news about stars like Janet and/or Michael Jackson, the-artist-formerly-known-as-Prince, Ice Cube, Snoop Doggy Dog, Whitney Houston, Queen Latifah, and many more.

How
Email

Where
majordomo@afrinet.net

Message
subscribe electronic-urban-report

White Punks on the Web

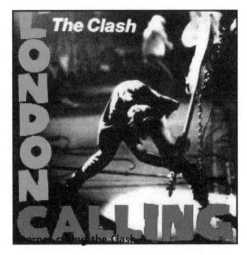

You don't need Freud to tell you that the whole punk music scene evolved (or is that *devolved*?) out of a need for alienated and disaffected youths to band together and shock and intimidate. Okay, it worked. Now take that ring out of your nose and quit smashing the furniture.

While much of punk rock is appreciated—and intelligible, for that matter—by only hard core followers, millions of others around the world enjoy the more "mainstream" punk the original movement spawned. You'll find both at the World Wide Web Punk Page.

The Punk Page includes lyrics, photos, sound files you can download, and information about punk's biggest bands, like:

- Dag Nasty
- Lagwagon
- Combustible Edison
- Screeching Weasel
- Black Flag
- Rancid

How

World Wide Web

Where

turnpike.net/metro/punk/punk.html

Where to Find Way More Goodies

The "Play It Again, Sam" section in *Movies and Television* contains a huge collection of movie soundtracks, with links to magazines related to film music, audio clips, information about the composers of your favorite soundtracks along with interviews, and—of course—music you can download.

For free updates to this book via FTP or the Web, go to: coriolis.com

Way More! FREE $TUFF

There is a theory which states that if ever anybody discovers exactly what the universe is for and why it is here, it will instantly disappear and be replaced by something even more bizarre and inexplicable. There is another theory which states that this has already happened.

Douglas Adams

Science and Nature

Weather's Here, Wish You Were Beautiful

So which of these locations would you prefer—Phoenix in the summer or autumn in New York? Okay, so that's an easy one. How about Miami in May versus San Diego in September? Hmm. Now that's a tougher call.

Here's a program that'll help you decide. U.S. Weather Atlas for Windows lets you graph the weather for over 80 cities in the U.S., including average temperatures, sunshine, rainfall, and humidity. Plus, you can display information for up to three cities at a time to help make your comparisons just a little easier.

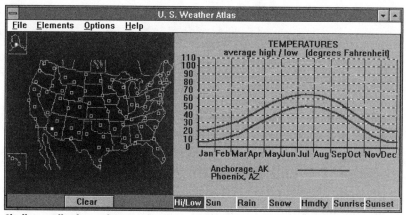

Shall we talk about the weather?

How
FTP

Where
gatekeeper.dec.com

Go To
pub/micro/msdos/win3/misc

Download
uswthrwn.zip (113 K)

Look at the Birdy

About the closest I've come to birdwatching is scaring the cactus wrens off my back porch so they'll quit eating my dog's food. I admit it, I'm not a back-to-nature kind of guy. Sure, fresh air, sunshine, and lots of quiet are okay if you like that sort of thing, but personally I prefer viewing nature from the comfort of my living room, cable TV, and the Discovery Channel. I'm afraid somebody would try to lock me up if I were to go meandering through the woods with binoculars, making strange warbling sounds and looking for yellow-bellied double-breasted sear suckers—or whatever.

But if birding is your thing, the Internet can help make your hobby a high-tech adventure. At the Tweeters Web site, for example, you'll find plenty of information on bird watching in the Northwest United States and British Columbia. In addition, you'll find links to over 14 birding mailing lists, the Washington Ornithological Society, regional hot line reports, and much more.

How

World Wide Web

Where

weber.u.washington.edu/~dvictor

Web-deprived Internauts can still get lots of birding bits by Gopher (simon.wharton.upenn.edu, then go to BIRD THINGS) and FTP (BirdData 3.04 at ftp.csusm.edu/pub/winworld/database/bdata304.zip).

Don't forget that the Big Three online access services—America Online, CompuServe, and Prodigy—all provide Internet access, including the World Wide Web. To access the Web, log on to your service, then:

AOL—Keyword *Web* from the Go To menu
CompuServe—Go *Web*
Prodigy—Jump *Web*

Your Mac Can Watch Birds Too

If you take birdwatching seriously, then you already know how important it is to keep track of your findings. But how organized can you really be if all of your records are scattered throughout several different notepads?

Now you can gather all of your notes together into one happy flock with Bird Stack, the Birdwatcher's data manager for Macintosh. Bird Stack lets you create a record of each bird sighting. For each bird, you can record the common name, scientific name, and the family of the bird along with a list of sightings. Sightings are recorded by date, location, and you'll even be given an area to enter on optional comment. The program automatically indexes birds by common name, scientific name, and year of sighting, and the database is searchable.

How
FTP

Where
ftp.sunet.se

Go To
pub
mac
info-mac
sci

Download
bird-stack-27-hc.hqx (100 K)

 This program requires Hypercard.

This Gopher Won't Ruin the Crops

Ask any farmer—or groundskeeper on a golf course, for that matter—and they'll tell you gophers and cultivation do *not* mix. There are exceptions to every rule, though, and it's not surprising that the National Agricultural Library (NAL) Gopher is no exception (if you know what I mean).

At the NAL, you'll find links to hundreds of agriculture- and veterinary-related Gopher sites around the world, including:

- Missouri Botanical Garden
- National Biological Impact Assessment Program
- NetVet Gopher
- Ohio Agricultural Research and Development Center
- Veterinary and animal legislation, regulations, and organizations
- African Gophers
- European Gophers
- The Electronic Zoo

How

Gopher

Where

gopher.nalusda.gov

The Science of Email

The Internet traces its roots to the scientific community, and there's no shortage of science-related discussions, newsgroups, and mailing lists on the Net today. Here's a handful of my favorite science- and nature-related mailing lists:

Alternative Energy

The Alternative Energy mailing list discusses the current state and future direction of renewable and sustainable alternative energy sources like solar, wind, geothermal, and tidal.

How

Email

Where

listserv@sjsuvm1.sjsu.edu

Message

subscribe ae *Your Name*

Sea Shepherd Conservation Society

This mailing list was created as an information collection and distribution tool for the Sea Shepherd Conservation Society, a direct-action conservation organization concerned with investigation, documentation, and enforcement of international conservation laws and treaties.

Where

nvoth@igc.apc.org

Message

subscribe

Park Rangers

This list is primarily for anyone working—or interested in working—as a ranger for the U.S. National Park Service. Rangers from state and county agencies as well as other countries are also welcome.

Where

60157903@wsuvm1.csc.wsu.edu

Message

subscribe

Student Solar Information Network

This list provides information, news, resources, and conference details free to anyone studying solar and renewable energy.

Where

m.e.thornton@bham.ac.uk

Message

subscribe

Cryonics

The cryonics mailing list (CryoNet) is a forum for topics related to cryonics, an experimental procedure in which patients who can no longer be kept alive with today's medical abilities are preserved at low temperatures for treatment in the future. CryoNet covers technical reports of cryonic suspensions, low temperature biology, biochemistry of memory, legal status of cryonics and cryopreserved people, and more.

Where
majordomo@cryonet.org

Message
subscribe

Electric Vehicle
The Electric Vehicle mailing list discusses the current state and future direction of electric vehicles.

Where
listserv@sjsuvm1.sjsu.edu

Message
subscribe ev *Your Name*

Skeptic
This mailing list discusses and examines paranormal topics, such as psychic claims, UFOs, reincarnation, the occult, and pseudosciences. In connection with paranormal claims, issues involving science and philosophy in general are often raised.

Where
listserv@jhuvm.hcf.jhu.edu

Message
subscribe skeptic *Your Name*

Earth and Sky
Earth and Sky is a weekly online publication about earth science and astronomy. It consists of transcripts of radio programs aired daily on the Earth & Sky Radio Series, hosted by Deborah Byrd and Joel Block and broadcast on more than 500 stations around the world.

Where
majordomo@lists.utexas.edu

Message
subscribe earthandsky *your_email_address*

NASA Info

This mailing list provides information from NASA about space missions, especially those of interest to the amateur radio space program.

Where

listserv@amsat.org

Message

subscribe

The Universe According to Lentz

The major FTP archives for Mac software include dozens—nearly hundreds—of programs related to science and astronomy. I've downloaded more of these packages than I care to admit, and frankly, when I test the programs, I'm usually disappointed. The applications are often either buggy, amateurish, highly specialized (get the latest organic compound modulation predictor for imprecise precipitation patterns), or just plain outdated.

But Robert Lentz has also been there and done that—at least in the category of astronomy—and has chosen to make only four Macintosh astronomy programs available at his Astro Resources Web page. As you might expect, all four programs are winners.

MoonTool

This little utility displays information about the previous new moon, and about the upcoming first quarter, half moon, full moon, and new moon. It also uses the current system date to

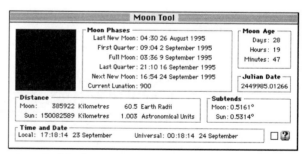

Moon Tool is the best tool for lunar learning.

display the distance of the moon and the sun, updated every second—great for amateur astronomers!

How
World Wide Web

Where
www.astro.nwu.edu/lentz/astro/home/astro.htm/#software-mac

Download
MoonTool 1.01 (95 K)

MacAstro
MacAstro 1.6 calculates the appearance of the sky at any time and any point on earth. It displays the position of the 8 major planets, the Sun, the Moon, and the 2,500 brightest astronomical objects (stars and Messier's objects). You can also view the sky in animation mode, and you can get ephemeris information about the moon, the planets, and hundreds of stars. The graphics in MacAstro are simple black-and-white images, but the versatility of this program definitely makes it a must-have for amateur astronomers.

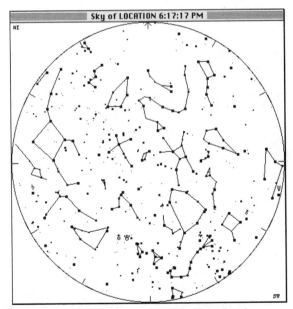

Well sure, it looks like a connect-the-dots drawing to the untrained eye, but any amateur astronomer would recognize this accurate representation of the night sky viewed from the West Coast, U.S., at 6:17 P.M. You did recognize that, didn't you?

How
World Wide Web

Where

www.astro.nwu.edu/lentz/astro/home/astro.htm/#software-mac

Download

MacAstro 1.6 (450 K)

SkyChart 2000
SkyChart 2000 is one of the most colorful, graphically appealing, and feature-rich astronomy programs available for the Mac. When you start the program, it reads a "Sky Data" file for current information, then gives you a view of the sky overhead at the present time. (If the time and/or location displayed at the bottom of the chart are grossly wrong, you may need to adjust your Mac's system time and location.)

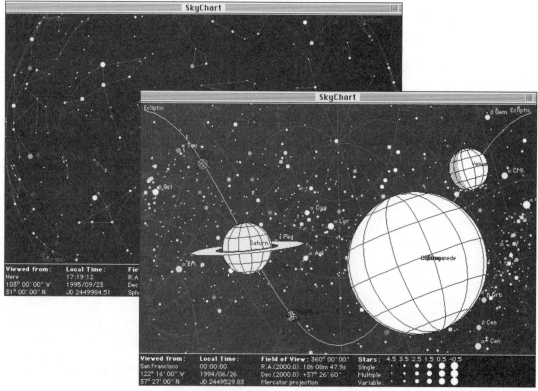

SkyChart 2000 provides dozens of views of the night sky in full color.

348

To identify any object in the chart window, simply click on it. To give you a better idea of SkyChart 2000's capabilities, several sample settings files are included in a Demos folder that's provided with the download. Settings files contain a time, viewer location, and various other program options. You can use them to save particularly interesting views or simulations, as well as your own personal program preferences.

How

World Wide Web

Where

www.astro.nwu.edu/lentz/astro/home/astro.htm/#software-mac

Download

SkyChart 2000 2.1 (650 K)

Paving the Way to a Greener Planet

Environmentalists can try appealing to your conscience until the polar ice caps melt, but any economist will tell you that, if you want to get people to help with something, appeal to the pocketbook. And if the Global Recycling Network (GRN) is any indication, maybe the environmentalists are starting to catch on.

At GRN, it's garbage in, a cleaner planet out.

GRN, one of the most comprehensive recycling information resources on the Net, is showing businesses and individuals that recycling can be profitable. You'll find the latest quotes of major public recycling companies, information to help your company save money by recycling, a directory of companies around the U.S. that recycle everything from auto parts to

wood products, technical updates and new regulations, market insights and international news, a calendar of recycling events, and much more.

How

World Wide Web

Where

grn.com/grn

Give Greenpeace a Chance

What would lead a handful of protesters to sail into atomic test zones or risk their lives by coming between a whaling ship's harpoon and the largest mammals in the world? Only the belief that determined individuals can alter the actions of even the most powerful governments and corporations by drawing the world's attention—whatever the risk—to environmental abuses being wreaked around the globe. Either that or being one sandwich short of a picnic.

Greenpeace: saving the environment through peaceful protest.

Created in 1971, Greenpeace is on a mission to create a green and peaceful world by protecting the environment through nonviolent protests. At the Greenpeace Gopher site, you'll find lots of information about the organization, including:

• Worldwide Greenpeace office addresses and phone numbers

• Worldwide job vacancies

- Ships' movements
- Pictures you can download
- Newsletters
- Scheduled events

How

Gopher

Where

gopher.greenpeace.org

Great Software, Period

Any possibility of me becoming a world-famous scientist ended abruptly around seventh grade—the first time I saw the periodic table of the elements. Finding the cure to some exotic and unpronounceable disease had some hint of glamour, but memorizing the properties of chemical elements? I don't *think* so.

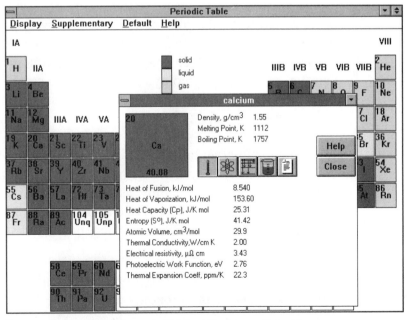

For anyone who feels they need just a bit more excitement: the periodic table of the elements.

For those of you with a little more cerebral interest in science, check out these two periodic table programs. Just click to get classifications, definitions, years of discovery, boiling points, and lots more information about each element.

How

FTP

Where

ftp.csusm.edu

Go To

pub/winworld/chem

Download

element3.zip (96 K)

ptable.zip (120 K)

Astronomical Odds 'n' Ends

Webheads seem to love space and astronomy. So, if you're into astronomy or would like to be, the good news is that just about any program, image, or reference on astronomy is available on the Internet and the Web. And it doesn't matter whether you're a novice astronomer, an experienced amateur, or a pro. Astronomy information and software on the Internet runs the gamut from beginner level on up to stuff that would challenge even the most experienced Ph.D.

But using the Internet to locate information and software on astronomy can be a lot like finding a needle in a galaxy far, far away. Fortunately Robert Lentz has unearthed just about every astronomy-related site on the Internet and collected them as a set of links on his Astro Resources Web site. Here's a brief list of the categories of links he provides:

- Recent news on events and discoveries in astronomy
- Links to dozens of sites that provide information about many categories and specialties in astronomy
- Online tours of the universe

- Encyclopedic astronomy sites
- Interest groups
- Image archives
- Software for Windows, Unix, and Mac users

How

World Wide Web

Where

www.astro.nwu.edu/lentz/astro/home-astro.html

Be sure to click on the Astro FTP List link, located in the Image Archives section. This site provides additional links to several dozen FTP sites that are devoted to astronomy.

The Nature of the Net

Living in Arizona, I can generally predict the local weather with amazing accuracy: hot and dry. Any variance is considered an act of God and cannot therefore be foreseen.

If your local climate has a bit more variety, check out the easy-to-use weather forecaster here that you can download. Just enter a few simple facts, and WEATHER 5.1 will tell you if it's a great day for a picnic or if it's going to rain on your parade. While you're here, download some of the other software available, including:

- A collection of agriculture programs
- Bird songs with species descriptions and sonographs
- A sunrise/sunset almanac for the whole year

How

Gopher

Where

gopher.ed.gov

Go To

Educational Software

IBM Computers and Compatibles

Download

agprgs.zip (173 K)

birdsong.zip (18 K)

sunrise.zip (56 K)

wx51.zip (69 K)

If any of the files stored here do not include the .ZIP extension, simply add it before you unzip, and the file will uncompress successfully. Also, be sure to read the weather.com file included here for help in using the program.

Laboratory to the World

Mother Earth is the biggest scientific laboratory in—well—the world, with every living thing part of some cosmic experiment. At the Earth and Environmental Science Web site, you'll find information on world climates, environmental issues, oceanography, and many other topics related to earth science.

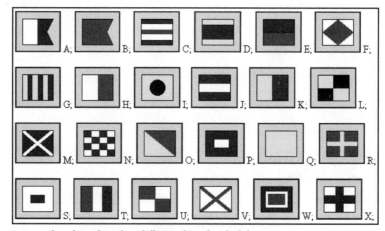

International marine signal flags, downloaded from one of the many oceanography links at the USGS Web site.

Maintained by the good guys at the U.S. Geological Survey (USGS), this site includes links to USGS and non-USGS Web sites, containing the latest scientific data on subjects like:

- Seismology
- Hydrology
- Oceanography
- Volcanology

How
World Wide Web

Where
info.er.usgs.gov/network/science/earth/index.html

The Big Boom

How many nuclear explosions do you think have been triggered since 1945? 300? Guess again. 500? Not even close. Since 1945, there have been over *1900* confirmed nuclear explosions detonated by the U.S., United Kingdom, Soviet Union, France, India, China, and Israel. That's one every three weeks for 50 years. I'm amazed we don't all glow in the dark by now.

This Gopher site includes a comprehensive list of detonations that, sadly, keeps growing. Keep in mind, also, that these are just the ones that are confirmed. How many more have been detonated is anybody's guess.

How
Gopher

Where
wealaka.okgeosurvey1.gov

Go To
CATALOG OF KNOWN NUCLEAR EXPLOSIONS
Catalog of 1900+ known nuclear explosions

Paint Your Computer Green

Maybe ozone depletion, global warming, and the destruction of the rain forests are old news to you. If so, you can thank an environmental journalist for getting the word out. In fact, if it weren't for environmental journalists, most of us wouldn't know about the polar ice caps melting until we were treading water. These potential environmental catastrophes would have been swept under the rug if these environmental watchdogs weren't spreading the word of doom—and what can be done to avoid it.

Read all about it at the Society of Environmental Journalists home page.

At the Society of Environmental Journalists (SEJ) Web site, you'll find links to the U.S. Environmental Protection Agency as well as information on air pollution, pesticides, the ozone layer, water supplies, and much more.

In addition, there's information on SEJ, a list of Internet resources for environmental journalists, SEJ announcements, copies of *SEJournal* and other newsletters on the environment and environmental journalism, and pointers to other information sources from air pollution to wildlife.

How

World Wide Web

Where

www.tribnet.com/environ

Hobnobbing with Hubble

So you'd like to travel the universe, but just don't seem to have the time. Believe me, I understand. But now with the Hubble Solar System Simulator, you can explore strange new worlds and still be home in time for supper.

View the universe through the eyes of this Hubble simulator.

This program lets you display planets, stars, and other astronomic bodies from different viewing angles and at different magnitudes, and includes many other customizable features as well. Outer space has never been closer!

How

FTP

Where

ftp.csusm.edu

Go To

pub/winworld/educate

Download

hubble14.zip (392 K)

Something Worth Howling At

Forget all those fairy tales you read as a kid. Those wolves in *The Three Little Pigs* and *Little Red Riding Hood* were framed! Far from being the evil schemers they're portrayed as, wolves are family-oriented, intelligent predators that do not eat grandmothers or girls wearing red capes. Okay maybe the occasional pig, but only in a pinch.

Here's a Web site that'll help clear up some of the myths surrounding wolves. You'll also learn about how they live and about recovery efforts being waged around the U.S. to help increase their numbers.

You'll have a howling good time at this site.

How

World Wide Web

Where

usa.net:80/WolfHome

For even more wolf info and pictures, try the Desert Moon Web site at wwwnncc.scs.unr.edu/wolves/desertm.html.

Scientifically Speaking

"Simulation of highly turbulent compressible convection showing the vorticity (localized spin) of fluid motions concentrated into an evolving network of vortex tubes and rings near the upper surface." Hello, is anybody still reading this? If *you* are, this site's definitely for you.

Scientists and propeller heads in general will love browsing this online edition of *Science Magazine*, published by the American Association for the Advancement of Science (AAAS). Billed as a forum for the presentation and discussion of important issues related to the advancement of science, *Science Magazine* on the Net contains the current hard-copy issue's table of contents, editorials, *This Week in Science* columns, plus the classified ads and information on how to become a contributor.

How

Gopher

Where

gopher.aaas.org

Go To

SCIENCE Magazine

Don't forget that many Internet addresses are case-sensitive, so be sure to type them *exactly* as shown.

Go Fish

When President Teddy Roosevelt first designated three-acre Pelican Island as a bird sanctuary in 1903, he probably didn't realize he had started a major trend. Today, there are over 500 national wildlife refuges stretching from the Arctic Ocean to the South Pacific, encompassing more than 92 million acres of the United States' best wildlife habitat.

The U.S. Fish and Wildlife Service's mission is to protect that land for the continuing benefit of American picnickers. With over 7,500 employees at facilities and field offices across the country, the Service is still understaffed when it comes to the huge task of maintaining so much land.

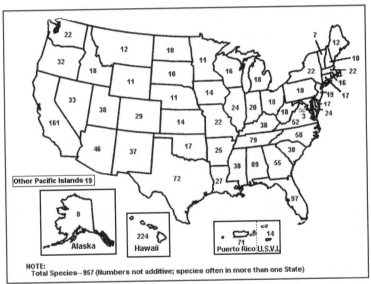

NOTE:
Total Species--957 (Numbers not additive; species often in more than one State)

Every state in the Union has more than it's share of endangered species.

In addition to information on its conservation programs and recreational activities, the Fish and Wildlife Service Web site includes information on:

- Conservation programs
- Endangered species
- Environmental contaminants
- Fire management

- Fisheries
- Migratory birds and waterfowl

How

World Wide Web

Where

www.fws.gov

You can also get the latest weather maps via Gopher at thorplus.lib.purdue.edu, then go to Weather Reports and Maps.

Martians Among Us

For anybody who just can't get enough of our Red Planet neighbor, MarsIcon can help. This Windows program displays the current view of Mars as an icon on your desktop. You can specify the current Central Meridian longitude, the number of hours and minutes in a "Martian" day, and the time and date in different formats.

You can also change the icon's background color and rotation direction, adjust MarsIcon for daylight savings time, and more. And while you're here, download copies of MoonIcon, as well as a program that displays Jupiter and its moons.

How

FTP

Where

gatekeeper.dec.com

Go To

pub/micro/msdos/win3/icons

Download

marsic27.zip (83 K)

gredsp37.zip (90 K)

moonic10.zip (144 K)

What a Discovery

THE WORLD OF SCIENCE

Discover

M A G A Z I N E

Discover the fun of reading DISCOVER magazine online.

Do you want to read about new ideas and new products, the latest breakthroughs in science, and discoveries that are changing the world we live in? Neither did I, but one look at *Discover* online and I was hooked.

Covering the entire world of science, including space, biology, health, medicine, computers, the environment, astronomy, and more, *Discover* uncovers breakthroughs on the origin of life, the evolution of the universe, the inner workings of the human brain, and the mass extinction of the dinosaurs. Written for those who do not necessarily have a background in science (like me), *Discover* is the only magazine that covers the entire world of science.

How

World Wide Web

Where

www.enews.com/magazines/discover/index.html

The Sites and Sounds of Space

Space may be the final frontier, but it's got to be the most photographed, written about, and generally observed frontier ever. And here's a site that adds to the hype.

You'll find a huge collection of images from space, including pictures of stars, planets, comets, the space shuttles, maps of solar eclipses, and much more. In addition, there are lots of animations and movies for PC and Mac users to download, including clips of the Hubble Telescope repair, animations about the Apollo missions, and even clips of Star Trek movies.

There are also lots of sounds from outer space (sort of), including audio clips from *Blade Runner*, *Dune*, *Moonraker*, *Superman*, and more.

How

Gopher

Where

sir.univ-rennes1.fr

Go To

Astro Gopher

In a Galaxy Far, Far Away...

Look up at the night sky and what do you see? Relatively speaking, not much. But magnify things a few thousand times and watch out! Space may be the Great Void, but you'd never know it from the pictures available here.

You'll find hundreds of otherworldly images to download, including galaxies, globular clusters (no, they're not candy bars), planetary nebulae, and supernova remnants. And if you're not sure what all this space-oddity mumbo jumbo means, not to worry. There's also lots of online help for nebulae newbies.

Reflection nebula NGC 7023 (in case you didn't recognize it).

How

World Wide Web

Where

seds.lpl.arizona.edu/billa/twn

An Englishman's Guide to the Universe

It used to be that the sun never set on the British empire, which must have made its subjects' love of stargazing very difficult to pursue. Now that things have shrank down to a more manageable size on the other side of the Atlantic, amateur astronomy is once again flourishing in the United Kingdom.

At the UK Amateur Astronomy Web site, you'll find information and links to astronomy societies throughout the U.K., astronomy magazines, computer bulletin boards devoted to stargazing, and much more.

Links for amateur astronomers in the U.K.

How

World Wide Web

Where

www.emoticon.com/emoticon/astro

Where to Find Way More Goodies

If you really want to get back to nature, stroll over to *Sports and Leisure* to find out about the Appalachian Trail, a 14-state, 2,140-mile nature hike across the U.S. In the same chapter, budding aerospace engineers will have a blast with The Greatest Paper Airplanes shareware program. They'll learn about the history of air flight, what makes that plane stay up there, and how to build some great paper models.

For free updates to this book via FTP or the Web, go to: coriolis.com

Way More!
FREE $TUFF

Anybody who watches three games of football in a row should be declared brain dead.

Erma Bombeck

Sports and Leisure

Hog Heaven

Some people say that jazz is America's only art form. But true hogheads know that Harley bikes represent the *real* American art form. So, put on your helmet and leathers, fire up your engine, and come experience the Harley-Davidson lifestyle with the Harley-Davidson of Stamford Connecticut Web site. Harley enthusiasts can check out the Harley-Davidson and Buell motorcycle lines, get valuable service tips, purchase clothing and collectibles, and learn about upcoming rumbles, er, events.

Live to surf, surf to live.

In addition, you can submit a picture of yourself on your Harley to win a Harley-Davidson T-shirt, download Harley audio files (really) and video clips, and much more. You may not be able to smell the rubber burning, but you'll be able to hear it.

How

World Wide Web

Where

www.hd-stamford.com

Taking Up a Collection

Coin collecting isn't nearly as popular as it once was—although the IRS still seems to enjoy it. Fledgling collectors probably can't resist the temptation to cash in their coinage to buy the latest Sega game cartridges. But

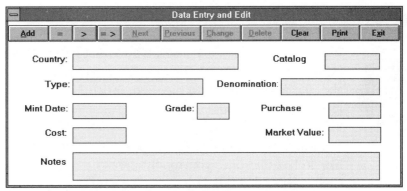

A penny saved...just might be worth something someday.

for true coin hobbyists who appreciate the value of a red cent, dBCoin for Windows is right on the money.

This easy-to-use inventory system helps you keep track of your collection. You can store an unlimited number of records with information about each coin, including country, catalog number, type, denomination, mint date, grade, purchase date, cost, market value, and comments.

How
FTP

Where
ftp.csusm.edu

Go To
pub/winworld/database

Download
dbcoin.zip (345 K)

Remember, shareware is *not* freeware. Try it out, and if you like it, be sure to follow the developer's instructions on how to register the software.

Organized Your Stamps Philately?

If you think stamps are just a way to get an envelope from Point A to Point B, then you're not thinking like a true philatelist. Stamps are probably the world's smallest pieces of artwork, and some of them are truly remarkable creations.

But if you're a philatelist (the insider's term for stamp collector) or you'd like to become one, you might already realize that one of the biggest challenges with this hobby is keeping your stamps organized. That's where PhilateLISTER can help.

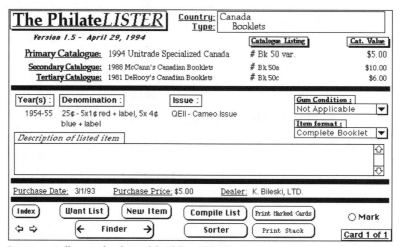

Stamp out disorganization with PhilateLISTER.

This Mac software program lets you enter information about individual stamps and stamp books, including their value (based on published catalogs), year of issue, denominations in which they were issued, gum condition, purchase date, purchase price, dealer name, and more. The program is available as a full-blown application or as a Hypercard stack. Both versions are included in the main file that you download.

How

FTP

Where

ftp.sunet.se

Go To

pub

mac

info-mac

app

Download

philate-lister-15-hc.hqx (590 K)

Walk, Walk, Walk Till You Drop, Drop, Drop

From Georgia to Maine, The Appalachian Trail winds through 14 states along the eastern U.S. in a continuous, marked footpath totaling over 2,140 miles.

At the Appalachian Trail Web site, you'll find maps and descriptions of this historic trail, a state-by-state breakdown of it, and links to various hiking clubs and other scenic trails on the Net. In addition, you can subscribe to an Appalachian Trail mailing list, get weekly reports and advice from veteran hikers, and more.

How

World Wide Web

Where

www.fred.net/kathy/at.html

Whaddaya say we go for a little walk?

Sporting News

If you're the kind of person who turns right to the sports page before you even read the morning headlines, well, you're probably male and you're probably used to your significant other making snide comments at you from the other end of the kitchen table. Anyway, whether you're male or female, if you love sports you'll love some of the sports-related mailing lists you can subscribe to on the Net. Here are some examples of what's available—with a few catering to other leisure activities, as well:

Baseball History Newsletter

This list is for anyone interested in all-things-baseball, including its history and what's to come. A newsletter will be mailed to you every other Monday, and you'll get more information with your first issue.

How

Email

Where

godux@teleport.com

Message

Please send me an introductory issue of the Baseball History Newsletter (be sure to mention how you heard about it—they appreciate that kinda thing).

Motorcycle Racing News

RacEMail is a mailing list that brings you the latest motorcycle race results every Sunday evening (during race season, of course). You'll get results from the FIM 500cc, 250cc and 125cc GPs, as well as World Superbike, AMA Superbike, and the American Supercross series.

Where

majordomo@motorcycle.com

Message

subscribe racemail

Cavers Digest

This mailing list is a great resource and forum for anyone interested in spelunking (if you need to ask, then you're not one of 'em).

Where

listproc@speleology.cs.yale.edu

Message

subscribe cavers-digest *Your Name*

Martial Arts

The martial arts mailing list discusses various aspects of the, well, martial arts, including teaching and training techniques, martial arts philosophy, self-defense, and traditional and non-traditional styles.

Where

martial-arts-request@dragon.cso.uiuc.edu

Message

subscribe

Base Jumping

This mailing list is for the altitudinally insane, and discusses fixed-object skydiving. It's open to anyone who has made at least one base jump or skydive. Topics include equipment, sites, packing techniques, and publications.

Where

base-request@lunatix.lex.ky.us

Message

subscribe

Balloon Sculpting

This list discusses balloon sculpting, new sculptures and suggestions for improving old ones, how to entertain with balloons, health issues, and more. Anyone with an interest in balloon art is welcome.

Where

balloon-request@cvs.rochester.edu

Message

subscribe

Horse Racing
The Derby mailing list discusses the various aspects and strategies of horse racing, primarily dealing with—but not limited to—handicapping.

Where

derby-request@inslab.uky.edu

Message

subscribe

Obedience Training
Different aspects of dog obedience training and related dog topics are discussed here.

Where

listserver@reepicheep.gcn.uoknor.edu

Message

subscribe

Exotic Cars
Discussion of Ferraris, Maseratis, "Testosteronis," and other power cars. This mailing list is for owners and admirers of exotic cars who want to talk about all aspects of their hobby, including buying, selling, maintaining, driving, styling, and more.

Where

exotic-cars-request@asl.hitachi.com

Message

subscribe

Let's Go Fly a Kite
This mailing list is for people interested in making, flying, or just talking about kites, kite activities, construction techniques, reviews of commercially available kites and plans, and any other aspect of kite flying.

Where

kites-request@harvard.edu

Message

subscribe

Wings of Paper

Despite the intrusion of video games, VCRs, cable TV, and other high-tech adventures, paper airplanes are still popular with kids. And here's a program that merges the time honored tradition of making these little pulp gliders with today's computer technology. The result is sort of a cross between Japanese origami and Boeing aerospace engineering.

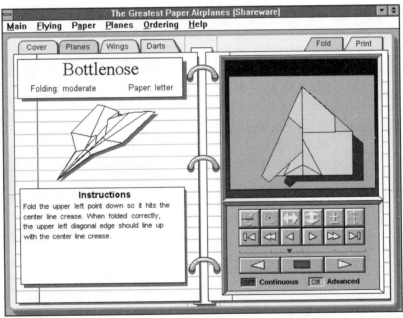

Create great paper airplanes with The Greatest Paper Airplanes 3D shareware.

The Greatest Paper Airplanes shareware program lives up to its name—and then some. This is arguably the best shareware program I've seen for the PC. The shareware version of this interactive 3D program comes with plans for building five paper airplanes, information about the history

and principals of flight, lots of great graphics and animation, and much more. Adults will love this one as much—or even more than—kids will.

How
FTP

Where
ftp.csusm.edu

Go To
pub/winworld/graphics

Download
gpa.zip (717 K)

A Very Popular Web Page

For over 90 years, *Popular Mechanics* has documented the dreams and deeds of those who believe technology will transform the world. Now, the magazine itself has been transformed in cyberspace. At the PM Zone, you'll

You've just entered the PM Zone.

find quality as well as quantity, with a huge collection of more than 1,000 pages of information to help make the mechanically complex easier to understand.

Offering the latest in technology news, the PM Zone features a searchable archive, where to go for the best free software on the Web, tech support for your computer woes, help on home improvement projects, and much more. Also, look for the Tech Update Of The Day, the Movie Of The Week, and the Feature Of The Month.

How

World Wide Web

Where

popularmechanics.com

Drive for Show, Putt for Dough

Golf is one sport that, try as I might, I've never quite been able to get the hang of. It's too quiet, for one thing—at least no one's ever applauded after one of *my* shots. But if golf is your game, check out Golf Budde.

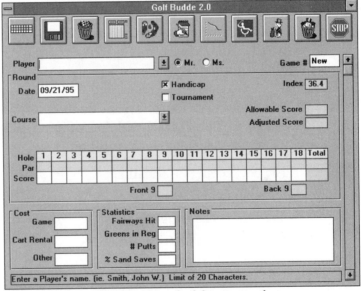

Golf Budde does everything but schedule your tee time.

This easy-to-use Windows program allows multiple golfers to keep track of scores, dates played, courses played, money spent on games and equipment (not to mention bets), statistics, and divorces caused by staying out on the links all weekend (okay, maybe in the upgrade). It even calculates your handicap after each round. You can also add course ratings and par scores for up to three different tee boxes, and stats can be displayed in tabular or graphical formats.

How

FTP

Where

ftp.csusm.edu

Go To

pub/winworld/database

Download

golfbd20.zip (400 K)

To Bee or Not to Bee

Originating in Asia centuries ago, beekeeping was introduced in America by its first colonists in the 1600s. Today, about 150,000 beekeepers manage over three million colonies in every state of the U.S. That's a lot of bees.

If you've got a taste for honey, and don't mind the occasional bee having a taste of you, here's a site with lots of information on how you can get started in this sweet hobby. You'll find:

- Basic beekeeping information
- Beekeeping publications
- Sources of beekeeping supplies
- Information about Africanized bees
- Bees and beekeeping newsletters

How

Gopher

Where

sun1.oardc.ohio-state.edu

Go To

Biological and Agricultural Resources
Bees and Beekeeping

C'mon, Take a Chance

Any Web site that uses thousand-dollar bills for wallpaper can't be all bad, and that's exactly what you'll find at the Internet Virtual Casino—at least Netscape users will. You'll also find links to online casinos around the world, including Switzerland, Italy, Japan, Germany, and France. Bon chance!

FREE JACKPOT

SLOT MACHINE

Congratulations! You won 0.12!

Looks like we have a winner at the Internet Virtual Casino.

How

World Wide Web

Where

www.casino.org/cc

Here's a couple of other gambling-related sites:

- www.vegas.com/wagernet
- www.virtualvegas.com

Baseball and Softball Stat Keepers

Put some big league power behind your little league baseball or softball team with Baseball Stats for Windows. This excellent baseball coaching software helps you keep track of batting averages, on-base and slugging percentages, pitching and fielding stats, and much more.

Plus, when you input new figures after each game, all your stats are updated automatically. You can even use it to keep track of your players' names and telephone numbers.

How

FTP

Where

ftp.csusm.edu

Go To

pub/winworld/database

Download

stat36.zip (371 K)

Check out the SportServer Web site at www2.nando.net/baseball/ bbmain.html for the latest stats, standings, team info, schedules, photos, and stories in pro baseball, football, hockey, and basketball.

How Crafty Are You?

Do you love free crafting, sewing, cross-stitch, tole painting and needlecraft offers? Then, you'll love the book *Free Stuff For People Who Enjoy Crafting, Sewing And More* (no relation). This site includes over a dozen samples from the book, including Rainy Day Ideas for Kids and a free cross stitch kit for beginners.

In addition to information about this book with the clever title, look for information on ordering free patterns, iron-ons, booklets, Christmas ideas, project sheets, samples, newsletters, puzzles, and more.

How

World Wide Web

Where

www.craftnet.org/prime/freestf2.html

Email Your Way to a Better Body

If hitting the Return key on your keyboard is your idea of exercise, your body's probably in big trouble, so you don't have a moment to lose. It's time to get in shape, and Better Bodies can help. This free email service lets Internauts around the world get online advice about health and fitness from professional personal trainers.

Created by Better Bodies, an upscale health club with locations in New York and Los Angeles, this service lets you get fast answers to your workout questions from certified fitness consultants.

How

Email

Where

betbodies@aol.com

Message

Ask away. Fitness consultants are standing by.

What Goes Up...

Information on aerobatic flying is just one of the numerous links you'll find at the World Wide Aviation Server.

I don't have a fear of flying; at 30,000 feet, it's *not* flying that scares me. The jumbo jets aren't so bad—at least they give you a magazine and some stale peanuts to keep your mind off the fact that the laws of physics prove beyond a doubt that flight is impossible (which is why you never see physicists flying)—it's airplanes the size of Volkswagens with wings that make me nervous.

But if your nerves are a little steadier than mine, here's a great aviation site to check out on the Web. The General Aviation Web server provides a huge assortment of flight-related information and links for amateur and professional pilots. You'll find:

- Weather information
- Piloting tips
- Model airplanes (more my speed)
- Simulator information
- Help on learning to fly
- Web and Gopher links

- Newsgroups and FAQs
- Flight-planning software

How

World Wide Web

Where

aviation.jsc.nasa.gov

A list of general aviation servers worldwide is also available on the Web at acro.harvard.edu/GA/ga_servers.html.

...Must Come Down

I'm sure that more than one atheist who has leapt from a plane has developed a personal relation with Jesus, Buddha, or Jehovah before reaching the ground, but I personally prefer to participate in sports that keep my feet firmly planted on Mother Earth. Thrill seekers and death defyers, however, will love "Skydive!," a thrill-a-minute Web site espousing the virtues of stepping out of a plane with 12,000 feet between you and ground zero.

The surf's up—to about 10,000 feet.

You'll find lots of tips, pictures, and links to other skydiving Net sites, as well as information on how to get started in skydiving, newsgroups for skydivers, and where the best jumps are.

How

World Wide Web

Where

www.cis.ufl.edu/skydive

Crazy for Sports

Are you a sports nut? Here's a simple test:

1. Have you ever painted any part of your body with your favorite team's colors before watching a game?

2. Can you remember every play from last night's game, but not what you had for dinner?

3. Were you overjoyed when TV coverage started including reverse-angle instant replays—in golf?

If you answered yes to any of these questions, you should seek immediate psychiatric help—on second thought, maybe you should wait until halftime.

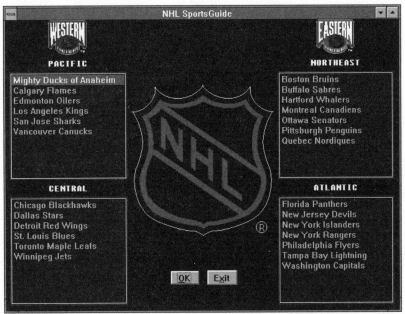

All your favorite NHL and NFL team logos are ready for you to download.

And while you're at it, maybe you should wait until you download these cool NFL and NHL screensavers for Windows. In addition to your favorite team logos, these screensavers come with team and league schedules, lots of sports trivia, wallpaper bitmaps, and much more.

FREE $TUFF from the Internet

How
FTP

Where
gatekeeper.dec.com

Go To
pub/micro/msdos/win3/desktop

Download
nflsg1.zip (305 K)

nhlsg1.zip (250 K)

You can also get dozens of sport-related icons by FTPing to gatekeeper.dec.com/pub/micro/msdos/win3/icons and downloading the file sprtico1.zip. Here's how to change an existing icon to a new one:

1. In the Program Manager, click on the icon that you want to change.
2. Select File|Properties, then click on the Change Icon button in the Program Item Properties window.
3. In the File Name box of the Change Icon window, enter the path to the icon (for instance, c:\software\icons\76ers.ico).
4. Click on OK twice.

Gophers and Golf Do Mix

To a *real* golf nut, reading about golf is the next best thing to actually playing it—either of which is better than eating or sleeping. And at the Golf Archives Gopher site, you'll find plenty to read about. Check out the Golf FAQ, get the latest information on custom-built clubs (golf clubs, not country clubs), download GIFs and bitmaps, and get course descriptions around the country.

How
Gopher

Where
dunkin.Princeton.EDU

Go To

Dunkin GOLF Archives

Fire up your Web browser for even more golfing info by accessing GolfWeb at www.golfweb.com.

What Are You Running From?

It makes sense, I suppose, for a guy named Peter Ferrett to be into running. Peter's an Australian who developed this simple but very useful Macintosh software tool for runners who like to race. The program includes two utilities.

The first utility takes your best time for a race of a particular length and then calculates what your expected time should be for a different-length race. For instance, suppose your best time for a 10K is 34:15. When you're ready to try your first half-marathon, you just enter your 10K time and the program will calculate your expected time for the half-marathon—in this case, 75:52:18. You can choose race lengths of 5K, 8K, 10K, half-marathon, and marathon.

The second utility tells you how to pace yourself for half-marathon and full-marathon races. You enter your target completion time for the race, and the pacer utility tells you what your times should be at 5K, 10K, 15K, and 20K checkpoints. For instance, for a half-marathon completion target time of 75:52, you should reach the 5K mark at 17:58:48, you should have run to the 10K mark by 35:57:36, and so on. This is a great program for both recreational and serious runners, and takes only minutes to learn how to use it.

How

FTP

Where

ftp.sunet.se

Running Times – Predictions

Known Distance: `10 km ▼`   Best Time (hr:mins) : `34:15`

Predicted Distance: `1/2 mar... ▼`   Predicted Time: 75:52:18

[Calculate Predicted Times]

Running Times – Predictions

Running Distance: `1/2 marathon ▼`

Completion Time: `75:52`

Distance:	Expected time:
5 Km:	17:58:48
10 Km:	35:57:36
15 Km:	53:56:24
20 Km:	71:55:12
Finish:	75:52:00

[Calculate Pace]

When it's time to pick up the pace, Runner's Helper will tell you exactly what that pace should be.

Go To
pub
mac
info-mac
app

Download
runners-helper.hqx (34K)

Hoop Dee Doo! NBA Schedules!

With the NBA strike averted, the season is on! Access the NBA Interactive Schedule Web site to find out who's playing where, when, and against whom. You'll also get up-to-the-minute NBA news and game dates, as well as links to lots of other sports pages around the Net (no pun intended).

How

World Wide Web

Where

wintermute.unh.edu/cgi-bin/nba-page.pl

 College fans can get the March Madness NCAA Mens Basketball Pool Manager by FTP at gatekeeper.dec.com/pub/micro/msdos/win3/misc and downloading marchmad.zip (371 K).

Get in the Zone

Top sports news? SportsZone! ESPNET, baby!

Zone out at ESPNET's SportsZone.

Lots of scores! Lots of news! And features? You better believe it! Columnists? Like you wouldn't believe!

Check it out! SportsZone on ESPNET, baby! Like my Dick Vitale impersonation? No? Well, TOUGH LUCK, BABY!

How

World Wide Web

Where

espnet.sportszone.com

Where to Find Way More Goodies

Ask couch potatoes what goes great with a day of watching sports, and they'll tell you...*beer*! Check out the "Suds by Mail" section of *Food and Cooking* for information on home brewing, including getting started, recipe ideas, and competitions you can enter.

Also, I can't think of anything more leisurely and relaxing than blasting a few space aliens back to whatever black holes they crawled out of. Check out the *Games* chapter for loads of gaming software to download.

You'll find lots of sports-related humor in the *Humor* chapter—in particular, the "Cat's Out of the Bag" section.

For free updates to this book via FTP or the Web, go to: coriolis.com

Way More! FREE $TUFF

Thanks to the Interstate Highway System,
it is now possible to travel from coast to
coast without seeing anything.

Charles Kuralt

Travel

This Is the Life

Money SEARCH FOR YOUR BEST PLACES

Create Your Own *Best Places* List

There's no place like home.

Whether you're a SINK (single income, no kids), DINK (dual income, nerdy kids), or DORK (divorced orphan, rotten kids), there's an ideal place for you to live in the U.S. It's just a matter finding it. And with *Money* magazine's Your Best Places Search Page, finding it has never been easier.

Simply rate each of the 78 criteria displayed on a scale from one to ten, and the database will display the 300 best cities in the U.S.—custom-tailored for your lifestyle, income, and interests.

How

World Wide Web

Where

www.pathfinder.com/money/best-cities/searchopener.html

Heavy Reading for the Adventurous

Whether you're setting out on safari, hiking the Himalayas, or biking the outback of Australia, your first step should be to check out the Adventurous Traveler Bookstore. This online catalog offers an extensive collection of outdoor adventure books and maps for the entire world.

You'll find over 1,700 titles, with much more to come. You can search the entire database by keyword or browse the geographically organized folders to view the books and maps profiled here.

How

World Wide Web

Where

www.gorp.com/atbook.htm

You can also request a paper catalog by sending email with your name and address to books@atbook.com.

Are We There Yet?

Here's some software to load onto the family laptop computer (don't *all* families have laptops these days?). It'll help keep the kids busy in the back seat on your cross-country trip next summer vacation. These fun and educational programs (hey, they *can* be both) teach U.S. geography, the state capitals, maps and countries of the world, and more. It sure beats counting license plates.

How
Gopher

Where
gopher.ed.gov

Go To
Educational Software
IBM Computers and Compatibles

Download
alfgeo.zip (171 K)

bh.zip (46 K)

bounty.exe 73 K)

capitals.zip (19 K)

capitols.zip (22 K)

cartog.zip (16 K)

flags.zip (99 K)

geobase.zip (103 K)

geochron.zip (55 K)

geograph.zip (102 K)

Fly the Friendly Skies

In the airline industry, there are two things you can always count on: your luggage being lost when you need it the most and fare wars between rival companies. And when one of these wars heats up, the only ones not bloodied are ticket buyers with an eye for a bargain.

Here's a Web site that'll help you keep abreast of events in the air, including information about dozens of major airlines worldwide, prices, contests and giveaways, incentives, flight schedules, and more.

You can access dozens of airlines on every continent at the Commercial Airlines of the World Web site.

How

World Wide Web

Where

w3.one.net/~flypba/AIRLINES/OAL/airlines.text.html

If you're using a slower modem, you might want to access the text version of this site at w3.one.net/~flypba/AIRLINES/OAL/airlines.text.html.

Getting There Is Half the Fun

Well, at least that's true if you're the pilot. But whether you fly your own plane or rent, you still have to file a flight plan for most destinations—probably the least glamourous part of being a pilot.

If you own a Mac, flight planning just got easier—thanks to Flight Master. Private pilots spend an average of 20 to 30 minutes creating a flight plan. With Flight Master, though, you can actually complete and print out a comprehensive flight plan in under a minute.

A	Air		Air		Speed		Fuel		Lit/h
	Date		Takeoff		Landing		Tot Time		

A	C O M								

A	N A V								

	MTOW				ATOW				

A		FIX	MR	ALT	L(NM)	TIME	ETO	RETO	ATO
		Dep							TkOff
A	01								
A	02								
A	03								
A	04								
A	05								
A	06								
A	07								
A	08								
A	09								

Create a complete, detailed flight plan in under a minute with Flight Master.

To help you save time, Flight Master does require that you spend a little time up front. Basically, you create "libraries" that contain information that you routinely use in planning your flights. The four major libraries are:

- AIR This library identifies the airplane that you usually use (although you can set up multiple libraries for different aircraft).
- COM Use this library to store the frequencies of all the COM stations you use in your flight zones.
- NAV This library contains the frequencies of all NAV stations (for VOR, DME, NDB, and locator stations).
- FIX Use this library to record the coordinates, latitude, and longitude of the fix points you use in your flights. Of course, you can set up multiple FIX libraries for several different common destinations.

The program also helps you calculate distance, time, and fuel consumption for the complete flight and for each flight leg. The documentation does a good job of walking you through the steps of the program, although with sentences like "Flight Master has been realized to allow you to be more productive," it's obvious that English is not the author's first language.

How

FTP

Where

ftp.sunet.se

Go To

pub

mac

info-mac

app

Download

For 68K Mac users (271 K): flight-master-108.hqx

For Power Mac users (271 K): flight-master-108-ppc.hqx

Driving Down the Freeway

At the risk of carrying an already overused metaphor too far, you can now use the "information highway" to help you get on the real highway. Freeways, Alamo Rent A Car's venture into cyberspace, lets you reserve your car, download rental forms, read about special offers, and much more.

For online car rental info, remember the Alamo—and the Freeways Web site.

This online reservation and travel information Web site lets you:

• Find the Alamo location nearest you

• Get handy travel tips and maps

• Access weather reports

You'll also find games for your kids, news about popular destinations, and lots of links with hundreds of helpful features for travelers.

How

World Wide Web

Where

www.freeways.com

Easing the Travel Travails

Long business trips wouldn't be so bad if it weren't for the crummy food, lumpy beds, crowded airports, and jet lag. While the Traveler's DataBook won't make your mattress more comfortable, it might help you sleep a little better.

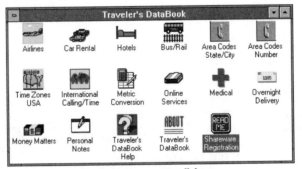

Travel information is just a mouse-click away.

Designed as a convenient way to access important information needed for business travel, Traveler's DataBook has many unique features for mobile computing professionals, including:

- Toll-free numbers for major airlines, car rental companies, and hotel chains
- Postal abbreviations, area codes, and time zones
- Metric conversions
- Telephone numbers for major credit card companies, traveler's checks, and money wire services

- Telephone numbers for international assistance with physicians or medications
- Telephone numbers for major overnight package delivery couriers
- Telephone numbers for major online sources of information, including Internet access

You can even include personal notes and important personal information, including frequently called numbers, user IDs, priority club numbers, travel expenses, and so on.

How

FTP

Where

ftp.csusm.edu

Go To

pub/winworld/educate

Download

traveldb.zip (98 K)

Takeoff to PCTravel

Check out PCTravel to purchase airline tickets for over 700 companies world-wide, find the lowest fares, and download flight schedules—all online. In addition, tickets you purchase are delivered to you the next day, free of charge. Just register to find out more.

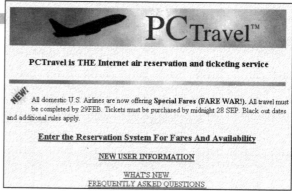

Getcher red-hot airline tickets at unbeatable prices at PCTravel.

How

World Wide Web

Where

www.pctravel.com

And the Reviews Are In

If you're ready to take a break from the Net and maybe do some *real* traveling (as opposed to the virtual kind), make the Web Travel Review your next stop on the Information Highway.

Web Travel Review brings you high-quality travelogs, including thousands of photographs and hundreds of pages of text. You'll find personal travel stories about Europe, North and South America, The Caribbean, Australia, and New Zealand. There are also dozens of links to other travel-related Net sites, book reviews, and more.

How

World Wide Web

Where

webtravel.org/webtravel

A Gopher for City Slickers

Did you know that, in addition to Glendale, Arizona (my home), there are 34 other Glendales scattered across the U.S.? Do you even care? It might not mean much to you now, but you'll thank me if it ever comes up in Trivial Pursuit.

If you're interested in less trivial matters, though, here's a Gopher site that gives you the hard facts on just about every U.S. city. This database lets you search by name or ZIP code, then displays data about each city, including:

• Area code

- ZIP code
- Population
- County
- Elevation
- Latitude and longitude

How

Gopher

Where

ccadfa.cc.adfa.oz.au

Go To

Library Services
Electronic Library
Resources by Subject
Science
GEOGRAPHY
US Geographical Location Service

Fun in the Sun—and Snow

I'm not exactly sure what snow skiing and scuba diving have in common, but if you're looking for the best of both, you'll find it at the TravelBase Web site. You'll find information about every ski area and

TravelBase is your home base for skiing and scuba info on the Net.

scuba shop in the U.S.—and I do mean *every*. There's information on over 500 ski areas and towns around the country, as well as a listing of over 1,000 scuba shops.

You'll also find in-depth info on Key West and Orlando, including hotels, restaurants, and attractions, and lots more.

How

World Wide Web

Where

www.travelbase.com

Destination Unknown

Vacation comes but once a year, I'm sad to say, so make the most of your next one by doing a little homework first. Sure, you could wade through the travel brochures and magazines, but who's got the time? And besides those are often outdated as soon as they're printed. Let TravelSeach come to the rescue.

TravelSearch sorts through competing and conflicting information to bring you the best, up-to-date data on the world's most visited cities and resorts. Once available only to travel agents throughout the U.S. and Canada, TravelSearch now offers the same information to you over the Web. These single-page destination sheets provide data on:

• The best shops, restaurants, and nightlife

• Sporting activities available

• What kind of weather to expect

• Where the interesting side trips are

How

World Wide Web

Where

www.bendnet.com/travelsearch.html

 If you're accessing the Internet using a Web browser, don't forget to key in the prefixes *http://* for Web sites, *gopher://* for Gopher sites, and *ftp://* for—you guessed it—FTP sites.

What in the World Is the Time?

Okay, so it's the night before your big trip to Europe, and you want to be sure that you're reservation's confirmed for that Bed and Breakfast in London. But if you call now, will you wake up the proprietors? Or maybe you want to make restaurant reservations in Paris. Is the restaurant still open?

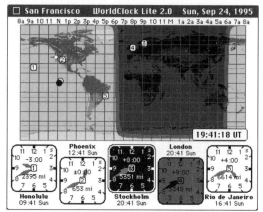

World Clock Lite gives telling time a whole new twist.

World Clock Lite makes it easy to get answers to these and lots of other questions about the time conditions in hundreds of cities throughout the world. The program automatically displays clocks for up to five cities around the world, and shows you which part of the globe is in daylight and which part is in darkness. It takes only a few seconds to switch to different clocks around the world.

World Clock Lite has a very nice graphical display, and provides lots of options for customizing its appearance. The author also makes a commercial version available, so if you find this version of the program useful, you might want to order the complete version. In any case, this program is great for frequent travelers. If you have a Power Book, you can load it and use it while you're on the road.

How

FTP

Where

ftp.sunet.se

Go To

pub

mac

info-mac

app

Download

Worldclock-lite.hqx (140 K)

Fly Me to the Moon

Keeping track of your frequent flyer miles may sometimes seem like more trouble than it's worth—until you get that free trip to Hawaii. Hmm, maybe it wasn't that much trouble after all.

Now with WinFly for Windows, tracking your miles has never been easier. WinFly tracks and updates your frequent flyer mileage for most major airlines, including TWA, American, and Delta, and even lets you keep track of mileage you've already redeemed.

How

FTP

Where

gatekeeper.dec.com

Go To

pub/micro/msdos/win3/misc

Download

winfly.zip (120 K)

Maybe You CAN Get There from Here

Before you head off to Point B, spend a few extra minutes at Point A and check out the University of Michigan's Geographic Distance Calculator.

Just enter where you are and where you're going, and the distance is automatically calculated (as the crow flies), longitude and latitude are displayed, as well as information about each city. You can even download maps to help you get there—wherever you're going.

How far is it?

This service uses the University of Michigan Geographic Name Server to find the latitude and longitude of two places, and then calculates the distance between them (as the crow flies). It also provides a map showing the two places, using the Xerox PARC Map Server.

This service was inspired by the spiffy Geographic Name Server/Xerox Map Gateway at Buffalo.

Various input formats are allowed. Very few places outside the U.S. are included.

From `Anchorage, Alaska`

to `Carson City, Nevada` (optional)

submit or clear

If you've got a long ways to go and a short time to get there, check out the Geographic Distance Calculator first.

How

World Wide Web

Where

gs213.sp.cs.cmu.edu/prog/dist

Breakfast Inn Bed

If you're tired of being treated like just another room number when you stay in a hotel or motel, maybe it's time you tried a bed and breakfast. Hotels and motels just can't match the charm and uniqueness of a quality bed and breakfast, and at the Internet Guide to Bed & Breakfast Inns Web site, you'll find a huge guide to bed and breakfasts around the country.

In addition, you'll find links to thousands of country inns and private homes you can stay in. You also get pictures, rates, reservation information, minimum stay requirements, and more.

How

World Wide Web

Where

www.ultranet.com/biz/inns

Just Checking

If you're a veteran traveler, you know that the importance of a travel item is inversely proportional to how likely you are to forget it. A perfect example: While I always remember to pack six extra razors when one is plenty, once I actually forgot to pack the front wheel of my bicycle for a mountain biking trip. I rest my case.

Anyone who travels—especially out of the country—will want to check out the Traveler's Checklist Web site first. While it won't remind you to pack an extra bike wheel, you will find lots of essential products and accessories you may not have considered, like:

- Electrical adapters
- Travel irons
- Money belts
- Travel alarms

There's also lots of information on travel safety you won't want to miss.

How
World Wide Web

Where
www.ag.com/travelers/checklist

Where to Find Way More Goodies

Whether your next vacation is to Monte Carlo or to Vegas, order your free pocket-sized blackjack crib sheet to help you shave the odds down to something a little more favorable. Turn to the *Games* chapter for more information.

Don't get caught in a strange town with a strange illness without knowing how to find the right doctor for you. Go to the *Health and Nutrition* chapter for information on finding a doctor anywhere in the U.S.

If you're more the world traveler, turn to the *International* chapter for lots of information on world happenings, as well as the *Language and Linguistics* chapter for lots of foreign language programs.

Kids traveling to Disneyland will be begging you to read the *Kid Stuff* chapter for tons of Disney-related sites, sounds, and mailing lists to get the latest information on Disney theme parks, upcoming projects, and Disney TV.

Predicting how fun your vacation will be is like predicting the weather. Help put the odds a little more in your favor by downloading the U.S. Weather Atlas for Windows, which lets you graph the weather for over 80 cities in the U.S., including average temperatures, sunshine, rainfall, and humidity. You'll find it in *Science and Nature*.

For free updates to this book via FTP or the Web, go to: coriolis.com

Index

FREE $TUFF from the Internet